THE FORTY-NINERS

THE OLD WEST

THE FORTY-NINERS

By the Editors of

TIME-LIFE BOOKS

with text by

William Weber Johnson

TIME-LIFE BOOKS, NEW YORK

TIME-LIFE BOOKS

Founder: Henry R. Luce 1898-1967

Editor-in-Chief: Hedley Donovan
Chairman of the Board: Andrew Heiskell
President: James R. Shepley

Vice Chairman: Roy E. Larsen

Managing Editor: Jerry Korn
Assistant Managing Editors: Ezra Bowen, David Maness, Martin Mann, A. B. C. Whipple
Planning Director: Oliver E. Allen
Art Director: Sheldon Cotler
Chief of Research: Beatrice T. Dobie
Director of Photography: Melvin L. Scott
Senior Text Editor: Diana Hirsh
Assistant Art Director: Arnold C. Holeywell
Assistant Chief of Research: Myra Mangan

Publisher: Joan D. Manley
General Manager: John D. McSweeney
Business Manager: Nicholas J. C. Ingleton
Sales Director: Carl G. Jaeger
Promotion Director: Paul R. Stewart
Public Relations Director: Nicholas Benton

THE OLD WEST

EDITORIAL STAFF FOR "THE FORTY-NINERS"
Editor: Ezra Bowen
Picture Editor: Grace Brynolson
Text Editor: Peter Wood
Designer: Herbert H. Quarmby
Staff Writers: David Lawton, Philip Payne, Suzanne Seixas, Bryce Walker
Chief Researcher: Joan Mebane
Researchers: Loretta Britten, Lea G. Gordon, Peggy Jackson, Mary Leverty, Mary Kay Moran, Ann Morrison, Wendy Reider, Jane Sugden
Design Assistant: Anne B. Landry

EDITORIAL PRODUCTION
Production Editor: Douglas B. Graham
Assistant Production Editors: Gennaro C. Esposito, Feliciano Madrid
Quality Director: Robert L. Young
Assistant Quality Director: James J. Cox
Copy Staff: Eleanore W. Karsten (chief), Barbara H. Fuller, Ricki Tarlow, Florence Keith, Pearl Sverdlin
Picture Department: Dolores A. Littles, Barbara S. Simon
Traffic: Carmen McLellan

©1974 Time Inc. All rights reserved.
Third printing. Reprinted 1976.
Published simultaneously in Canada.
Library of Congress catalogue card number 73-88997.

THE AUTHOR: William Weber Johnson, who wrote the text of *The Forty-niners*, lives and works as a freelance writer in Warner Springs, California—the very town where many forty-niners coming West used to stop for a meal at the Juan José Warner ranch and a dip in the hot mineral springs. The author of three previous TIME-LIFE volumes (*Mexico*, *The Andean Republics* and *Baja California*), Johnson is a native of Illinois and was a TIME-LIFE correspondent in Europe during World War II. From 1945 to 1958 he served as chief of TIME-LIFE News Bureaus in Mexico, Buenos Aires, Dallas and Boston. He was a correspondent in the Los Angeles bureau until 1961 when he began a decade as a professor in the graduate department of journalism at UCLA. During his last four years there he was department chairman and is now professor emeritus. He has been a Guggenheim Fellow and in 1969 received the gold medal of the Commonwealth Club, a San Francisco civic organization, for *Heroic Mexico*, one of 10 books he has written.

THE COVER: The forty-niners of the 1854 painting on the cover, with their gold-washing pan and pack mule, are authentic to the last detail—as well they might be. The man with the pan is the artist himself, Alburtis del Orient Browere. A self-taught New York painter, Browere twice visited California during the gold rush and portrayed the Argonauts in a series of realistic canvases. Equally authentic—despite the gaudy retouching—is the frontispiece photograph of the mustachioed miner holding an eight-pound lump of gold taken from a mine near Sierraville, California. Whoever made the photograph later tinted the anonymous Argonaut's neckerchief and then added a glowing aura to his precious trophy.

Valuable assistance was provided by the following departments and individuals of Time Inc.: Editorial Production, Norman Airey; Library, Benjamin Lightman; Picture Collection, Doris O'Neil; Photographic Laboratory, George Karas; TIME-LIFE News Service, Murray J. Gart; Correspondents Jane Estes (Seattle), Martha Green (San Francisco), Leslie Ward (Los Angeles), Sue Wymelenberg (Boston).

THE TIME-LIFE LIBRARY OF BOATING
HUMAN BEHAVIOR
THE ART OF SEWING
THE OLD WEST
THE EMERGENCE OF MAN
THE AMERICAN WILDERNESS
THE TIME-LIFE ENCYCLOPEDIA OF GARDENING
LIFE LIBRARY OF PHOTOGRAPHY
THIS FABULOUS CENTURY
FOODS OF THE WORLD
TIME-LIFE LIBRARY OF AMERICA
TIME-LIFE LIBRARY OF ART
GREAT AGES OF MAN
LIFE SCIENCE LIBRARY
THE LIFE HISTORY OF THE UNITED STATES
TIME READING PROGRAM
LIFE NATURE LIBRARY
LIFE WORLD LIBRARY
FAMILY LIBRARY:
   HOW THINGS WORK IN YOUR HOME
   THE TIME-LIFE BOOK OF THE FAMILY CAR
   THE TIME-LIFE FAMILY LEGAL GUIDE
   THE TIME-LIFE BOOK OF FAMILY FINANCE

CONTENTS

1 | Gold, gold, gold in California!
6

2 | Sailing for El Dorado
40

3 | The rough realities of grubbing for gold
72

4 | The sprouting shantytowns
114

5 | Boomtown on the Bay
154

6 | Wondrous end of a wild quest
203

Credits 234   Acknowledgments 236   Bibliography 236   Index 238

1 | Gold, gold, gold in California!

It lasted barely a decade. But the California gold rush was a grand, gaudy adventure for a generation of brash young men, most of them citizens of a brash young nation. They took their name —the forty-niners—from the year the rush began. In 1849 the East was electrified by the news that across the continent, on land newly wrested from Mexico, golden nuggets were lying around loose on the ground. Abandoning farms and apprenticeships, deserting their families and fiancées, the Argonauts swarmed West by the thousands. In California, they heard, a man could take a fortune out of the hills and streams with little more equipment than a shovel, a tin pan and a wooden, boxlike contraption called a cradle *(far right, below)*. And if he did not strike it rich in that fabulous El Dorado—and most did not—who cared? For most of the forty-niners the adventure alone was treasure enough to last a lifetime.

An idealized 1850 view of a digging records the methods miners used to wash out gold.

Typical Sunday morning activities in the diggings — a fight *(upper left)*, a horse race, a drunken spree, Bible reading beside the cabin and miners washing their clothes *(far right)* — were recalled by Charles Nahl in this scene he painted 22 years after his own arrival in California in 1850.

A toiling six-mule team hauls supplies to a mining town from Stockton. After dropping their loads of tools at the diggings, these wagons often carried quartz and other raw ore to refineries, where rockcrushers and smelters separated out the gold. The painting is by artist Eugene Camerer.

A moonlit evening at the diggings finds six miners in their cabin. While one cooks over a fire and a companion sleeps in the shadows, three others perform the night's ritual: weighing the day's take. Oblivious to it all, a sixth miner finds solace in a whiskey bottle at the end of a long day.

Having scoured the Sierra mine camps for authentic material, Alburtis Browere of Catskill, New York, then used the faces of his own family to create this sentimental depiction in 1854 of the joyful homecoming of a forty-niner.

A GOLD HUNTER ON HIS WAY TO CALIFORNIA, VIA, ST. LOUIS.

The giddy start of a grand adventure

For eons the little streams, sluggish trickles in late summer and early autumn, roiling torrents in the spring, had drained the High Sierra. Tumbling over steep scarps and rushing down the canyons, they sliced through sand and gravel and decaying rock, abrading the harder granites and quartz and carrying bits of the mountains with them into the valleys below.

At first the streams were known only to Indians. Later, Spaniards and Mexicans found them. Then came the hunters and trappers, hardy mountain men who courted loneliness, looking for beaver, muskrat and otter. The taste of the streams was sweet, particularly to desert-parched throats, and the sound of running water was loud in an otherwise hushed world.

Then, late in the fifth decade of the 19th Century, the streams were muddied and the calm shattered in one of the great mass adventures of all time, perhaps the greatest since the Crusades. The event that triggered that adventure was first reported in a four-sentence item on the inside page of an obscure California newspaper *(above)*. Several months passed before the significance of the little news story impressed itself on the world. Then hysteria radiated outward from the Sierra like waves from a deep-sea eruption. From all parts of the globe—North and South America, Europe, Asia, Australia—came all kinds of men: doctors, lawyers, preachers, ribbon clerks, farmers, mechanics, scholars, illiterates, merchants, wealthy men, ne'er-do-wells, brave men, cowards. A polyglot horde, dreamers all, hurrying toward the valleys, toward the streams and mountains of California. They were noisy, eager, impatient for the vast wealth that was there for the taking —or so they had heard.

For these streams, pouring down toward the central valleys of California, carried a precious burden of gold washed out of the granite mountains above. Some of the gold was deposited as powdery dust, some as thin flakes. Some of it had been worn and rolled to the shape of grains of wheat or melon seeds, and some took the form of heavy nuggets. Right there—in the stream beds, the gravel banks, the sandbars and ledges. Right there—in the Feather River and the Yuba and the American, in the Stanislaus, the Tuolumne, the Merced and in the smaller streams that fed them. All a man had to do was pick it up, the dreamers heard, and some came armed with nothing more than a jackknife or a horn spoon to dig the treasure out. A man would get rich in no time. Each day would bring a golden harvest, each day new wonders.

It was a great, exciting and in some ways fearful venture into the unknown, a challenge to enterprising manhood. Enos Christman, a printer's apprentice from West Chester, Pennsylvania, already seven months outward bound from Philadelphia around the Horn, wrote to Ellen Apple, his fiancée back home, that California would be "a poor place indeed to regret the undertaking. Every difficulty should be met with manly fortitude, and my intention is to meet them in such a manner that I need never be ashamed. I now boldly

---

CALIFORNIAN.

SAN FRANCISCO, WEDNESDAY, MARCH 15, 1848.

GOLD MINE FOUND.—In the newly made raceway of the Saw Mill recently erected by Captain Sutter, on the American Fork, gold has been found in considerable quantities. One person brought thirty dollars worth to New Helvetia, gathered there in a short time. California, no doubt, is rich in mineral wealth; great chances here for scientific capitalists. Gold has been found in almost every part of the country.

A contemporary caricature of a forty-niner —with cooking pot on his head, tools under his arms, pan and provisions over his shoulder, weapons in his pocket—spoofed a typical Argonaut's conglomeration of gear.

In 1849, General Bennet Riley led a survey party out of headquarters in Monterey. Their assignment was to locate a site for a fort that would ensure order in the gold-mining areas of the interior. Riley's topographical engineer made this map, which roughly indicates the party's circuitous route and the dates on which they reached the locales where mining activity was most hectic: along the Merced, Tuolumne, Stanislaus, Mokelumne and American rivers and the lower slopes of the Sierra Nevada.

turn my face toward the celebrated Sierra Nevada. What we may have to encounter I cannot anticipate; perhaps we shall have to engage with the native Indian in bloody conflict, or be hugged to death by the fierce and savage grizzly bear. But, should the worst come and I be fated to leave my bones to whiten on the bleak plains of this golden land, I can never forget you. Should you not hear from me for a long time do not despair. That happiness may be found in your footsteps is the prayer of your devoted ENOS CHRISTMAN."

Apprehension, yes, but bounding optimism, too. Some disembarked from their ships in San Francisco Bay staggering under the weight of iron strongboxes, in which they planned to put at least part of their gold. One man was more sensible. He had whiled away the monotonous months on shipboard making 15 sturdy buckskin bags that, empty, could easily be carried to what the miners called the "diggins." He calculated each would hold 20 pounds of gold; that would be 300 pounds of gold, worth about $76,000. If he found more gold than that, he would figure out something else. Some were more modest in their hopes, and above all did not want to appear foolish. One character declared himself prepared to disbelieve exaggerated stories. "If I don't pick up more than a hatful of gold a day," he allowed, "I shall be perfectly satisfied."

Illusions diminished — and discomforts increased — as they neared the diggings. Hiram Pierce of Troy, New York, a blacksmith by trade and an elder of the Second Presbyterian Church, worked his way up the American River toward Auburn and wrote: "The Senery at the river is wild in the extreme. The water appears to have forced its way through a perfect Mtn. of Granite boulders of imence Size, 20 or 50 tons. There is, I judge not more than 100 men at work in this place, averageing perhaps $10 per day. Prices high. Molasses $1 per bottle, 1½ pints. Vinegar the same. Pork $5, flour 40 cts a lb. At night the Wolves and Kiotas give us plenty of music. I would gladly warn my brethren & friends against comeing to this place of Torment. Verry much fatigued, my back getting lame in consequence of getting my feet wet & sleeping on the ground nights. A great many are laid up about us, some with sore hands & feet caused by poison & some with disentary."

But physical misery, high prices and fear are no match for gold fever. The gold seekers came, first by the doz-

John Sutter's hankering to be an Army officer was partly assuaged when he was appointed a major general in California's militia. The honorary office enabled him to wear a glittering uniform for this portrait.

ens, then by the hundreds, the thousands, the ten thousands — and they continued to come. Until 1848, California, a somnolent, Mexican frontier colony, had been thinly populated. There were a few coastal settlements where whalers and merchantmen put in for wood and water, where trading ships picked up cargoes of hides and tallow, the only exports. Other thinly populated areas surrounded the old Franciscan missions. Cattle ranches, where life was lonely and simple, dotted the interior. Then, almost overnight, all that changed.

The upheaval came to be known as the California gold rush and the participants as forty-niners, in recognition of the year the rush got underway in earnest. Actually, gold seekers had gone into the field the year before, in 1848, while latecomers continued to trickle into California all through the 1850s. The peak of the rush, in terms of mineral output and mining population, was 1852, when $81 million worth of the precious metal was taken from the California earth. By that time 100,000 miners and would-be miners were swarming through the central valleys of the newly admitted state and up the western slopes of the Sierra. Whether they arrived in '48, '49 or '52 — distinctions that those who

The adobe walls of Sutter's Fort, 18 feet high and two and a half feet thick, impressed John Hovey, a miner who did this watercolor in 1849. Within the walls were Sutter's house, barracks, a bakery, workshops, a mill and two prisons; planted outside was a splendid two-acre rose garden.

were there might make among themselves—to the outside world they were simply the forty-niners, and they were all a little crazy.

But what of the inert metal with the property to warp human reason and precipitate so extraordinary a stampede? It bears some description. Compared with more homely and practical metallic elements like iron, tin and copper, gold was relatively useless in a functional sense. Aside from false teeth, there was little in 1849 that could be made from it that would help man in the performance of his tasks. But, being rare, beautiful, easily worked by hand and highly resistant to oxidation, tarnish and decay, it has been esteemed through the ages for the measurement, storage and display of wealth. Thus, the hope of finding gold—or stealing it —has launched, since far back into antiquity, some of man's most frenzied and colorful pilgrimages and migrations, picturesque myths and bloody wars.

Gold washing is depicted on Egyptian monuments nearly 50 centuries old. Searches for the legendary gold regions of Ophir and Punt, mentioned in the Old Testament, led to many early voyages of exploration by the Greeks. The legend of the Argonauts tells about the adventures of these Greek gold seekers voyaging to the Black Sea in search of the Golden Fleece. Supposedly the fleece was the skin of a supernatural ram that carried Phrixus, cousin of the Argonaut leader, Jason, to Colchis from Thessaly. The legend probably originated in the method Armenian natives used to extract gold from their streams by trapping the particles in the fibers of sheepskins. And there were the golden sands of the River Pactolus, where, mythology reports, the Phrygians' King Midas bathed himself to get rid of the curse by which all he touched turned to gold. (The Pactolus, like the rivers draining the Sierra, probably did carry some alluvial gold.) Efforts by magicians and alchemists to convert base metals into gold and gold into an elixir of life led to the sciences of chemistry and metallurgy at about the dawn of the Christian era.

The 16th Century Spaniards' lust for the treasures of the Aztecs and Incas and their discoveries of rich mines of gold, silver and mercury helped speed the exploration and settlement of the New World.

These same Spaniards believed there was abundant gold on a mythical island situated "on the right hand of the Indies." In fact, the island was the invention of a medieval romancer, Garcí Ordóñez de Montalvo, who peopled the place "with black women without any men. Their arms were all of gold, and so were the caparisons of the wild beasts which they rode after having tamed them; for in all the island there is no other metal." Montalvo gave the name Calafía to the Amazon Queen and called her kingdom California.

The Spaniards were very susceptible to tales of women without men and islands full of gold; and in dispatches to the King, Cortez used the name California when referring vaguely to the northwesternmost part of the New World. And so the name California was linked to gold even before the first explorers arrived.

Cabeza de Vaca, a 16th Century Spanish colonial official and also a notorious liar, told of great wealth in the region, while the more reliable Sebastian Vizcaino, who arrived from Spain a century later, merely reported rumors of gold. After Sir Francis Drake touched the California coast in 1579, his chaplain, Francis Fletcher, who kept a diary of the voyage, described the country as seeming "to promise rich veins of gold and silver."

But, rapacious as the Spaniards were for gold — and expert as they usually were at finding it in faraway places — they never prospected in California. After Mexico (including California) won independence from Spain in 1821, California remained a remote and neglected province. Even the discovery of a modest deposit of alluvial, or, as it was commonly called, placer gold, just north of Los Angeles in 1842 did not alter the central government's indifference to this isolated part of the re-

The discovery that triggered California's gold rush was tersely noted by Sutter's mill hand Henry Bigler in a diary entry for January 24. In the preceding entry, he wrote more fully of the crew's feud with a cook.

public. Gold, silver and copper mines of proven wealth already were producing satisfactorily in the districts of Sonora and Guanajuato and other parts of New Spain, so why bother to develop a new and questionable find? This indifference contributed to the ease with which Mexico ceded California to the United States by the treaty of Guadalupe Hidalgo in 1848. And, ironically, the gold rush started immediately thereafter.

The stampede into California in 1849 could not have been better timed. The national economy, depressed since the end of the Mexican War, badly needed a jolt. Then, at exactly the right moment, thousands of Americans flooded into the Pacific wilderness, adding millions of dollars in gold to the national income and helping to ensure the manifest destiny of the young, expansionist nation. But the gold rush was not planned as a national boon. Ironically, its origin lay in the boundless ambition of a German-born Swiss, John Augustus Sutter, whose dreams of a personal empire bore no relation to the vision of America's founding fathers.

An amiable, gregarious man, Sutter was a bankrupt merchant who had fled Germany to escape his creditors. He had crossed the Atlantic in 1834 at the age of 32. After much restless wandering back and forth in the New World — and one more bankruptcy — he arrived in California in 1839 by way of the Hawaiian Islands.

Using letters of introduction from the commander of the Hudson's Bay Company's headquarters of Fort

Vancouver and from the American consul in Honolulu, plus his considerable charm and infectious enthusiasm, Sutter persuaded the Mexican governor of California, Juan Bautista Alvarado, to award him a grant of some 50,000 acres of land. To qualify, Sutter became a Mexican citizen. The grant lay in the marvelously fertile but little-populated central valley east of San Francisco Bay, at the confluence of the Sacramento and American rivers. Here Sutter built a stockade and fort, and was known as Captain Sutter, a rank he had bestowed upon himself for imaginary service in the Swiss Guard of Charles X of France. His riverbank establishment he called New Helvetia—although everyone else called it Sutter's Fort.

Most of the workers on the large farming-ranching-mercantile empire he built were Indian. By local standards Sutter was good to his Indian workers, cordial with the few Mexican ranchers in the region, extraordinarily kind to his riding mule, Katy, and magnanimously hospitable to travelers in that part of the world—particularly to American overland immigrants who naturally gravitated to his fort after making the final grueling march across the Sierra. He was, in fact, unusually well thought of by practically everyone except his creditors (the Russians sold him the fur-trading outpost they had established at Fort Ross, but were never able to collect more than a fraction of the sum agreed upon). His multiple ventures appeared to prosper, but he was almost constantly and disastrously in debt.

Sutter needed a sawmill to provide lumber for his many projects. In 1847 he took into partnership James Wilson Marshall, a 35-year-old carpenter and Jack-of-all-trades who had come to California from New Jersey by way of Oregon. Marshall was a gentle man, able enough, but given to fits of gloom. Sutter thought him to be somewhat strange. Marshall found a promising location on the south fork of the American River, 50 miles northeast of Sutter's Fort. Here there were good stands of pine and plenty of water to drive a mill. The land belonged to no one, for the rights of the Coloma Indians were ignored.

For labor, Marshall took with him 10 of Sutter's domesticated Indians. He also hired 10 Americans, six of them veterans of the Mormon Battalion that had gone West to fight Mexicans but, arriving too late, had been disbanded in California. Timber was cut for cabins

James W. Marshall was born to failure. He lost a homestead in Kansas through illness; another in California was ransacked. And though he found the gold at Sutter's Mill, he never made a dollar in the diggings.

and the mill, and a race was laid out to carry water over the mill wheel. Once the millrace had been dug, the river was periodically turned into it by opening wooden sluice gates so that the current would widen and deepen the channel. A delta of mud, sand and gravel accumulated at the lower end of the race.

Marshall was in the habit of inspecting the watercourse each morning to see how much the current had accomplished during the night. On Monday, January 24, 1848, Marshall was making his daily inspection. "I went down as usual," he recalled, "and after shutting off the water from the race I stepped into it, near the lower end, and there upon the rock about six inches beneath the water I discovered the gold. I picked up one or two pieces and examined them attentively. I then tried it between two rocks and found that it could be beaten into a different shape but not broken."

Henry Bigler, one of the Mormon veterans on the mill job, made a succinct note in his diary: "Monday 24th this day some kind of mettle was found in the tail race that looks like goald first discovered by James Martial the Boss of the Mill."

"Martial" made no secret of his belief that the mysterious substance was gold. A piece was pounded on an anvil. It flattened out (iron pyrites, or fool's gold, would have shattered). Mrs. Jenny Wimmer, a bossy woman who cooked for the mill crew, put a piece of

23

A rare lithograph, copied from an 1850 painting by William S. Jewett, shows Coloma, a town that was to burgeon around Sutter's sawmill on the American River. It became home to 10,000 miners, then by 1870, as the diggings gave out, dwindled to a hamlet of 200. Jewett, a forty-niner, struck it rich as California's first portrait artist.

the metal in her soap kettle and boiled it with lye and baking soda. The metal was unchanged.

On the 28th, Marshall saddled his horse and set off for Sutter's Fort, where he arrived in a rainstorm. He sought out Sutter and conspiratorially insisted that they lock themselves in a room. "He was a singular man," Sutter later recalled, "and I took this to be some freak of his. I only supposed, as he was queer, that he took this queer way to tell me some secret."

Marshall unrolled a piece of cotton cloth and showed Sutter what he had found. They consulted an encyclopedia to ascertain the qualities and properties of gold. Sutter fetched some aqua fortis (nitric acid) from the fort's apothecary stores, treated the metal with the acid and found it had no effect. The men then placed some silver in one tray of an apothecary scale and an equal weight of the yellow metal in the other tray. When the trays balanced, they submerged them in two bowls of water. The yellow metal, being more dense, sank. Sutter was convinced and promised to visit the mill and inspect the phenomenon firsthand.

When Sutter, accompanied by two Indians, set out several days later for the sawmill, he was outwardly the same optimistic, expansive man he had always seemed to be. He sat his mule proudly, carried his walking stick under one arm and carried gifts of jackknives for the mill hands and a jug of *aguardiente,* the fiery brandy that he distilled from grapes at the fort and often shared with his workers. He was a man of grand manners and great property. His fortunes seemed powerfully on the rise. He had his fort and his stores. He had hundreds of acres under cultivation and expected a harvest of 40,000 bushels of wheat in the coming season. He had 12,000 head of cattle, 2,000 horses and mules, 10,000 sheep, 1,000 hogs. His Indian field hands were so numerous that he had to slaughter four or five steers a day to feed them.

But inwardly Sutter was troubled—or so he would claim in the bitter years to come. The Indians had told him that gold was bad medicine; it belonged to a jealous demon who lived in a mountain lake with gold-lined shores. This, he told himself, was superstition. Nonetheless, he was to recall that, on the night before he started for the sawmill, "the curse of the thing burst upon my mind. I saw from the beginning how the end would be, and I had a melancholy ride of it to the sawmill. Of course I knew nothing of the extent of the discovery, but I was satisfied, whether it amounted to much or little, that it would greatly interfere with my plans." A gold rush would prove an irresistible lure to the many workers he needed to man his vast operations. Outsiders would trample his fields, violate his property, destroy his stock, make it impossible for him to complete his ambitious undertakings.

These forebodings, as Sutter would find, erred only in being too mild. Had the captain known the true impact the discovery would have on his dream of a pastoral empire, he might well have turned Katy around then and there, and sold out to the first bidder. Still, when he arrived at the mill Sutter wore his usual air of affability and confidence.

The mill hands, at Marshall's suggestion, had pooled the particles of gold they managed to pick up. The gold had been given to Bigler who then scattered pieces along the millrace so that "Old Cap" (Sutter was then 45) could find some gold for himself. It would not be many years before the practice of baiting mineral deposits to attract investors would become commonplace in California, but this was the state's first recorded case of salting a mine. By this stratagem, Marshall hoped so to please Sutter that he would share with all hands the jug of *aguardiente,* which he usually carried.

But before Sutter and Marshall could reach the millrace one of Mrs. Wimmer's sons had been there, seen the gold, gathered it and had run back shouting joyously. Sutter examined the boy's find, pounded the ground with his walking stick and said, "By Jo, it is rich!" Later he picked up some of the pieces the boy had missed. The *aguardiente* presumably was shared, and Sutter asked the mill hands to keep the secret to themselves, at least until he could deal with the obvious problem that presented itself.

Sutter and Marshall had no formal title to the real estate their mill sat on. So far as they knew, the gold-rich land all around them was public domain and, with the outcome of the Mexican War still unknown in California, no competent authority existed to decree otherwise. In that vacuum Sutter did the only thing he could think of. He summoned the local Indians and, in exchange for an assortment of clothing and food, he negotiated a lease of the mill land and surrounding area,

In 1852 a photographer posed James Marshall at the Coloma sawmill he built for Sutter. By then, thousands of miners—but neither Marshall nor Sutter—had profited from Marshall's gold strike in the millrace.

about a dozen square miles, for a period of three years.

Henry Bigler, the diary keeper and gold salter, made another entry the following Sunday: "Sunday 30th clear. Our metal has been tride and proves to be goald it is thought to be rich we have pict up more than a hundred dollars woth last week."

Bigler, in addition to being the most faithful and reliable chronicler of the event, was also the first prospector, the first man to go out deliberately searching for more gold. He was, he admitted, the only one of the sawmill crew to be seriously afflicted with gold fever. On Sundays and at every other opportunity, he went off looking for gold, not in the millrace but in other streams, gullies, ravines and sandbars in the area. On Sunday, February 6, he and James Barger, another of the Mormon crew, crossed the river and dug in rock crevices with jackknives Sutter had given them, picking the gold out speck by speck. By nightfall they had collected $10 worth. They made themselves a simple wooden scale to measure their take. In one pan they would put a Mexican *real,* or bit, as it was known locally, a silver coin worth 12½ American pennies. At the ratio of 16 to 1, which was the going differential in price between the two metals, gold dust enough to balance the real was worth two dollars.

More and more often Bigler went off by himself, saying he was going to hunt for deer or ducks. Instead he sought out new gold locations. Picking and scratching

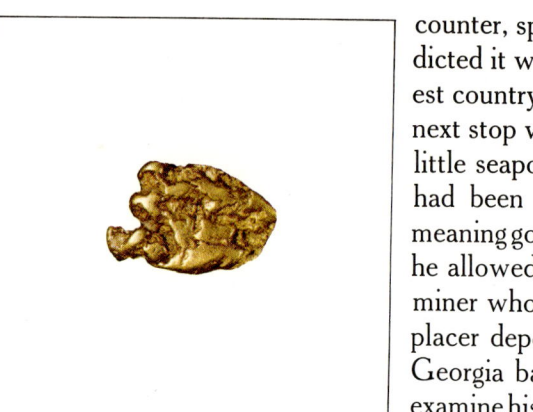

Among the bits of metal James Marshall found in Sutter's millrace was this quarter-ounce nugget, shown full size. The nugget survived a day's boiling in a kettle of lye, a test that convinced Marshall it was gold.

among the rocks with his knife, he would collect anywhere from a few dollars' worth in a day's work to an ounce and a half of gold ($24).

Bigler also let out the secret. He wrote about the discovery to other Mormons—buddies of his in the Mormon Battalion—who were working on the new gristmill Sutter was building on the American River, near the Indian village of Natoma, a few miles from his fort. It was for completion of this gristmill, among other projects, that Sutter needed lumber from the sawmill. Sutter hoped that the gristmill would in time grind all the grain that could be produced both by his own farmhands and by the emigrants who would soon be pouring into the Sacramento valley. It never did because the mill was never finished. One of the reasons it remained unfinished was the word of gold that Bigler had passed to his friends.

But this was not the only leak. When Jacob Wittmer, a Swiss-born teamster in Sutter's employ, carried a load of supplies from the fort to the sawmill on February 11, another of Mrs. Wimmer's children showed him some particles of gold he had found in the millrace. Wittmer scoffed at the child, but the strong-minded Mrs. Wimmer came to her offspring's defense. Insisting that it was indeed gold, she gave some to Wittmer, and on his return to Sutter's Fort, he tested the metal by offering it in payment for a bottle of liquor. Sutter himself was consulted as to the value of the strange material. In his usual forthright manner, the captain confirmed that it was gold—and his secret was broken again.

Anticipating the ceding of California to the U.S., Sutter dispatched one of his employees with a message to Colonel R. B. Mason in the provincial capital at Monterey, asking Mason, the new military governor of California, to confirm the lease he had negotiated with the Indians for the land around the mill. The messenger, one Charles Bennett, carried with him in a buckskin bag six ounces of gold dust that he had collected in his spare time. En route Bennett stopped at Ed Pfister's store in Benicia. Some hangers-on were discussing a deposit of coal that was thought to exist nearby. Bennett laughed at their interest in such base material as coal. He poured the contents of his buckskin bag on the counter, spread out the gold and predicted it would "make this the greatest country in the world." Bennett's next stop was San Francisco, a quiet little seaport that only a year earlier had been known as Yerba Buena, meaning good herb in Spanish. There he allowed Isaac Humphrey, an old miner who had dug gold in the rich placer deposits in his home state of Georgia back during the 1830s, to examine his secret bag. The Georgian said that the bright yellow powder was indeed gold.

Finally reaching Monterey, Bennett approached Colonel Mason about approving Sutter's lease. Mason declared that "the United States does not recognize the right of Indians to sell or lease lands." Bennett consoled himself for the failure of his mission by displaying his buckskin bag of gold and talking of it freely.

Sutter himself, as mercurial as he was good natured, lacked the very caution he had urged upon his employees. He bragged about the gold discovery in a February 10 letter to General Mariano Vallejo, a prominent member of the Mexican community. With the grace for which his people were noted Vallejo commented: "As the water flows through Sutter's millrace, may the gold flow into Sutter's purse."

Within a month of the discovery, the news of the gold find at Sutter's sawmill had captured the local imagination. Within six weeks, Sutter reported that all of his staff, laborers and bosses alike, had deserted his stores, his farms and ranches, and headed for the gold fields, leaving behind only the ailing and the lame.

But, while knowledge of the gold spread quickly, gold fever was surprisingly slow to develop except in the immediate vicinity of the mill and the fort. Reports of Sutter's gold circulated freely in San Francisco and other California cities but little attention was paid to them. The prevailing attitude seemed to be: "I'll believe it when I see it."

And it was right there that Sam Brannan, a burly, loud-mouthed man, stepped in to become the key figure in all the excitement that was to follow. Brannan was a Mormon elder, and even before the gold hysteria he had never been an obscure or retiring sort. At the very time that the U.S. was in the act of wresting California from the Mexicans, he had conducted a shipload of 238 migrating Mormons around Cape Horn and up to Yerba Buena. Their arrival increased the population of that modest little settlement by about sixfold. Brannan preached the first English-language sermon there, performed the first white marriage ceremony and was the defendant in one of the earliest jury trials (some of his recent shipmates had accused him of misuse of church funds; the jury was unable to reach a verdict). He was also the founder of San Francisco's first newspaper, the *California Star,* having brought around the Horn a printing press as well as other useful equipment and salable merchandise. And above all, he was among the first of a long line of California boosters. He had been disappointed, in July 1846, when his ship, the *Brooklyn,* sailed through the Golden Gate, to see that the American flag already floated over the old customs house. Captain John B. Montgomery and the crew of the U.S. sloop *Portsmouth* had raised it upon receiving dispatches that war had been declared with Mexico. Sam Brannan was an empire builder at heart and had counted on raising the flag himself.

But Brannan forgot his disappointment in great surges of enthusiasm for his new-found home and its predictable future as a metropolis of the West. He made an arduous trip inland to eastern Utah to meet the Mormons who were migrating overland under the leadership of Brigham Young. Having been hounded off their farms in Caldwell County, Missouri, the Mormons were in search of a home free from persecution, and Brannan tried to persuade Young that California would be just such a spot. He marched west with his coreligionists and was bitterly disappointed when Young, catching his first glimpse of the Great Salt Lake Valley, declared firmly, "This is the place." Brannan and Young never were reconciled, and Brannan was later excommunicated by the Church of Jesus Christ of Latter-day Saints. But not before Young tried, unsuccessfully, to recover from him the tithes Brannan continued to collect from the Mormon faithful in California. It was, Young reminded Brannan, the Lord's money. To this Brannan is said to have replied, "I'll give up the Lord's money when he [Young] sends me a receipt signed by the Lord, and no sooner."

On his return from Utah, Brannan had stopped at Sutter's Fort and, in partnership with C. C. Smith, a trader from San Francisco, rented space in which to set up a store inside the massive adobe walls. One asset of this new business was a contract to furnish supplies to the sawmill Sutter was building on the south fork of the American River and to the gristmill at Natoma. Another asset, unrealized at the outset, was that his operations at the fort put Brannan in an excellent position to garner firsthand information on the feverish events that were to follow. It was at Brannan's store that Jacob Wittmer, the teamster, presented gold dust in payment for a bottle of liquor.

But, although Brannan had early indications of the gold strike, the editor of his own newspaper, the *Star,* tended to ignore the scattered reports. A rival paper, the *Californian,* which had recently been moved from Monterey to San Francisco, was the first in the whole country to acknowledge the strike in print *(page 17).* On March 15, 1848, the *Californian* reported: "GOLD MINE FOUND—In the newly made raceway of the saw-mill recently erected by Captain Sutter, on the American fork, gold has been found in considerable quantities. One person brought thirty dollarsworth to New Helvetia, gathered there in a short time. California, no doubt, is rich." But, while the *Californian* scooped the world on what turned out to be one of the biggest news stories of the age, it gave a more prominent position in the paper to a discussion of the slavery issue in California.

Young Edward C. Kemble, then only 20 years old, who edited the *Star,* resorted to the journalistic tactic of first ignoring and later ridiculing a rival's story. When he did finally take note of the news of gold he declared it was "all sham—a superb take-in as was ever got up to guzzle the gullible."

In mid-April, Kemble and two other San Franciscans, George McKinstry and P. B. Reading, both of whom had formerly worked for Sutter, decided to go see for themselves. They cruised up the Sacramento River to Sutter's Fort and from there rode overland to Sutter's Mill, accompanied by Sutter himself astride his saddle mule, Katy. At the mill both James Marshall and the Mormon crew, still mindful of Sutter's desire for secrecy, were somewhat closemouthed. The investigators looked for gold and found very little. They were not impressed and soon left. When Kemble wrote about the trip in his paper on May 6, he dwelt on the

When French-born Victor Prevost painted 13-year-old Yerba Buena in 1847, U.S. settlers were already trickling into the port. That year the newcomers founded a newspaper and changed the town's name to San Francisco—but the metropolis-to-be still had only 300 inhabitants.

beauty of the trees, flowers and streams, but he said very little about gold.

But in the same week that this issue of the *Star* appeared on the streets of San Francisco, so did Sam Brannan, also just returned from a visit to the gold region. His clothes were travel-soiled and his mane of black hair was unruly. But he rushed through the streets waving a quinine bottle full of gold dust and shouting in his bull voice, "Gold! Gold! Gold from the American River!" Brannan, ever the consummate businessman, was drumming up trade for a brand-new store, built right next to the sawmill on the south fork of the American River and stocked with an ample supply of picks, shovels and pans.

Brannan's voice was authoritative, his enthusiasm contagious and his tactic faultless. So, finally, four months after the discovery at Sutter's sawmill, San Franciscans saw for themselves, and gold fever at last infected their drowsy little port. The outbreak was moderate only in comparison with the epidemic that came later. At the time it seemed cataclysmic. Workmen put aside—or simply dropped—their tools. Stores and shops closed. Houses were locked, fields deserted—as everyone took off in search of gold. Within a fortnight San Francisco's population dropped from several hundred to a dozen or so (though it would shortly soar into the thousands). The *Californian,* faced with loss of readers, advertisers and staff, ceased publication with a sad note: "The whole country resounds with the sordid cry of gold! GOLD! GOLD!!! while the field is left half-planted, the house half built and everything neglected but the manufacturers of shovels and pickaxes."

Sam Brannan's *Star* noted its rival's demise: "Gone to ———. The *Californian* ceased issue Tuesday last. Verdict of inquest—fever." And then shortly afterward, the *Star* also suspended; "We appear before the remnant of the reading public with the information that we have stopped the paper—that its publication ceased with the last regular issue. We have done."

Editor Kemble, who had scoffed at reports of gold, now decided that he had better go, too. On his way he stopped at a hardware store. The owner had gone gold hunting, but his wife was there. Kemble said he had heard that an iron pan was useful in finding gold and he would like to buy one. The woman said she did not have a single one, nor was any to be found in San Francisco. Why? Simply because Sam Brannan had bought them all. The iron pans, originally priced at about 20 cents, were selling at Brannan's new store and in the gold fields for as much as a half ounce to an ounce of gold apiece—or, from eight dollars to $16.

There probably were no more than a few hundred gold seekers in the fields in May. By midsummer there were about 4,000. And by the year's end there were between 8,000 and 10,000. Sutter's Swiss gardener wrote: "Exciting rumors began to spread with the rapidity of a great epidemic. Everyone was infected, and, as it spread, peace and quiet vanished. To all appearances men seemed to have gone insane, or to have suddenly lost some of their five senses; they were, apparently, living in a dream. Each man had to stop and ask himself: 'Am I mad? Is this all real? Is what I see with my own eyes actually gold, or is it merely my imagination? Is it a Chimera? Am I delirious?'"

One San Franciscan described a friend who had returned from the gold fields with so much treasure that he "became crazy and now goes about crying 'I am rich! I am rich!'" Army Captain Joseph L. Folsom wrote to a colleague, future Civil War General William Tecumseh Sherman, who had been stationed in Monterey, that he expected soon to be the last person left in San Francisco, and that "only lunatic asylums can effect a cure of the present ills of the body politic—at least until hunger drives all the visionary fools from the gold 'diggins.'"

Something like a quarter of a million dollars in gold was taken from the rich California earth in 1848. Most of it, carried in bottles, tins, buckskin bags, even old shoes, found its way to San Francisco, and much of it was shipped out. Since the gold-carrying ships stopped at various points—Hawaii, Mexico, Peru, Chile—knowledge of California gold was at first more widely disseminated abroad than among the new proprietors of California, the people of the United States. And there was a quick response.

Experienced miners in South America began looking for ships to carry them north. Natives and foreign-born residents of the Hawaiian Islands crowded every ship bound for San Francisco. In addition to these Argonauts from overseas, thousands of Mexicans headed for California, either trekking overland from the mining state of Sonora or sailing from the west coast port of Mazatlan.●

A deserter heads for the diggings in an engraving from *Three Years in California,* an 1850 book by Walter Colton, a magistrate of Monterey.

A lopsided struggle between duty and the lure of the diggings

In the early days of the gold rush, soldiers in towns like Monterey and San Francisco felt doubly aggrieved. Victors in the Mexican War (though few actually had seen combat), they were pulling garrison duty while civilians got rich overnight in nearby diggings. Worse yet, by mid-1848 a rocketing local inflation had made a private's pay, six dollars a month, worth about three pounds of flour.

"No time in the history of our country has presented such temptations to desert," wrote California's acting governor, Colonel R. B. Mason, to the War Department. His soldiers agreed. "The struggle between *right* and six dollars a month," said one, "and *wrong* and $75 a day is rather a severe one."

A soldier who lost the struggle wrote: "A frenzy seized my soul; piles of gold rose up before me at every step; thousands of slaves bowed to my beck and call; myriads of fair virgins contended for my love. In short I had a violent attack of gold fever."

Whole platoons deserted with their arms and horses. In the 18 months beginning July 1, 1848, the Army in northern California lost 716 men of a total 1,290. So many sailors jumped ship that the Pacific Squadron's commander, Thomas Ap Catesby Jones, advised the Secretary of the Navy: "for the present and I fear for years to come, it will be impossible for the United States to maintain any naval establishment in California."

Army Lieutenant William Tecumseh Sherman complained: "None remain behind but we poor devils of officers who are restrained by honor." He worked as a surveyor to make ends meet. He also zealously pursued deserters, once capturing 27 of a band of 28—18 of them at one swoop when he stormed alone into a cabin with a cocked musket.

But most got away. "Others were sent to force them back to duty," wrote historian Zoeth Skinner Eldredge, "and all, pursuers and pursued, went to the mines together."

33

POSITIONS
of the
Upper and Lower Gold Mines
on the
South Fork of the American River,
CALIFORNIA.

July 20th, 1848

After a June 1848 tour of the first gold fields, Colonel R. B. Mason, military governor of California, sent a report to Washington, along with some gold samples and a map showing Sutter's Fort and the area where James Marshall found gold. President James K. Polk included the map in a message to Congress officially confirming the discovery.

An 1849 *History of an Expedition to California* spoofs the hopes and despairs of a forty-niner. In succeeding pages of the cartoon *History,* hero Swapwell goes West, fails as a gold miner but prospers as a grocer and finally comes home to settle down.

| The first discovery of Gold at Suter's Mill. | The report reaches San Francisco. The inhabitants are much moved thereat. | The sailors desert the vessels in the harbor. |

In the U.S. perhaps as many as 3,000 men from Oregon Territory had started south before the end of 1848—many of whom had earlier refused military service because they did not want to leave their wives and children alone in the wilderness. Mormons, some of them veterans of the Mormon Battalion and some discontented members of Sam Brannan's California colony, arrived in Salt Lake City bearing shining specimens of California gold. That set off still another migration for many of the far-traveling Latter-day Saints. A Mormon elder noted: "Many have become weak in the faith, choosing the things of this world and are starting to the gold mines."

The *New York Herald,* on August 19, carried a letter from a New York soldier serving in California. He reported that gold had been found in a tributary of the Sacramento River and predicted for California a "Peruvian harvest" of the sort the conquistadors had found in the Andes. Other newspapers began to pick up odd, inclusive stories about gold in California.

Thomas O. Larkin, who had been U.S. consul in Mexican California and was now U.S. Naval agent in Monterey, kept the State Department advised as well as he could as to what was going on. He sent letters on June 1 and 28 with considerable information regarding gold: "I have to report one of the most astonishing excitements and state of affairs. There has been discovered a placer, a vast tract of land containing gold, in small particles. This gold, thus far, has been taken on the bank of the river, from the surface to eighteen inches in depth, and is supposed deeper, and to extend over the country. It is now two or three weeks since the men employed in these washings have appeared in this town with their gold, to exchange for merchandise and provisions. I presume nearly twenty thousand dollars of this gold has been so exchanged. I have seen the written statement of the work of one man for sixteen days, which averaged twenty-five dollars per day; others have with shovel and pan, or wooden bowl, washed out ten to even fifty dollars a day."

Larkin's first letter reached Washington in September, carried by Lieutenant Edward F. Beale, USN. Beale also bore a dispatch from Commodore Jones, commander of the Pacific Naval Squadron, giving more details about California gold. There was a renewed flurry of stories in newspapers, but they did not yet attract widespread attention. It remained for another official reporter to cause a real stir back in the States.

The reporter was Colonel Mason, Governor of the newly acquired territory and the man who had ruled

| The news reaches New York. | And creates an excitement. | Jonathan Swapwell, of Swapville, hears the news, and resolves to go to California. | Having taken leave of his mother, Deacon Twist advises him to remain, as the report is a snare of the devil. |

Sutter's lease of Indian land invalid. In June 1848, Mason, accompanied by Lieutenant William Tecumseh Sherman, went on a tour of the gold fields. Ascending the Sacramento valley, he found farmhouses vacant, mills idle, fields abandoned, livestock wandering loose. He paused at Sutter's Fort long enough to observe Independence Day, and then proceeded up the American River to the lower mines, or Mormon Diggings, where Bigler's buddies had commenced operations. Several hundred men were hard at work with pans, tightly woven Indian baskets (which could be used like pans to separate gold from gravel) and improvised gold-washing machines called rockers, or cradles. Mason visited Sutter's sawmill — now in operation — and heard stories of Marshall's discovery. He ascended Weber's creek and saw one ravine which had yielded $17,000 in gold in a week and another which had produced $12,000. He was told that most of the men were averaging about two ounces per day. He learned about diggings elsewhere, on the Feather, Yuba and Bear rivers to the north of the American, on the Cosumnes to the south.

Colonel Mason estimated that "upwards of four thousand men were working in the gold district, and that from $30,000 to $50,000 worth of gold, if not more, was daily obtained." One company worked seven weeks on the Feather and produced 273 pounds of gold (worth almost $70,000) and, Mason added, "I see no laboring man from the mines who does not show his two, three, or four pounds of gold."

Mason also noted that the principal store at Sutter's Fort, owned by "Brannant & Co." (i.e., Sam Brannan and C. C. Smith) "had received in payment for goods $36,000 worth of this gold from the 1st of May to the 10th of July." And, while nearly everyone else was out looking for gold, Captain Sutter was not. Instead, he was "carefully gathering his wheat, estimated at 40,000 bushels. Flour is already worth at Sutter's $36 a barrel, and soon will be fifty."

The colonel was also aware that California and its mining region constituted a political anomaly. "The entire gold district, with very few exceptions is on land belonging to the United States. It was a matter of serious reflection with me how I could secure to the government certain rents or fees for the privilege of procuring this gold; but upon considering the extent of the country, the character of the people engaged, and the small force at my command, I resolved not to interfere, but permit all to work freely, unless broils and crimes should call for interference. I was surprised to learn that crime of any kind was very unfrequent, and that no thefts or

A Hartford *Courant* article, printed the day after Polk's 1848 message to Congress, shows how the Presidential revelations turned widespread skepticism about the tall tales from California into all-out credence.

HARTFORD DAILY COURANT

WEDNESDAY MORNING, DECEMBER 6.

The Gold Fever.

The California gold fever is approaching its crisis. We are told that the new region that has just become a part of our possessions, is El Dorado after all.—Thither is now setting a tide that will not cease its flow until either untold wealth is amassed, or extended beggary is secured. By a sudden and accidental discovery, the ground is represented to be one vast gold mine.—Gold is picked up in pure lumps, twenty-four carats fine. Soldiers are deserting their ranks, sailors their ships, and every body their employment, to speed to the region of the gold mines. In a moment, as it were, a desert country, that never deserved much notice from the world, has become the centre of universal attraction. Every body, by the accounts, is getting money at a rate that puts all past experience in that line far in the shade. The stories are evidently thickening in interest, as do the arithmetical calculations connected with them in importance. Fifteen millions have already come into the possession of *somebody*, and all creation is going out there to fill their pockets with the great condiment of their diseased minds.

robberies had been committed. All live in tents, in bush houses, or in the open air, and men have frequently about their persons thousands of dollars-worth of this gold; and it was to me a matter of surprise that so peaceful and quiet a state of things should exist. Conflicting claims to particular spots of ground may cause collisions, but they will be rare, as the extent of the country is so great, and the gold so abundant, that for the present there is room and enough for all."

Mason acknowledged that many letters had been sent East describing the vast wealth to be had in California. "It may be a matter of surprise why I have made no report on this subject at an earlier date. The reason is that I could not bring myself to believe the reports I heard of the wealth of the gold district until I visited it myself. I have no hesitation now in saying there is more gold in the country drained by the Sacramento and San Joaquin rivers than will pay the cost of the war with Mexico a hundred times over."

Colonel Mason completed his report in Monterey on August 17. During his trip he had bought samples of gold weighing 230 ounces, 15 pennyweights and nine grains—$3,900 worth according to the assay of the U.S. Mint in Philadelphia. The collection was carefully packed in a tea caddy. The tea caddy and one copy of Mason's report were entrusted to Lieutenant Lucien Loeser for delivery to Washington.

Loeser sailed from Monterey on the schooner *Lambayecana* to Payta, Peru, and from there to Panama on a British steamer. He crossed the Isthmus and shipped again, this time to New Orleans. From there he telegraphed a report to Washington and then proceeded by stagecoach to the capital, always conscious of the contents of Colonel Mason's precious tea caddy.

The Mason report provided welcome substance for President James Knox Polk's opening message to the second session of the 30th Congress, December 5, 1848. Polk had overseen a period of almost explosive expansion of the boundaries of the United States. The growth was hard to translate into terms comprehensible to a public that had no very clear idea of geography and that had considered the recent war with Mexico both useless and a shameful drain on the federal treasury. In his message Polk said that at the time of California's acquisition it was known that "mines of the precious metals existed to a considerable extent. Recent discoveries render it probable that these mines are more extensive and valuable than was anticipated." And then he added, "The accounts of the abundance of gold in that territory are of such an extraordinary character as would scarcely command belief were they not corroborated by authentic reports."

The $3,900 worth of gold from Colonel Mason's tea caddy was put on display in the War Department. The presence of California gold in the national capital, the Presidential message and the details from Colonel Mason's report made headline news around the world.

Gold fever, until now only a local outbreak in a remote and almost-unheard-of place, all at once became an international epidemic. California, the United States and the world would never be quite the same again.

Gold fever fills a Long Island, New York, post office in William Mount's 1850 painting *California News*. Amid ship-sailing notices, the artist *(right foreground)* and friends read reports from the gold fields.

2 | Sailing for El Dorado

Fortunes in gold lay waiting to be picked up in California—but a man had to get there first. Some gold seekers simply hitched up their farm wagons and started walking west. Others traveled over faster, but more complicated routes across Mexico or the Isthmus of Panama. But most of the forty-niners who lived along the Eastern Seaboard made a 13,000-mile voyage all the way around the coast of South America. In the month of February 1849 alone, over 50 ships—sleek clippers, reconditioned hulks, even coastal freighters—left New York Harbor for the gold fields. Among them was the little steam packet *Hartford (below)*. A dangerously small ship for the trip around the Horn, she made it after a harrowing voyage that took almost 12 months.

Argonauts jam the rail of the steam-sailer *Hartford* as she departs for the gold fields.

The long trail to the mother lode

William Downie, 30, who had knocked around the world as seaman, trader and lumber dealer since leaving his boyhood home in Scotland, was staying in the Lovejoy House in Buffalo, New York, when he was struck by gold fever. Everyone, he would recall later, caught the contagion: "I among the rest. Some of the tales were fabulous, and the reports of treasures found were enough to entice any man of grit and daring to challenge fortune. Many, even, who had neither quality, ventured upon the search for gold, prompted merely by the lust for gain, and the hope of escaping the yolk of poverty and the discomfort of narrow circumstances."

President Polk's message in December confirming the California gold strike galvanized the nation as no official utterance had since the Declaration of Independence. By early 1849 gold fever was raging all along the Atlantic seaboard, through the South and across the broad Mississippi valley—the areas that contained most of the nation's 22 million people. Men sold their businesses and farms and quit their jobs. They borrowed money, pawned their belongings, studied maps and, as soon as they could, took off by sea and by land, glowing with optimism but also anxious lest they be too late. They were the forty-niners.

Only a few months before, many of them had regarded the reports of California gold with skepticism.

Anxious to set off for the diggings, a pair of amply equipped Pennsylvania lads show off their travel togs before embarking on the voyage around Cape Horn. Their impressive weaponry had a real purpose: to protect the claim they expected to find.

Whatever it was that had been found there, it wasn't gold. Mica, maybe. Or perhaps the whole thing was just a real-estate promotion for the vast lands that had been acquired from Mexico. It was, they said, humbug, or, alternately, moonshine. But, just as the man who soberly resists buying an ounce of magic snake oil may, in the end, buy a gallon of the stuff and worry later about exhaustion of the supply, they changed—almost overnight. Doubters became believers in infinite riches and instant wealth. Journalists, preachers, lecturers, publishers, song writers and entertainers: all fanned the flames.

News editor Horace Greeley, soon to become a passionate advocate of the westward movement, was deeply stirred by the excitement in California. "We are on the brink of the Age of Gold," his *New York Daily Tribune* thundered on December 9, 1848. "We look for an addition within the next four years equal to at least One Thousand Million of Dollars to the general aggregate of gold in circulation."

Two days later Greeley was at it again: "We are all fairly afloat. We don't see any links of probability missing in the golden chain by which Hope is drawing her thousands of disciples to the new El Dorado, where fortune lies abroad upon the surface of the earth as plentiful as the mud in our streets, and where the old saying 'a pocket full of rocks' meets a golden realization. The perilous stuff lies loose upon the surface of the ground, or only slightly adheres to rocks and sand. The only machinery necessary in the new Gold mines of California is a stout pair of arms, a shovel and a tin pan. Indeed many, unable even to obtain these utensils, are fain to put up with a shingle or a bit of board, and dig away quietly in peace of mind,

The long trip to the distant mine fields stimulated some outlandish suggestions for speedy ways of getting there. Here a cartoonist pictures an immense rubber band stretching across the continent; when the eastern end is cut, the gold seekers straddling the band will zip through the air to California.

pocketing their fifty or sixty dollars a day and having plenty of leisure."

The *Washington Daily Union* was moved by a firsthand look at Colonel Mason's treasure-laden tea caddy to observe: "However skeptical any man may have been, we defy him to doubt that if the quantity of such specimens as these be as great as has been represented; the gold in California must be greater than has hitherto been discovered in the old and new continents; and great as may be the emigration to this new El Dorado, the frugal and the industrious will be amply repaid for their enterprise and toil."

Preachers preached about gold and economists and editorial writers wondered what this abundance of gold was going to do to the world. In January 1849 James Gordon Bennett's *New York Herald* was somewhat worried: "The actual circulation of money in the world, so far as we can arrive at it, is ten hundred and thirty millions of dollars. In the event of the mines of California producing one-half as much as is estimated it will be seen that the amount of gold in circulation will be doubled within the next ten years. Fifty millions of dollars in gold added to the currency of the World in each year will create a revolution in financial and commercial affairs."

There were eager audiences for lectures on gold. In New York a Dr. Boynton, "distinguished lecturer, engaged for many years in mining," spoke on the subject of "Geology, Mineralogy, Structure and Formation of the Rocks in which precious metals are found, with practical instructions for detecting, testing and washing Gold." In Washington a Mr. Atherton gave a "Gold Lecture" in which he said the reports were not exaggerated, that 100,000 persons could not exhaust California's gold resources in 10 or 12 years, that California miners were making up to $1,000 a day, that one man had obtained 36 pounds ($9,000) in one day, that another had made $12,000 in six days, that he himself had seen a lump weighing seven pounds. And that the gold region was as large as New York State, and in some places a handful of dirt would yield a half ounce of pure gold.

Clairvoyants were much in demand to advise prospective gold seekers as to what kind of luck they were likely to have. One, in Amsterdam, New York, after a session of "magnetic sleep," advised an audience of clients that they would have a "glorious success." Another, in Milwaukee, Wisconsin, laid down rules that would ensure the health of the forty-niners and also predicted that vast amounts of gold would be found in the bed of the Sacramento River. An Argonaut in Rochester, New York, hired a personal clairvoyant to accompany him in the search for gold.

A bumper crop of gold-oriented advertisements echoed the euphoria, many under the heading "Ho for California!" There were offerings of arms—revolvers, pistols, even cannon; of tents, clothing, boots and collapsible boats made from India rubber; of patent medicines, such as Mrs. Frazier's Compound Vegetable Cough Remedy and Gay's California Cachalangua ("for what is wealth compared with health?"); of a variety of machines ostensibly designed for gold mining, ranging from "Leavenworth's patent gold washer" to the brainchild of "an experienced engineer and practical mechanic who has invented an apparatus upon philosophical principles that will separate gold from 40 to 60 tons of sand and gravel by the aid of two men per day"; and of provisions—"Pilot and Navy bread kiln-dried for shipment," flour, lard, hams, beans, butter, sugar, cheese, Malaga raisins, Zanta currants.

An instantaneous rash of guidebooks appeared: *California, from Its Discovery by the Spaniards to the Present Time, with a Brief Description of the Gold Region; California: Her Wealth and Resources.* Most of the publications were scissors-and-paste jobs, seasoned with fiction. Guidebook authors borrowed heavily from newspaper files, from the reports of Colonel Mason and Consul Larkin, from hearsay and from the earlier travel journals of Richard Henry Dana and John C. Frémont. The *Emigrant's Guide to the Gold Mines* told of riverbeds "paved with gold to the thickness of a hand," from which "twenty to fifty thousand dollars of gold" could be "picked out almost instantly." One of the better guidebooks was compiled by a St. Louis newspaperman, Joseph E. Ware, who, somewhat later, attempted to follow his own advice and died of cholera on the trail.

For what they lacked in substance and reliability many publishers tried to make up by appending sentimental poems and lively songs about gold and California. The music publishers were not far behind, bringing out such topical numbers as "The San Fran-

A primer for the overland route

For gold seekers traveling overland, Joseph Ware's 1849 guide served as an invaluable source book. Its title page *(above)* indicates the range of its contents; examples of its pithy, practical advice appear below.

Start at 4—travel till the sun gets high—camp till the heat is over. Then start again and travel till dark.

After the upper Platte Ford, for over fifty miles, the water is impregnated with poisonous matter. If you would avoid sickness, abandon its use.

TRUCKIE'S PASS, You will be tried to the utmost. Pack everything over the summit, then haul your wagons up with ropes. You will certainly save time, and perhaps hundreds of dollars.

cisco Waltz," "The Sacramento Gallop" and "The Gold Diggers Waltz."

P. T. Barnum, an acute judge of American susceptibility, recognized the irresistible lure of gold. His offerings of the moment—Mr. Hales, the eight-foot, quarter-ton English giant; Major Littlefinger ("much smaller than General Tom Thumb") and a live orangutan—were not enough for the spirit of the times. So Barnum wrote to Lieutenant Edward F. Beale, one of the military couriers who had brought back gold from California: "Dear Sir: Mr. Harding of the *Philadelphia Inquirer* has just informed me that you have in your possession an eight pound lump of California gold. As I am always anxious to procure novelties for public gratification I write this to say I should be glad to purchase the lump. If not that, I should like to procure it for exhibition for a few weeks. Your ob't. servant, P. T. Barnum." The eight pound lump was actually only a few ounces, of which half went to the government and the other half to make an engagement ring for Beale's fiancée, Mary Edwards. Not even Barnum, it appeared, was immune to the exaggerations of the day.

"Fleecing the Golden Fleecers" became a lively and profitable business. Young men—and the forty-niners were predominantly young—bought outfits consisting of what enterprising merchants said was proper for a gold miner: red or blue woolen shirts, homespun flannel drawers, wide-brimmed felt hats of a black or rusty hue, knee-length coats, high boots, baggy trousers of Kentucky jean, trunks and rubber bags for their gear.

Most overequipped themselves. Enos Christman, the young man from West Chester, Pennsylvania, took 17 pairs of new heavy pantaloons, 12 new flannel shirts, 18 new checked shirts, 5 white muslin shirts, 7 coats and 5 waistcoats—almost all of which he either gave or threw away in California. Some of the modern-day Argonauts hopefully took evening clothes. For supplies they bought jars of pickles, candied fruit and berry syrups (all useful to combat scurvy), jugs of brandy, all-healing salves, purgatives, camphor, quinine, sulfur, brimstone, laudanum (a Britisher marveled at the way the American forty-niners were constantly medicating themselves and anyone else who would hold still).

There was much interest in weapons: revolvers for the belt, small pistols for the vest, stout bowie knives, walking sticks with dirks concealed in the handles, blackjacks for hip pockets. "As if," Dr. William McCollum of Lockport, New York, recalled later, "we were so many sons of Mars instead of what we really were—soldiers and devotees in the ranks of Mammon." Already dressed for the goldfields with their new slouch hats and their stiff new boots, the Argonauts, waiting for transportation, tramped the streets of New York, Boston, Philadelphia and Baltimore, frequently drinking too much and constantly talking, with great authority, of the "Auriferous Zone." They paid elaborate attention to young ladies, since they wouldn't see any for a long time to come. And the young ladies, in turn, held sewing bees to prepare what they called bachelors' companions—rolls of cloth containing the needles, thread, buttons and scissors that the young adventurers would need to keep their splendid outfits in working order.

They sang minstrel songs like "Oh Susanna," which, with new verses ("I'm bound for California with my washbowl on my knee"), became the anthem of the gold rush. And they learned new songs. One went:

> *Then blow, ye breezes, blow!*
> *We're off to Californi-o*
> *There's plenty of gold,*
> *So I've been told,*
> *On the banks of the Sacramento.*

They were to be the most articulate migrants of all time. They bought writing paper, notebooks, journals, ledgers, portable writing desks, ink and pens of steel, gold or quill. Even before departure many of them had begun diaries or undertook the first in a series of long, romantic letters home. They unburdened themselves of such exuberant sentiments as "Ho for California and the Gold Regions—Westward the Star of Empire takes its Way!" and "I firmly believe in *manifest destiny,* that we shall yet overrun the whole continent and spread out on the islands and into Asia." The Reverend John D. Gardiner of Sag Harbor, Long Island, celebrated the departure of his son Howard with a premature lamentation, published in the *New York Journal of Commerce* and including this verse:

> *Then, if beneath the evening star*
> *Beside the great Pacific's wave*
> *Thou find'st an early tomb afar*
> *His grace will there thy spirit save.*

In Nebraska one of the six groups into which former West Pointer Bruff divided his uniformed, quasi-military company cooks a meal.

Vivid record from the journey of a brave and lonely man

Bruff tersely describes his passage over a Nebraska creek that stank of marsh grass.

One of the most vivid records of the overland journey to California was compiled by a traveler named Joseph Goldsborough Bruff. Bruff began his career as a West Point cadet. He later served as a sailor, then became a U.S. government draftsman in Washington, D.C. But in 1849, when he was 44, gold fever inspired Bruff to give up drawing official maps and designing buttons for officers' tunics. He organized the Washington City and California Mining Association and led 63 men in 13 wagons across the Plains. On the way, he filled his notebooks with a narrative of the journey, including observations of topography, plants, animals and weather. Bruff embellished his text with quick sketches bearing his own laconic captions, and later elaborated some drawings in haunting watercolors.

On a knoll in the Nebraska prairie, one wagon upset and its mules bolted. Bruff caught the mules, repaired the wagon and went on.

On July 20, 1849, Bruff and his fellow travelers crossed the North Platte River on a raft of planks supported by cottonwood dugouts.

49

The Desert

The mules has got through, but the owner aint,— by a long ways.

When a mule gave out on the trail, as Bruff's sketch shows, its owner shouldered the load.

In 120 days Bruff's party trekked from the Missouri River to the Sierra Nevada, losing only two men to illness and none to Indians, accidents or harsh deserts shown here. Then his luck failed. In the Sierra he stayed with his snowbound wagons and sent his men ahead; despite their promises, none hiked back from the gold fields to help him. Ill and alone, he staggered 30 miles to the nearest settlement carrying his notebooks, which he hoped to publish as a gold-seekers' guide. He found no gold himself and went home via Panama. Then, in New York, thieves took all of his possessions except his journals. But Bruff was able to find no market for them; almost a century passed before his great adventure story became the book that he had planned.

In an especially effective watercolor, Bruff painted a hot, dry Wyoming defile and the "rugged, bare and harsh-looking Rattle-Snake Mts."

50

Bruff found this steep drop in Nevada littered with wrecked vehicles. Slowed by double-locked wheels, his own wagons inched safely down.

Under the ironic title *Pilgrim's Progress,* Bruff depicted travelers on the Nevada desert trudging past debris cast off by earlier expeditions.

51

Many of the Argonauts joined companies or associations whose members would share the cost of transportation and whatever equipment and supplies they fancied might be useful in the gold country. They would also share the fruits of whatever could be won in the West from mining or trading.

Some outfits had dashing names, such as Cortez, the Buckeye Rovers and the Helltown Greasers. But most were named for their place of origin—the Hartford Union Mining & Trading Company, the New York Overland Mutual Protection Association for California. The companies were usually organized for a term of five years and often were quasi-military, with uniforms, drills, captains and lieutenants.

These associations were very popular in Massachusetts; during 1849, 102 companies comprising some 4,200 men departed the commonwealth. Many members had obtained, for two dollars, a passport signed by the governor, George M. Briggs requesting "all whom it may concern, to permit safely and freely to pass [name of emigrant], a citizen of said Commonwealth, going to CALIFORNIA and elsewhere, and in case of need to give him all lawful aid and protection."

The companies ranged from a few members to several hundred. Prior to departure, either overland or by sea, frequent meetings were held. They discussed travel arrangements, oversaw stocks of provisions and equipment, brushed up on drill, assigned responsibilities and drafted more bylaws. Some of the bylaws revealed the ignorance that abounded about the gold fields. Members of the Hartford Union planned that, after arriving in California, they would return to the ship each night and deposit the day's take of gold in the company strongbox—although, as it later turned out, the ship's anchorage was hundreds of miles from the diggings.

One of the most elaborately conceived and equipped companies was the Boston & California Joint Mining & Trading Company, which sailed from Boston on January 13, 1849, aboard a fast ship, the 700-ton *Edward Everett,* named for Harvard's president. In recognition of the honor, President Everett presented the 150-man company with a library of 100 volumes and this stern admonition: "Take your Bible in one hand and your New England civilization in the other and make your mark on that country." Everett did not explain how a man so encumbered might also dig gold, but little else was overlooked. The group included merchants, manufacturers, artisans, medical and divinity students, eight sea captains, a mineralogist, a geologist and four doctors. The ship was equipped with lightning rods and two brass cannons. There was a large dormitory and social hall with berths in triple tiers. Corridors between the berths were named for Boston streets. A band was organized to give nightly concerts. Sunday services and mid-week prayer meetings were scheduled. The scientists were to deliver regular lectures in their fields of expertise. There was a dispensary well stocked with drugs and 25 gallons of whiskey for medicinal purposes.

The *Everett* also carried trade goods, food for two years, wagons, wheelbarrows, shovels, picks, a steam-operated launch, several steam engines, building supplies and lumber enough for two houses, one of which was to be the company's headquarters and office in San Francisco. The building was never erected, for this company, like most of the rest, was dissolved soon after reaching California. There was something about the gold rush that seemed to render rational considerations, careful planning and orderly organization null and void.

But companies continued to set off on the great adventure. Often there were predeparture prayers and hymn singing. The three companies leaving on the 650-ton vessel *Sweden* in March 1849 were presented with a gold-fringed, white satin banner bearing the word "Excelsior" and under it a painting depicting the *Sweden* already moored in California waters, the Argonauts heading ashore to climb a golden mountain. The air of optimism was radiant and contagious. There was a general feeling that gold mining would be no more arduous than gathering wild berries or digging clams—and far more pleasant and profitable. One man embarking from New York stood at the ship's rail and tossed his last five-dollar gold piece into the dockside crowd, shouting, "I'm going where there is plenty more."

The first big decision either a company or an individual forty-niner had to make was how to get to California. There were three principal ways. One was overland, across the continent, by any of several trails. Another was the all-water route, down the Atlantic coasts of North and South America, around Cape Horn and up through the Pacific to California. And a third, with several variations, was by sea and land—to Panama, Nicaragua or Mexico by ship, cross-country to the Pacific and then by ship again north to the destination. There were also fanciful ways: Mr. Rufus Porter, editor of *Scientific American,* announced plans to build an "aerial locomotive" with which he intended to sail over mountains, plains and deserts, carrying freight and passengers at $200 a head to California in three days (the actual time required was four to eight months).

The most obvious and direct route and, in many ways, the most hazardous and demanding was overland. Hunters and trappers had been crossing the western wilderness for several decades. But these mountain men were almost animal-like in their ability to live off the land. Few of the forty-niners were so adaptable.

By the early 1840s emigrants had begun using the overland trails, joining together for safety in great wagon trains. In 1840 a Western Emigration Society had been organized in Independence, Missouri, with 500 enthusiasts who hoped to start new lives in California. Before the departure in late May, 1841, all but 69 of the would-be emigrants had changed their minds about going. In the end, only half of those actually reached California, the remainder splitting off and heading for Oregon. In 1846 there was a considerable flow of emigrants into California in anticipation that the Mexican War would soon make this territory part of the United States. It was during this migration that the luckless Donner party was trapped by snow in the Sierra Nevada and lost nearly half of its 87 members by starvation before being rescued. There had also been a movement of Mormon pioneers from Illinois and Missouri to Utah between 1846 and 1848 and they added considerably to knowledge about the West.

The journey was still perilous. The sea of land that bounded California on the east was less charted, less known to the white man than the true sea that bounded it on the west. But the various overland routes had their attractions for the eager forty-niners. For one thing these routes were shorter — about 10,000 miles shorter, for example, than the trip around Cape Horn. Easterners could travel almost halfway across the continent by steam trains and river boats; and many of the forty-niners already lived near the established departure points for the overland trek.

And going overland could be cheaper. The average traveler by the sea routes needed at least $300 to start with and might spend many times that, depending on his tastes. By contrast, midwestern farmers already owned much of what they needed for the overland trip — wagons, teams, stores of food they had raised themselves. All they required was time, energy, determination, enough cash to buy necessities they could not get by barter and, as many would learn, luck.

There were a number of southwestern routes — from Missouri, Arkansas or Texas westward to Santa Fe, after which the forty-niner could swing to the north along the Old Spanish Trail or go south along the Gila River to Southern California. Or he could dip farther south still and cross the border into Mexico, proceeding overland or to the port city of Mazatlán, where he could take passage by ship north to San Francisco. Some 9,000 Argonauts tried these southwestern routes in 1849 by way of Santa Fe.

But far more — at least 22,500 in 1849 — chose to follow the more familiar emigrant trail across the West. Leaving the Missouri River around the vicinity of Council Bluffs they followed the Platte and the Sweetwater to South Pass, then around Great Salt Lake, along the course of the Humboldt River and finally across the desert to the foot of the great Sierra, last barrier to California. Because of the popularity of this route, little towns along the Missouri River — Independence, St. Joseph and Council Bluffs — became staging areas and during the spring of 1849 rapidly developed the air and appearance of vast gypsy encampments.

Early in the month of May, Benjamin Burt Jr. of the Boston-Newton company wrote that there were 5,000 emigrants at Independence and 10,000 at St. Joseph. "Gold fever is on the increase," he noted, and added, "From three-fourths to seven-eighths are temperance, steady men." Saloons, nevertheless, were doing a booming business; there were many thirsty miles ahead.

At the Missouri River the wagons were made ready. Many were farm wagons or smaller variations of the rugged, classic freight wagon. New iron rims were fitted to the wheels, spokes tightened, axles greased, bolts secured, harness reinforced. Bows were raised over the wagon bed and canvas — often weatherproofed with a mixture of linseed oil and beeswax — stretched over the bows. Frequently the wagon body was painted blue, the wheels red — and with the white canvas above they presented a patriotic and festive picture. The name of a

GLIDDEN & WILLIAMS' LINE
FOR SAN FRANCISCO.
FROM LEWIS WHARF.
The Elegant, First-class, Extreme Clipper Ship
ARCHER
E. R. POWER, COMMANDER,

Is now loading. She is in fine order for the voyage, and being of small capacity, and very fast, will be quickly loaded. Shippers will much oblige by early delivery of their engagements.

For Freight, apply at the California Packet Office, 114 State St., Boston.

Agents at San Francisco, WILLIAMS, BLANCHARD & CO.

Watson's Press, 21 Franklin Street, Boston.

---

112 DAYS TO
SAN FRANCISCO.
MERCHANTS' EXPRESS LINE OF CLIPPER SHIPS.
Dispatching the Greatest Number of Vessels!
SMALLEST, SHARPEST AND FASTEST VESSEL NOW UP!

THE MAGNIFICENT OUT-AND-OUT CLIPPER SHIP
WHITE SWALLOW
BUNKER, Commander, is now rapidly loading at PIER 16 E. R.

This splendid vessel, having made *very short passages*, and delivered her cargo in *unexceptionable order*, has established a reputation that will ensure *immediate dispatch*.

RANDOLPH M. COOLEY, 88 Wall Street,

Agents in San Francisco, Messrs. DE WITT, KITTLE & CO.   (TONTINE BUILDING.)

NESBITT & CO., PRINTERS.

MERCHANTS' EXPRESS LINE OF CLIPPER SHIPS FOR SAN FRANCISCO.
Passages 106 & 117 Days.

THE WELL-KNOWN   EXTREME CLIPPER SHIP
EAGLE WING
LINNELL, Commander, is now loading at Pier 16 E. R.

For Freight, apply at once to RANDOLPH M. COOLEY, 88 Wall St., Tontine Building.

Agents in San Francisco, Messrs. DE WITT, KITTLE & CO.

NESBITT & CO., PRINTERS, N. Y.

Clipper ships to San Francisco guaranteed fast, clear sailing, according to the advertising cards put out by East Coast lines. None of the ads hinted at the gales and calms that plagued the long sea voyage.

joint stock company would be painted on the canvas, or the name of the owner's hometown, or the familiar "Ho for California!" or, simply, "Gold!"

Blacksmiths and harness makers did a lively trade. So did provisioners. There was constant buying and swapping of oxen, horses and mules. Traders were there with strings of unbroken Mexican mules, which they sold and then trained for the new owners in a few days time. The Mexican mules, accustomed to life in arid, stony, mountainous country, were regarded as more reliable for the trip ahead than the bigger, sleeker mules from Louisiana, Arkansas and Mississippi. Oxen were highly favored, too; they were slow, but they were also patient and very strong.

The time of departure was carefully calculated. It had to be early enough in the season for the voyagers to be able to reach the eastern flanks of the Sierra Nevada before autumn snows blocked the passes. But it also had to be late enough in the spring for grass to be up and flourishing for the livestock and for rivers and streams to be back inside their banks after the winter floods. Rivers that could not be forded had to be crossed by raft, and wagons lined up for miles waiting their turns. Such waits could consume precious days.

The forty-niners, like most amateurs, traveled overloaded. Wagon wheels stuck in prairie sand and mud, putting a strain on the draft animals and the wagon as well. Surplus goods—complicated mining machines, elaborate camping equipment, iron stoves and trunks full of extra clothing—began to be left behind. All the trails west would be littered with goods abandoned in the interest of mobility and safety. Firearms, tools, a few personal possessions and food were, in fact, the most the travelers could hope to haul across the continent. All else would be dumped to make space in the wagons for fodder and for water to keep the livestock going while crossing arid regions.

One of the companies in the vanguard of the spring migration up the Platte in 1849 was the Columbus & California Industrial Association, a group of 30 young men from Columbus, Ohio, equipped with 10 light wagons and 40 mules. The group's announced purpose was "operating in the gold regions of California." When the company left Columbus on April 2, 1849, the editor of the *Ohio State Journal* commented: "Impelled more by a desire for adventure than by a love of riches, they have this day bid adieu to their families and friends, to the sweets of society and appliances of civilization, and taken their departure for that country where the setting sun gilds with its rays mountains rich in the precious metals, and streams whose shining sands are impregnated with yellow gold."

Peter Decker, a religious young man of 26, was secretary of the group and a diligent diarist. At Cincinnati the company boarded the steamer *Hancock* with 400 other westward-bound voyagers for the trip down the Ohio and up the Mississippi and Missouri rivers. "A few snorts & puffs and we were off on our way to El Dorado," Decker wrote. Steamboats, he soon decided, "are wicked places," and he was troubled by his companions' "vulgarity & a too free use of *ardent.*" In addition to his concern over the inordinate consumption of alcohol, he was also worried about the epidemic of cholera that was sweeping the country and dosed himself with gunpowder ("its effect was cooling") and Dr. Zoril's "cure-all medicine," and on a string around his neck he wore a resinous lump of asafetida to ward off spasms. Many of the river steamboats were stopping at night to bury cholera victims in unmarked graves along the riverbanks.

The Columbus company disembarked at St. Joseph and spent almost two weeks getting its gear in order, laying in the supplies of food needed for the trek ahead —some 300 pounds per man. Finally, on a cold Monday morning, April 30, the young men set off, three to a wagon. Decker, a vegetarian, had not eaten meat in 10 years. Soon, however, he became inured to fat bacon, either fried or raw, which with sea biscuit was the staple diet for the company. He found it harder to accept the fact that none of the forty-niners—or at least none in his company or in others he encountered —would interrupt the drive west to observe the Sabbath. He also discovered that such travel tried men's tempers. Nine days out he wrote: "Some of our men are dissatisfied & talk of 'disunion' &c. Much occurs on the way to stir men's baser passions & little to influence favorably the better feelings." Later he noted: "Men hard to please, our captain thinks they could not be all pleased were the Good Being to direct affairs."

The company had their first Indian scare just after leaving the valley of the Blue River: "The shout was given 'Buffalo ahead' perhaps two miles. All hands but

Battered by hurricane winds, the California-bound *Comet* wallows in heavy seas off Bermuda in October 1852, as shown in a contemporary painting. Storms off Cape Horn were equally fierce; there, passengers heading for the gold fields often endured 100-knot winds for days at a time.

In a journal he kept while rounding the Horn in 1849, Argonaut Isaac Baker made light of the monotonous shipboard fare: pork from live hogs slaughtered aboard and a glutinous pudding called plum duff.

Fresh pork once more,—
One more "Plum Duff"
Take hold, take hold, sure there's enough;—
Eat—Eat your fill—don't look forlorn.
Here's roasted pig, & there's Cape Horn!—
So don't be making such a bother,
We'll eat up one, & pass the other!—

drivers ran for them until near enough to see that they were a lot of Indian Warriors on horseback. Our men all returned, the wagons had hurriedly drove up in coral form for defence. Mules unhitched and tied to wheels and all arms ready. Men drawn up in 'battle array' & with the enemy (36 in number) advancing on us all hands expected a fight. A large body on foot was approaching us on the rear through a ravine behind us. They had Rifles, Arrows, a few swords."

The Indians were Sioux but the encounter proved friendly enough, ending in a trading session. Decker said that he and "our men generally" had felt "cool and collected." Another diarist in the company, Dr. Charles Boyle, recorded a different version: 'D--- was discovered under a wagon. C--- was unable to get his gun in order until informed that he would be assisted into the rank by some of our men. F--- stole my pistols and drank half a pint of whisky to keep his courage and some few knees might be seen shaking and rattling as some supposed a battle was inevitable."

An average of 150 wagons a day were passing Fort Childs, on the south bank of the Platte River, at the time the Columbus men reached there on May 14. The number would grow to a maximum of 460 by the end of May when, with the season well advanced, it would begin to decline.

Beyond Fort Childs the country grew wilder and wilder, and beyond Fort Laramie in Missouri Territory, water, when it could be found, was often alkaline and grass was scarce. After their first encounter with the Sioux, the men learned to distinguish buffalo from other moving objects, and eventually learned to get close enough to shoot some for food. But mostly they amused themselves by taking potshots at badgers, ground squirrels, prairie dogs and skunks. Past Independence Rock on the Sweetwater River (where Decker carved his initials, as did most passersby) the company was joined by two men and a woman who had left another wagon train "on acct of rude fellows," and Decker noted "our whole camp is quieter. Obscene and improper language not heard just because a woman is in camp. This is the refining influence of woman. Without society men almost become desperados."

Off and on they were joined by the Delaware (Ohio) Company and the Iron City Rangers of Pittsburgh. For these and other companies that had got underway early, conditions were comparatively favorable. Later companies would find the spring grass gone and the water holes dry. At Fort Hall in Oregon Territory, which they reached at the end of June after two months on the trail, Decker was told that at least another 60 days of travel lay ahead, part of it over terrifying desert, and he commented: "There is surely no Royal road to California & traveling it is labor indeed." He also noted that he would have "given up my interest in the Gold mines" if he could only get rid of the mosquitoes.

After several hard, dusty days along the putrid, alkaline Humboldt River (alternately known as the Hellbolt and Humbug) during which they had seen a number of dead oxen and found a scribbled note warn-

During a later voyage in 1852, Baker noted an ingenious remedy for seasickness. Seated behind a sawhorse rigged with reins, queasy passengers pretended the ship's motion was the swaying of a horse carriage.

Quincy Sketches No 3

Lady passengers, being somewhat troubled with sea sickness, take one of our best horses, & a ride (in imagination) to the "Beach" to cheer their drooping spirits!—

ing travelers of a noxious weed that killed cattle in two hours time, Decker wrote: "It was my turn at guarding the mules last evening—a delightful starlight night & at 11 o'clock the moon in her third quarter rose in splendor over the mountain ridge. In camp the boys sing 'Old Ned,' 'Old Virginia Shore,' & the 'Carrier Dove.' The latter is beautiful in sentiment. I thought keenly of other days & better—of the unbroken family circle I once enjoyed on the other side of the great mountains. Yes, & of many friends & acquaintances, of the advantages of well organized & refined society. *All* these I bid farewell to. Reflections like these soften the asperities of even a heart on the plains where selfishness reigns supreme."

The most excruciating part of the trip was the Forty-Mile Desert, a wasteland stretching from the Humboldt Sink, where that miserable river disappeared in the desert sand, to the Carson River at the foot of the Sierra. A note left by an earlier traveler said: "Expect to find the *worst desert* you ever saw & then find it worse than you expected. Take water, *be sure* to *take enough.*" From the last available springs Decker and his companions filled every possible container—canteens, kegs, coffeepots, gum boots, waterproof sacks, even a rubberized blanket, good for the equivalent of five buckets of water. They traveled by night, the men helping the mules pull the wagons through the deep sand. The landscape was desolate with abandoned wagons and the stinking carcasses of mules and oxen.

Finally, 10 miles from the Carson, the mules were unhitched and taken ahead to recuperate. Decker and fellow diarist Dr. Boyle remained behind to guard the wagons. Decker spent his time reading John Charles Frémont's account of his explorations in California, and Dr. Boyle read Shakespeare. From time to time abandoned horses, mules and oxen, near death from thirst and exhaustion, would stick their heads in the wagon that sheltered the men, looking hopeful.

After two days the rest of the company returned with the mules and they made the last stage across the desert. On the banks of the Carson they camped under a cottonwood tree—the first tree they had seen, Decker said, since leaving Fort Hall, 700 miles back.

The climb up through Carson Pass and over the Sierra was dangerous, exhausting and painfully slow, but there was grass and water for the mules and berries, fruit and game for the men. Mules fell over cliffs and wagons were wrecked. More and more of the goods and supplies had to be packed on muleback or carried by the men themselves. En route they met a party of Mormons with ox-drawn wagons, leaving California for Salt Lake City. "We had many questions to ask them," Decker wrote. "Their account is favorable as to Gold. Provisions abundant & comparatively cheap. The mines crowded, much business done, liquor drank & cards played constantly. Hard Society. Say they never left a place without regret except that."

On August 6 the Columbus company reached the summit of Carson Pass, and by August 10 they were in Sacramento asking the usual question: Which way to the diggings? Decker wrote: "We are now in California, having been on the road since last April. A tedious, irksome and disagreeable trip, made in about 100 days without an accident. All came through lucky considering the exposures &c. We can only ascribe it to a providential goodness."

For gold seekers from New England and the middle Atlantic states it was natural to think of going to California by ship. Old whalers in New Bedford, Salem and other ports were hastily refurbished. They were scrubbed out, patched up, equipped with bunks, and re-rigged. The advertisements offering passage were enthusiastically phrased: "Superior, very fast sailing, coppered & copper-fastened bark, for the Gold Region direct, passengers well provided for."

The route most favored at the outset of the gold rush was by way of Cape Horn: south through the Atlantic to the tip of South America, northwest in the Pacific to California; a trip of some 13,000 nautical miles. It was a rough and sometimes dangerous voyage, particularly

ODYSSEY OF THE APOLLO
The voyage of the *Apollo,* one of the first ships to carry forty-niners to California, lasted nine wearisome months —and every day the owner's son, John Beach, marked the ship's position on a chart *(left).* Beach's personal log supplemented the chart's notations. "Very sea sick lay a bed nearly all day—whew!" he wrote on January 19, his fourth day at sea. The rounding of Cape Horn began May 8 in "a fine snow storm" that sent the *Apollo* skittering around the chart. In September, after languishing two weeks just off San Francisco waiting for a fair wind, Beach wistfully sketched in the shorter route across the Isthmus of Panama.

A party of forty-niners begins the short cut across Panama to the Pacific Ocean with a five-day trip up the Chagres River in a native dugout. On this leg of the journey travelers faced special hazards—a tumble overboard, a boat wreck or the threat of catching malaria from the mosquitoes that infested both the stream and the jungle on both banks.

in the stormy latitudes of the Cape. The trip took from four to eight months, with an average of about six months—and this at a time when everyone was in a hurry to get to California before all that loose gold had been picked up. Sleek, rakish clipper ships could sail from Boston to San Francisco in a little more than 100 days—the *Flying Cloud* eventually made it in 89 days—but they specialized in premium freight, not passengers. The blunt-bowed wide-beamed vessels that carried human cargoes took much longer, even without allowing for calms, contrary winds and other mishaps.

Still, the ocean route had advantages, if one could stand the tedium of endless days at sea, of seasickness and food that ranged from monotonous to dreadful to scarce. Large amounts of baggage—equipment, provisions, clothing and trade goods—could be taken along. And, unlike the overland travelers whose movements were governed by the seasons, the Cape voyagers could leave at almost any time—although the Southern Hemisphere's winter storms could be hellishly violent.

Nevertheless, before they reached California, all round-the-Horn Argonauts were heartily weary of the sea and ships. Most of them, whether traveling as individuals or in organized companies, were accommodated in tiered berths, usually three men sleeping abreast on platforms barely two feet apart, one above the other.

The inevitable cases of seasickness combined with the difficulty of getting out of such a bunk caused dismay, anger and, of course, more nausea. Once the Argonauts had their sea legs and could again bear the thought of eating, they became aware of the atrocious food. One passenger complained that the salt pork was rusty, the dried beef rotten and "there were two bugs for every bean." The pilot bread and navy biscuit were frequently full of weevils, and passengers on the French brig *Cachalot,* keeping count of the weevils, wryly bragged that theirs was "the only vessel on the California run serving fresh meat three times daily." There were repeated servings of a concoction called lobscouse, a hash made of salt pork, onions, navy biscuit, water and thickening. The rare desserts—plum duff, mince turnovers and a pudding called dandy funk—had a pasty, greasy sameness. Water stored for months on end in the ship's vats developed a remarkably foul taste. Diluted with liberal portions of molasses and vinegar, it became a potable concoction known as switchel, whose only virtue was that it could be swallowed (and sometimes kept down).

As the miserable passengers grew more accustomed to life at sea, their tempers grew shorter and their pa-

Argonaut George P. Clarke drew this map of his own journey in 1850 across Panama en route to California. Starting by small boat from a settlement at the mouth *(far left)* of the Chagres River, Clarke floated past Indian thatch huts as far as the village of Cruces. There he rented a mule for the last 21 miles of steep hill country. Because the Isthmus curves, Clarke's route to the Pacific ran from west to east.

tience with captain and crew diminished. When embarking on the schooner *Europe* on July 3, 1849, Enos Christman, the former printer's apprentice and now a member of the California Gold Mining Association of Philadelphia, had first thought the skipper, one Addison Palmer, an admirable man, "a whole-souled sort of fellow." Six months later, after a stormy passage around the Cape and with food and water running low, he thought the captain had "hardly capacity enough to take proper charge of a canal boat, let alone a vessel that plows the oceans. He is colleagued and identified with the mean and rascally owners."

The Cape passage was enough to change anyone's mind. Even worse were the shortcuts through the Strait of LaMaire or the even more perilous Straits of Magellan. Either way the seas were monstrous, the winds adverse and the weather bitterly cold. One captain was described coming off the bridge and leaning over the galley stove to thaw the ice from his whiskers. Passengers donned all their clothing and lay shivering in their bunks, remembering all the tales of harrowing shipwrecks in this lonely, miserable corner of the world.

Boredom was even more constant than physical misery. Few of the companies and none of the individuals had given as much forethought to the voyagers' need for entertainment and stimulation as had the Boston & California Joint Mining & Trading Company. A few of the forty-niners had thought to bring books along and these, no matter whether they were novels or treatises on theology, were passed from hand to hand until they were in tatters. Less bookish souls found relief in gambling and alcohol. The latter might run out but the former was always present. Profanity rose sharply, both in incidence and intensity.

Still, there were pleasures in the long journey. A Maine farmer was in a group that landed briefly on the island of St. Catherine's, off the coast of Brazil. He recorded that they had found "benaners growing wild & et our fill; you eat only the core first peling of the skin which is bittr & contains little nurisshment." Others marveled at the Juan Fernández Islands off the coast of Chile, Robinson Crusoe's rumored refuge, where good fresh fruit was available, and the Galápagos Islands, where great turtles and tortoises could easily be captured to vary the dreadful shipboard diet.

One small group sailing from New York aboard the bark *George Emory,* read from a library of 150 volumes, played cards, chess and backgammon, and sang to the accompaniment of two violins and two flutes. They went ashore at Rio de Janeiro and attended a the-

Travel by ship from Panama to California was unreliable, expensive and, as this etching shows, miserably uncomfortable. Argonauts paid as much as $1,000 for space in the cramped hold of a Panama coaster.

ater. One of them, wearing a white coat, was admitted only on the condition that he stand in the shadows where he could not be seen. The Brazilian emperor, Dom Pedro II, was in the audience and everything was very formal. "Luckily," said Franklin Buck of Bucksport, Maine, the narrator of the incident, "the rest of us were in full dress." The same group vastly enjoyed themselves in the Peruvian port city of Callao and the nearby capital, Lima. The fresh beauty and lively manners of the Peruvian women enchanted them. They talked of returning to Peru—after they had made their fortunes in California gold, of course—and choosing mates for life. None of them did any of those things.

Forty-niners too impatient to round the Cape might go partly by sea, partly by land. California-bound emigrants could take a ship to the Caribbean side of Central America, go overland to the Pacific and take a chance on a northbound vessel. Panama was the most popular crossing. Since the traveler had to negotiate his passage on two ships on two oceans and, in between, was at the mercy of natives who soon learned the joys of inflated prices, this route also tended to be the most expensive. It was favored by government and military officials en route to assignments in California, by the wealthier forty-niners and, before long, by gamblers and prostitutes. An 1846 treaty between the United States and the Republic of New Granada, of which Panama was then a part, had given United States citizens freedom of transit across the Isthmus in return for recognition of New Granada's sovereignty there.

On the Caribbean side, passengers disembarked at the mouth of the Chagres River, a fever-ridden region of swamps with but one slight elevation. There stood the ruined fortress of San Lorenzo, where some 300 men had died in an attack by the pirate Morgan in 1670. The distance from Chagres to Panama City on the Pacific was about 75 miles. The journey's first 50 miles were made in long dugout canoes called bungos. These were paddled or poled by native boatmen who overcame fatigue with frequent siestas and long absences during which they stoked themselves with local rum. The passengers drank brandy and amused themselves by trying out their new firearms on alligators, iguanas, parrots and other wildlife along the river.

The boatmen, who knew no English, soon knew the words and tunes of "Oh Susanna" and "Yankee Doodle." They learned other things as well: the price for the boat trip from Chagres to Gorgona—or as far as Cruces in the wet season *(pages 64-65)*—soon rose from $10 to four or five times that. The emigrants grumbled, but Dr. William McCollum of Lockport, New York, more reasonable than the rest, observed: "I should like to see a community of genuine Yankees enjoy the monopoly of a few canoes, to transport a crowd of eager adventurers willing to pay almost any price to get ahead; I opine there would be such a fleecing and extortion as the Isthmus has not yet witnessed."

Bayard Taylor, a trained reporter who made the trip in June 1849 on assignment for the *New York Tribune,* was predictably more observant than most of his fellow travelers in Panama. He noted that his boatmen were "Ambrosio Mendez, of mixed Indian and Spanish race," and "Juan Crispin Bega, almost entirely of Negro blood." The latter, he said, "was a strong, jovial fellow and took such good care of some of our small articles as to relieve us of all further trouble about them."

The boatmen, Taylor said, expected to be given frequent portions of brandy which they would wash down with river water dipped up in a cocoa shell. "As a class," he noted, "they are faithful, hard-working and grateful for kindness. They have faults, the worst of which are tardiness, and a propensity to filch small articles, but good treatment wins upon them in almost every case. Ambrosio told me they would serve no one well who treated them badly. 'If the Americans are good, we are good; if they abuse us we are bad.' Many blustering fellows, with their belts stuck full of pistols and bowie knives, which they draw on all occasions but take good care not to use, have brought reproach on the country by their silly conduct. It is no bravery to put a revolver to the head of an unarmed and ignorant native, and the boatmen have sense enough to be no longer terrified by it."

Many travelers picked up aches and fevers—including cholera and malaria—particularly in the early stages of the Isthmus crossing. Health conditions were better in the higher altitudes inland and on the Pacific side. For those who remained well and lucky the trip across took about five days. The latter part, from Gorgona or Cruces to Panama City, was on muleback—or on foot. Accommodations were almost nonexistent in the interior of the Isthmus and not much better in Panama City, a decaying town of shacks and ruined buildings and grass-grown streets and plazas dating from the 17th Century, when Panama City was a major seat of Spanish power in the New World. But the discomfort was nothing compared with the frustrating uncertainty of securing passage for the remainder of the trip. In the first two months after President Polk's message to Congress, 8,098 Americans left East and Gulf Coast ports for Chagres, and most of them began to pile up in Panama City, anxious, angry and certain that all the gold would be gone before they could get there. The few ships plying the Panama-California run were wholly inadequate for the horde of gold seekers. Many vessels sailed for San Francisco and never returned—and the crowd of stranded California-bound adventurers multiplied at a staggering rate.

Occasionally, after waiting for weeks on end, passage up the Pacific Coast could be booked on whalers and merchantmen that had been rapidly converted for passenger trade. But these old sailing ships were slow and uncertain. Sometimes they had to reach out into the Pacific as far as Hawaii before a favorable wind could be found for the run back to San Francisco.

The advent of regular steamer service eventually helped, but steamer service was slow in coming. In 1847 Congress had voted mail subsidies of more than half a million dollars to induce private companies to establish regular steamship service between New York and Chagres, and between Panama City and California and Oregon. Contracts called for five mail steamers on the Atlantic side and three on the Pacific.

The first steamship built for the new service was the 1,000-ton sidewheeler *California.* She sailed from New York on October 6, 1848, to round South

In an 1849 cartoon President Zachary Taylor (*rattlesnake*) and General Winfield Scott (*eagle*) defy four gold-seeking European monarchs.

Barring the gold fields to hated foreigners

Of some 85,000 men who swarmed to California's gold fields in 1849, about 23,000 were not U.S. citizens. At the time, the mining camps were the most cosmopolitan spots in North America. But hardly the most tolerant. Few of the citizen-miners relished sharing the gold, even with English-speaking Britons and Australians—not to mention Germans, Frenchmen, Latin Americans in general and Mexicans in particular, or Chinese. Some even feared that territorial claims—especially from Europe—might follow the waves of immigrants. Others hated to think of gold leaving the country. But most U.S. prospectors had simpler feelings and ruthless solutions. The author of a letter to the *Panama Star* suggested that "the millions that might be shipped from the four quarters of the globe" could be put to useful labor. They could "till the soil and make roads, or do any other work that may suit them; but the gold-mines were preserved by nature for Americans only." This was a startling interpretation of nature's will, since California had been Mexican only the year before and Spanish before that.

Starting in 1850, the infant California legislature embodied this idea in a series of laws taxing what it piously called foreign miners. Such discrimination drove away some goldfield visitors; the declining prospects of quick fortunes discouraged others. As the diggings played out, most of the so-called foreigners moved on, but they left behind a heritage of hatred and prejudice that would plague the people of California for generations.

America and reach Panama City, which would be her home port. Although the *California* had accommodations for 60 saloon passengers and 150 steerage, she sailed almost empty — nobody was particularly interested at that point in where she was going. The *Falcon,* first ship to ply the Atlantic portion of the mail service, sailed for Chagres on December 1 by way of New Orleans. She carried only 20 passengers, most of them destined for intermediate points. When the *Falcon* was five days at sea (and the *California* 60 days) President Polk's message changed everything. When the *Falcon* reached New Orleans, the docks swarmed with people clamoring to get aboard. When she reached Chagres she discharged some 200 California-bound passengers.

The *California* had a stormy, slow trip through the Straits of Magellan. She had been scheduled to reach Panama January 4, 1849, but did not make it until January 17. By that time there were at least 1,500 Argonauts waiting for berths, their anxiety mounting every minute. To make matters worse, the *California,* during her stop at Callao, had taken on 70 Peruvian passengers bound for the California gold fields. The shortage of space on a United States ship headed for the United States' gold fields with a lot of foreigners aboard exacerbated the already aroused feelings of the American Argonauts in Panama. There were protests, arguments, threats of violence.

Major General Persefor F. Smith, in Panama en route to California where he would replace Colonel Mason as the ranking American official, became a spokesman for the outraged Americans. He addressed a letter to William Nelson, U.S. consul in Panama:

"Sir: The laws of the United States inflict the penalty of fine and imprisonment on trespassers on public lands. As nothing can be more unreasonable or unjust than the conduct pursued by persons not citizens of the United States, who are flocking from all parts to search for and carry off gold belonging to the United States in California; and as such conduct is in direct violation of the law, it will become my duty, immediately on my arrival there, to put these laws in force, to prevent their infraction in future, by punishing with the penalties prescribed by law, on those who offend.

"As these laws probably are not known to many who are about to start to California, it would be well to make it publicly known that there are such laws in existence, and that they will be in future enforced against all persons not citizens of the United States."

General Smith's statement was cheered at a mass meeting of stranded Americans. It was one of the earliest expressions of a xenophobia that was to be distressingly apparent in the gold fields somewhat later.

The commander of the *California* eased matters by announcing that, while the Peruvians could not be deprived of passage, they would be forced to sleep on deck, thus providing accommodations for 250 Americans — well over the ship's rated capacity.

The *California* left Panama on February 1. Stephen H. Branch, a correspondent for the *New York Herald,* was aboard and reported the event: "We set sail, or steamed, or fired up, and started at 9 A.M., minus 15 minutes, amid nine tremendously hearty cheers from all hands, including the hens, chickens, cock-a-doodle-doos, sheep, goats, cattle, and especially the hoggies and little piggies, which made the welkin ring, and the natives stare." On the next day he reported, "Various eating clubs have been formed on the fore-deck, appointing captains, secretaries, vices, &c, the captain's duty being to get the grub from the cook, apportion it to his men, &c. Malichi Fallon, Esq., of the 6th ward, late keeper of the Tombs, is captain of the Knickerbocker Club, consisting of twenty members, among whom are Charles Hughes of the 15th ward, McCarty of the 16th ward, and a member of the democratic general committee last year, and also a defeated candidate for Alderman of the 3d ward."

The *California*'s arrival at San Francisco on February 28, almost five months after leaving New York, was a bench mark in the history of the gold rush, the beginning of the big influx of forty-niners. When the *California* dropped anchor in the bay there already were 30 vessels lying there. The *California*'s Argonauts disembarked and headed for the diggings as fast as they could. So did the crew of the *California* — just as had the crews of all the other ships. Only Captain Cleveland Forbes and a boy from the engine room were left. To get his ship back to Panama, Captain Forbes, whose monthly salary was $250, had to hire a chief engineer and a cook at $500 apiece, firemen at $250 and seamen at $200. Some skippers later adopted the expedient of putting the crew in chains upon arrival in San Francisco. It helped them resist the lure of gold.

A forest of ships' masts greeted new arrivals at San Francisco Harbor. Most of the vessels had been abandoned by passengers and crew rushing off to the diggings. By the mid-1850s more than 500 ships lay rotting at anchor, many still laden with cargo that nobody had taken time to unload.

3 | The rough realities of grubbing for gold

In 1851, not far from Sutter's Mill, sluicers process dust from ground already heavily worked over.

The eight-pound nugget and the single pan that yielded $5,000 in dust were popular subjects of gossip around the diggings, but in sober truth, separating gold dust from rock and sand usually meant backbreaking toil. A Missourian who panned along the Trinity River said he had made "an ounce a day damned easy—by working damned hard."

The minimal tool kit for that hard work was a shovel and a wash pan. But after the first heady spree of '48 and '49 no sane Argonaut would think of working a claim without a cradle or a long tom *(following pages)* to speed up the sorting of earth. Still more efficient was the sluice fed by water *(below)*, with which a crew of shovelers could process up to 100 cubic yards of gold-bearing gravel in a day. With such technological advances the character of the gold rush gradually changed from a madcap adventure to a full-blown—but still-chancy—industry.

A group of forty-niners displays the cradles, pans and gravel buckets used in placer mining.

A woman brings lunch to a team using a long tom, an outgrowth of the cradle, near Auburn, in 1852.

77

Lith. & Published by B.F.Butler, Post Office Building Clay St. San Francisco.

Seeing the elephant at the California circus

In the autumn of 1848, Edward Gould Buffum, until just a few weeks before a lieutenant in a regiment of U.S. Army volunteers, was on his way from San Francisco out to the California diggings. One morning, from the crest of a high ridge, he and a companion could see for the first time the meeting place of the Sacramento and San Joaquin basins and the "noble rivers which lend their names to these rich valleys," stretching "like a highly colored map" at their feet. Recalling the experience afterward, Buffum recaptured the lyrical excitement of that moment.

Through air that was "so pure and transparent as to render objects visible at a great distance," Buffum traced the courses of the rivers, "winding like silver threads through the dark lines of timber fringing their banks; now plunging amid dense forests, now coming in view sparkling and bright as the riches they contain. The intermediate plains were dotted with autumnal flowers and open groves of evergreen oak. Herds of elk, black-tailed deer and antelope browsed near the mountain sides. Far in the distance the massive peak of Shasta reared its snow-capped head from amid a dense forest, fourteen thousand feet into the sky."

About dusk "we arrived at Weaver's Creek: about a dozen log houses rudely thrown together and plastered with mud. This was the little town which was to be our winter home, where we were to be initiated into the mysteries, pleasures and sufferings of a gold digger's life."

Buffum's words preserve a fresh and innocent view of a lovely country that would soon be turned upside down—along with the lives of the men who came there in search of gold. Two days later he himself was eagerly at work in the dry diggings, removing a layer of loose stones, earth and gravelly clay to get down to the gold-bearing bedrock in one of the dry ravines that lay along Weaver's Creek.

"I shall never forget," he wrote, "the delight with which I struck and worked out a crevice. Getting down into the excavation I had made I commenced a careful search and at last found a crevice extending longitudinally along the rock. It appeared to be filled with a hard, bluish clay and gravel, which I took out with my knife, and there at the bottom, strewn along the whole length of the rock, was bright yellow gold, in little pieces about the size and shape of a grain of barley.

"Eureka! Oh how my heart beat! I sat still and looked at it some minutes before I touched it, feeling a sort of independent bravado in allowing it to remain there. When my eyes were sufficiently feasted I scooped it out with the point of my knife and an iron spoon. I weighed it and found that my first day's labor in the mines had made me thirty-one dollars richer than I was in the morning." Buffum was understandably impressed and exultant. His rate of pay as a young lieutenant in the U.S. Army had been less than one dollar per day.

The experience that Buffum recounted was known as "seeing the elephant," a phrase that in 1848 and the

---

A startled forty-niner catches his first glimpse of the dancing elephant — a symbolic beast standing for the unbelievable experience of the gold rush, with all its hopes and perils. The drawing heads a sheet of letter stationery printed in San Francisco.

THE
ILLUSTRATED CALIFORNIA NEWS,

A BREAKFAST IN THE MINES.—In order not to make a rush upon the trade, we divided ourselves into three parties, each going to a different store. Mac and myself went together, and made a breakfast from the following items ;—one box of sardines, one pound of sea-biscuit, one pound of butter, a half pound of cheese, and two bottles of ale. We ate and drank with great gusto, and when we had concluded our repast, called for the bill. It was such a curiosity in the annals of a retail grocery business, that I preserved it, and here are the items. It may remind some of Falstaff's famous bill for bread and sack.

One box of Sardines,	$16 00
One pound of hard bread,	2 00
One pound of butter,	6 00
A half pound of cheese,	3 00
Two bottles of ale,	16 00
Total,	$43 00

years following became securely rooted in the American language. It was said to originate in an old story about a farmer who had heard of elephants but had never seen one, and longed to do so. When a circus, complete with elephant, came to a nearby town, he loaded his wagon with eggs and vegetables and started for the market there. En route he met the circus parade led by the elephant. The farmer was enchanted but his horses were terrified. They bucked, pitched, overturned the wagon and ran away, scattering broken eggs and bruised vegetables over the countryside. "I don't give a hang," said the farmer. "I have seen the elephant."

The phrase became synonymous with the lure of California's gold, with the excitement of finding it and with the hardships and disappointments that usually came along with it. It was a concise description of the great American experience of the mid-19th Century, an experience that no spirited, venturesome man could resist.

By the time Buffum was well settled on Weaver's Creek other elephant viewers were streaming into California by the thousands. Those who came overland tended to gather at Sutter's Fort and the adjoining brand-new town of Sacramento, also on Sutter's land, where the American River flowed into the Sacramento. When Buffum went through there in November 1848 not a single house stood at the river's fork—there was, in fact, nothing on the spot but an abandoned riverboat beached on the bank and used as a store and warehouse. But a surveyor had been engaged to lay out a townsite, and two months later dozens of hastily erected buildings had sprung up.

By early 1849 speculation in building lots reached a furious pitch; before the year was out Sacramento had grown to 12,000 people. Even more Argonauts camped temporarily outside the town in a sea of tents, wagons and smoking cookfires. They were ragged, gaunt men who had crossed the deserts and mountains, who talked of what they had endured, how they had survived and what they should do next to get to the diggings.

The fast-growing, untidy, raucous village of San Francisco presented a similar scene. Ocean-going craft from all parts of the world—steamers, big sailing ships, schooners and brigs—discharged hordes of Argonauts. Many of them fetched up on a beach a mile east of the village proper, at a place wryly called Happy Valley. Here the more farsighted among the newcomers put up

On the shore of San Francisco Bay, Argonauts load gear into rucksacks and onto mules for the hike to the diggings. The lighters in the background have brought the gold seekers from ships anchored offshore.

in tents, while others crawled onto packing boxes or slept on their trunks or the bare ground while waiting to get their bearings and find their way to the gold fields.

Gradually, with the help of sketchy maps and haphazard conversations, the fortune hunters began to learn the lay of the country. The wide, brown Sacramento River, which emptied into San Francisco's huge bay, came down from the north, absorbing the waters of smaller, west-running rivers that drained the northern Sierra—the Feather, the Yuba and the American.

Each of the smaller rivers was fed in turn by a bewildering number of branches. So many that when mention was made of the east branch of the north fork there was no telling what river was meant unless the speaker happened to be standing right on it (or, as was often the case, in it). Along these mysterious forks lay gulches and bars where men found gold.

From the south, meandering through multiple channels across plains covered with bulrushes—generally called by their local nickname, tules—the San Joaquin River drained the Sierra. Before its meeting with the Sacramento in the north, 35 miles from San Francisco Bay, the San Joaquin absorbed various mountain-fed tributaries—the Cosumnes, Mokelumne, Tuolumne, Stanislaus and Merced—every one of them containing hidden caches of gold.

Sacramento was the staging area for the northern mines. And at the head of navigation in the San Joaquin, the equally raw new settlement of Tuleburg, later named Stockton, was the supply and departure point for the mines in the south.

Complicating the elementary geography of the gold regions was a grand confusion and bewildering number of picturesque place names. There were four gold camps named for the lost Biblical city of Ophir. There were four Poverty Bars, four Missouri Bars, three Long Bars. There were Angels Camp and Bidwell's Bar, Carson Hill and Cuteye Foster's. There were Coyote Diggings and Old Dry Diggings. There were Drunkards Bar, Dead Man's Bar, French Corral, Gouge Eye, Jimtown, Murphys, Melones (which was also known as Slumgullion Gulch), Murderers Bar, Mad Mule Gulch, Mokelumne Hill, Pilot Hill, Rattlesnake Bar, Red Hill, Rough and Ready, and Whiskytown.

There were many more, named for men, animals, recent local history, luck (both good and bad), mishaps and misbehavior. And pure capriciousness governed the naming of some. Yankee Jim's was named for an Australian. There were no volcanoes in Volcano. And Dry Bar was said at one time to have 26 saloons.

Fascinating names, but precise directions on how to get to the places they stood for were hard to come by. This vagueness might ordinarily have discouraged newcomers to Sacramento and San Francisco from trying to find their way to the diggings—had it not been for the stories of the miraculously easy ways in which gold had been discovered.

A Southerner brought his slave with him to Old Dry Diggings, near Coloma. The slave had a recurrent dream about finding gold under a certain cabin in the settlement. When the master had a similar dream, he bought the cabin and together the two men, master and slave, dug up the dirt floor and panned out $20,000 in gold. Another man in town took $2,000 from under his own doorstep. Three Frenchmen uprooted a tree stump from the middle of the Coloma road and dug $5,000 in gold from the hole. A man who had been sitting on a rock, moping in discouragement and homesickness, arose and kicked the rock in anger. The rock rolled aside, disclosing a nugget of shining gold. A little girl found a strangely colored rock and took it to her mother. The mother washed it off and saw that it was a seven-pound nugget. A prospector's mule was staked out for the night. When the stake was pulled up in the morning, there in the hole was the welcome glint of gold. Way up north above the Feather River a fellow claimed he'd found a lake whose shores were littered with big lumps of gold, but he could not remember exactly where it was.

Down on the Tuolumne a hunter shot a bear and the bear tumbled over the edge of a canyon, landing on a ledge at a lower level. When the hunter climbed down after the bear he found that the ledge was quartz, richly laced with gold. Another man found gold-bearing quartz after a gunfight in which a bullet missed him, but dug a crease in some quartz near his shoulder; there was gold in the quartz. Near Carson Creek a miner died, and his fellow diggers decided to give him a decent funeral instead of the usual quick burial. After drinks all around, the miners marched solemnly to the grave site. One of them, who had been a powerful preacher back in the States, preached and prayed while the miners

A notice scribbled by a latecomer to the diggings suggests how easy it was to stake a claim. Miners simply picked their land, drove wooden stakes at the corners and tacked up a sign.

knelt at the graveside. The praying and preaching went on and on, and the mourners became restless. Some began gathering loose dirt from the grave and letting it run through their fingers, as miners will. Suddenly one of them yelled "Color!" The dirt from the grave had encouraging traces of gold. "Congregation dismissed!" the preacher roared. The body was hastily removed from the hole and set aside. All—preacher and mourners alike—began digging. Profitably, too.

Some of the tales were clearly mythical—the kind of folklore that flourishes wherever wandering, lonely men get together. But some of them seemed to wear the trappings of truth and bore the names of real people. A man named George McKnight went chasing after a runaway cow at Grass Valley and stubbed his toe on an outcrop of quartz that was, sure enough, rich with the precious metal. And there was a man named Bennager Raspberry—nobody could invent that name—who worked as a storekeeper at Angels Camp. He was locally famous because of the time when he had in his stock a keg of brandied peaches that had spoiled on the long trip around Cape Horn and up from San Francisco. He threw out the peaches, and all the pigs in Angels Camp stayed squealing drunk for four days and nights. Bennager went hunting one day and got the ramrod stuck in his musket. He couldn't pull it out, so he fired it at a hillside and the ramrod went through the exposed roots of a manzanita, a shrub that grows in the mountains. To get his ramrod back he had to pull up the manzanita, roots and all, and there in the ground was lots of gold. Things had been quiet at Angels Camp for a while, but with this discovery a big new rush was on.

And there were many who prospered by digging and panning gold in the conventional manner. An ox-team driver named John Sullivan had, in the summer of 1848, discovered a gully—since known as Sullivan's Creek—near the Stanislaus River from which he took out $26,000 in dust. The same summer—on the Fourth of July, as a matter of fact—John Bidwell, who had once worked for Sutter, found the fabulously rich Bidwell's Bar on the Feather.

The following summer a young man from New York staked a claim in a gulch somewhere between Coloma and the middle fork of the American. He dug four feet to bedrock and found gold in large pieces, free and pure. In six weeks he cleaned up $20,000, including one nugget weighing 14 pounds. Four other young fellows diverted the channel of the Yuba River about 50 miles

83

Six miners assemble proudly before their sturdy log cabin and its most prized possession: a theater sign they had rescued from nearby Deer Creek after a washout and hung above the door. To work their rich strike in a Sierra ravine, these partners put up a camp that was especially durable.

85

above its mouth, and from the exposed riverbed took $15,000 in gold in less than two months. Two of them then went farther upstream, built another diversion dam and made $3,000 in two weeks. There was, in short, more gold in the hills and waterways of California than most of the world had ever seen.

The newcomers listened to the tales of quick and easy wealth, wide-eyed and slack-jawed. They met whiskered, dirty men returning from the mines, carrying buckskin bags and quart pickle jars packed with gold dust, men who paid for drinks with a pinch of gold (the origin of the phrase "how much can you get up in a pinch?"). And they met still others who were returning empty-handed. These men, bitter and often sick, told all who would listen that the big talk of easy pickings for California gold was pure humbug. But no one paid much attention to them.

For Argonauts who came overland, the gold-mining region was close at hand the moment they crossed the Sierra Nevada into central California. But for gold seekers who came by sea and landed at San Francisco, the approach to the mines was slower and more difficult. First, like Edward Buffum, they had to work their way inland to a meeting place of the Sacramento and San Joaquin rivers; from there, they went up one of the two rivers to Sacramento or Stockton. Although there was no steamer service on the rivers until the late summer of 1849, many sailing vessels bucked the current, depending on uncertain winds to get them past sandbars and mudbanks. Prices for passage upriver ranged from $15 to $100 and more, depending on accommodations and the amount of baggage carried, and many Argonauts could not afford such fares. Some pooled their dollars, bought old boats from among the ships that had been stranded in San Francisco Bay and rowed upstream through dense clouds of ferocious mosquitoes. Others knocked a few boards together into primitive rafts and paddled across the bay to Oakland Point. From there they went on by foot.

Once on land, travel became even more difficult. California had few usable roads and few wheeled vehicles. Most of the roads ran parallel to the coast, connecting the missions that had been built by Franciscan fathers back in the 1700s. In the interior the closest thing to roads were the cattle trails that wandered haphazardly through swamps and boulder-strewn canyons, uphill and down. Strings of mules expertly managed by Mexican *arrieros* could follow them well enough, but the rocks and gullies made hard going for the old trail-worn wagons pressed into service to supply the mines.

Only a few Argonauts could afford a seat in a wagon or the rental of a riding horse or mule. Most made deals to have their gear carried by wagon or mule train while they proceeded on foot. Walking was arduous. The Central Valley was muddy and cold in winter, blazing hot and baked dry in summer, and the months on shipboard had left most of the men in poor condition for the long walk.

Enos Christman and two friends who arrived with him in San Francisco in the winter of 1850 after 222 days at sea made a typical trek. They went as far as San Joaquin City, 110 miles below Stockton, by boat. There they arranged with a Mr. Cox, a teamster, to carry their baggage to the Mariposa Diggings for $50. Cox, his wife and five children had been 10 months driving their oxen from Iowa to California.

Soon after leaving, Christman and his companions met a group of "brokendown looking fellows" headed in the opposite direction. "They told us," he noted in his journal, "they had been at the mines five or six months without being able to make anything, and that hundreds were working for their board alone. This did not in the least abate our bright anticipations. We are determined to go and see for ourselves."

That night the group camped on the bank of a small stream, brewed cups of chocolate and soaked chunks of hard pilot bread in it for their supper. "Here are three tired boys," Christman noted. "Oh, how my poor legs ache! I think I could almost rest forever."

Next day they came to the San Joaquin River. Their freight was taken across in a whaleboat, the wagon was disassembled and carried across on a barge, and the oxen were swum across. Then the wagon was put back together again and reloaded, the oxen were hitched up and the party moved on. They came to many of the shallow backwaters called sloughs and, in crossing one of them, the boys' big camp kettle, containing all their food, was dislodged from the wagon guide pole and drifted away downstream. Luckily one of them spotted it; otherwise they would have bedded down that night hungry as well as sore from aching legs and blistered feet. They had by now walked 45 miles. But they had been

With a scoop of gold dust in his left hand, a scale at his right to weigh it and his gold pan on the floor beside him, William D. Peck of Rough and Ready, California, sits for a portrait in his miner's cabin in 1852.

The Oakland Museum

cheered by the sight of herds of elk and wild horses, deer, antelope, coyotes, jack rabbits, ground squirrels, coveys of quail and huge flocks of ducks, geese and brant, all against the snowy crests of the Sierra Nevada as a dramatic backdrop.

On the fifth day they crossed the Merced River and entered the foothills of the Sierra. Next day they camped at last in a community of miners, less than a mile from where men were digging for gold.

Like all Argonauts, Christman and his friends were dismayed by the price of food at the diggings. At a tent store they bought 12 pounds of pork at 50 cents a pound, 2½ pounds of bread at 75 cents, a pound of brown sugar at 62½ cents. Christman recalled that after selling their provisions, clothes and tools in San Francisco he and his friends had about $85 apiece. He was now down to $27 and his companions had even less. They needed to find gold in a hurry.

Christman and one of his friends, McGowan, took a shovel and wash pan and went to work. After some aimless prospecting they found a location where they began to uncover traces of gold. "We continued here a little while, washing out some four or five panfuls of sand from which I obtained about 75 cents and McGowan about 25 cents." Next day they went farther afield and dug, sifted and washed dirt for six hours. When they returned to camp Christman had about a dollar's worth of dust and McGowan less. At this rate they would not make enough to eat. Christman had an additional worry: to finance his trip he had pledged half his earnings in the gold fields to the printer to whom he had been apprenticed back in Pennsylvania. He and his friends decided to move on to Mariposa, 30 miles away, in the hope that their luck would improve.

Any number of gold seekers could have told the same story: a rough trip to the diggings, some days of disappointment there and the decision to pack up and move. John Doble, a young blacksmith from Shelby County, Indiana, walked into the mining country from Stockton after paying a wagon driver $1.37 to carry his carpetbag. He went to the little settlement known as Latimer's Store on the Calaveras River. "I went to work sinking a small hole near Latimer's," he wrote. "I worked all day but could get nothing but a few small specks which I did not save. I worked verry slow as I knew nothing about it & the ground was hard to dig being full of stones. By night I got a hole about 3 feet square & 4 feet deep & was verry tired at that. The next day I went and sunk the hole to the ledge but found nothing more. The Ledge or Bed rock is found almost everywhere among the hills at a few feet below the surface, and that is where most of the Gulch Gold is found. Washed several pans of dirt but got nothing more than the color & that in verry small specks. Returned to the house tired of prospecting." So, like Enos Christman, Doble moved on; a few days later he was at Angiers, near the Mokelumne River.

Howard C. Gardiner of Sag Harbor, Long Island, was one of a party of seven young men who came to California by sea via the Isthmus, bought a whaleboat in San Francisco and set off in August 1849 for Stockton. One night they moored their boat in one of the sloughs of the San Joaquin, using an iron cookpot as an anchor. When they raised the cookpot next morning, it was full of glittering sand; for a moment they thought they had already found gold. But one of the boys identified their find as fool's gold—iron pyrites—and they moved on. At Stockton they managed to sell their whaleboat to a man just returned from the mines and they were paid in gold dust: 13 ounces, 6 pennyweight and 16 grains, carefully measured out on a grocer's scale — the equivalent of more than $200 at $15 an ounce.

A wagon driver agreed to haul their gear at $20 per hundred pounds. They bought and cooked a quantity of salted beef tongue to eat on their journey and set off for the Tuolumne River, walking behind the wagon that carried their belongings. The young men soon regretted buying that tongue. The weather was hot, water was scarce and the salty meat aggravated their thirst.

Three days of walking brought them to Hawkins' Bar on the Tuolumne, where several hundred men were camped. It was still a new mining district, in which most men, if they worked hard, could pan out from six to ten dollars a day. But, Gardiner noted, "that sum did not accord with their preconceived ideas and was considered too little. Every few days reports would come in of 'big strikes,' when a general stampede occurred and away they would go in pursuit."

Three of Gardiner's young friends chose a riverbank that looked promising: tufts of grass pulled up from the bank showed flakes of gold among the roots, though not in the quantity the young men had confidently expect-

An expense account *(below)* of the T.K.L. Company does not add up properly; in the left-hand column, $200 spent for a mule was more than the total. But T.K.L.'s income account *(right)* still shows a profit.

ed. In a few hours they washed about 20 buckets of dirt, then brought a panful of sand back to camp with them and put it aside to dry while they ate supper and slept. In the morning, when they took their proceeds to the storekeeper to be weighed, they were amazed to discover that they had $20 in gold—a very good payoff for their short day of work.

The men rushed back to the riverbank—but by that time a miner named Gauly was working their digging. They had neglected to leave their tools on the site, the accepted way of establishing a claim. "We had forfeited the claim through sheer ignorance," Gardiner wrote later. "We were ready to howl with vexation. That claim, afterward known as the 'Gauly claim,' was the richest spot ever struck on Hawkins' Bar and yielded thousands of dollars before it was exhausted." (Gauly stayed at Hawkins' Bar all through 1849, and prospered; he was remembered best for an order he gave the local trader when he bought provisions for the winter of 1850: "A sack of flour, 10 pounds of bacon, 10 of sugar, five of coffee, three of tea, a peck of beans, a bag of salt —and a barrel of whisky.")

Gardiner and his friends did not let their first disappointment stop them. They continued to work, put-

O boys I've struck it heavy! runs the title of this watercolor by forty-niner Victor Seamon. By 1853, when Seamon painted this scene, the rich placers had been worked over, so such celebrations had become rare.

ting their communal collection of gold dust in a mustard bottle and governing their purchases of food and supplies by the quantity of gold on hand. To decide upon their menus, they pasted strips of paper on the bottle, marked from bottom to top with the names of foods available at the camp: pork stew; pork and beans; roast beef and potatoes; plum duff; canned turkey with fixings; and, at the very top, oysters with ale and porter. The dust seldom rose above plum duff, Gardiner noted sadly, "while the average height was pork and beans."

In October news reached Hawkins' Bar of a strike on Sullivan's Creek, 20 miles away. A year earlier, John Sullivan had made his fabulous find there. Now an 18-pound nugget had been found, and most of the miners at Hawkins' Bar took off for Sullivan's Creek.

Gardiner and his friends dug a hole at Sullivan's. At the end of a week they had made $150—a little over three dollars per day per man, and less than they owed for groceries. Finally they struck dense blue clay and abandoned the effort. Cursing their luck, they began working the creek bottom with no better results. But while they toiled in the creek, they learned that another miner had taken over their abandoned hole and, sticking his pick in the sidewall—which they had neglected to examine—uncovered a pocket of gold so rich that his first pan yielded $300. The young men were sick with disappointment. For the second time they had barely missed the great strike they had traveled thousands of miles to find. They continued digging in the creek bottom and bailing out the seeping water, looking for bedrock. Before they reached it they found an empty whiskey bottle—proof they were slaving on a site that had already been worked. At that point they gave up their futile efforts and headed back for Hawkins' Bar. ●

To ensure fair play at the diggings, miners drew up rules governing such matters as claim sizes and water rights. Regulations for the Springfield area were issued so hurriedly that the printer misspelled the name.

MINING LAWS
OF
SPINGFIELD

Springfield, April 13, 1852.

At an adjourned mass meeting of the miners of Springfield and vicinity; held at Mr. McClure's Hall, according to previous notice,

The following Resolutions and Bounds were adopted, viz.:

BOUNDS.

Commencing at a spring above and near Yaney's steam saw mill, the line running from thence in a westerly direction to the north side of Mr. McKenny's store, from thence to a spring at the head of Dead Man's Gulch, thence following the said gulch to the Stanislaus river, thence down the river to Horse Shoe Bend, thence in an easterly direction to Mormon Creek, intersecting it one hundred feet below the Illinois House, thence up the creek to Sawpit gulch, thence up the Sawpit gulch to the Sullivan's Creek Water Company's reservoir, thence in a straight line to the spring, the place of commencement.

BY-LAWS.

ART. 1. A claim for mining purposes within this district shall not exceed one hundred feet square to each man.

ART. 2. That no man within the bounds of this district shall hold more than one claim.

ART. 3. That each and every man holding a claim within the bounds of this district shall work one day out of every three, or employ a substitute; otherwise such claims shall be forfeited.

ART. 4. That any persons holding claims with dirt thrown up or excavations made on such claims, such claims shall be governed by articles 2 and 3.

ART. 5. That each and every man holding a claim within the bounds of this district, shall designate such claims by erecting good and substantial stakes at each corner of their claims, or dig a ditch around said claim, with a notice, signed by each person or individual of a company holding such claim.

ART. 6. Where two or more claims join together, and are worked by companies, such companies can work on any portion of such claims as they deem expedient, complying with article 3.

ART. 7. That when any dispute arises concerning claims, and either party shall refuse to refer such dispute to a committee of five, two to be chosen by each party and the fifth to be chosen by the four, the party so refusing shall forfeit all right to such claim in dispute.

ART. 8. That all water claims in dispute shall be settled by and according to article 7.

ART. 9. That a standing committee of ten be appointed, to whom complaints shall be made in all mining disputes, and it shall be their especial duty to see article 7 enforced, and that said committee be empowered to summon a posse at any time when necessary to assist them in the discharge of their duty.

ART. 10. That all laws passed by this meeting shall be retro-active.

STANDING COMMITTEE.

Chairman.—Mr. J. Swift, Jr.

Mr. James Eddy, Mr. J. Roberts.
"   Shields, " E. Smith;
Dr. Hughs, " W. Crocker,
Mr. Vincent. " J. Montgomery

W. Sudworth, *Secretary.*

Resolved, That the proceedings of this meeting be published in the Sonora Herald, and that 500 copies be printed in hand bills.

Resolved, That the Standing Committee have the supervision of printing the above.

J. HARRINGTON, President
W. L. Thayer, Secretary.

Simple tools for separating out the gold

Of all the contraptions designed to help the Argonaut separate his gold from the earth around it, the most popular was the lowly pan. The pan was simple to use and versatile: you could wash a shirt, feed a mule or fry bacon with it.

But panning meant hours of squatting in ice-cold water, rotating the pan until a man's arms were numb. To alleviate the struggle, the miners whacked together all sorts of ingenious gold separators. Though none proved less laborious than the pan, the three types shown here—the cradle, long tom and sluice box—did make the job move faster. Yet they were all simply extensions of the pan-washing method. And in the final cleanup, it was the pan that kept the last particles of gold from escaping.

THE WASH PAN

Usually made of tin or iron, the pan was flat-bottomed with gently slanting sides. The miner first filled it with dirt and then began swirling it around under water *(left, above)*. Next he raised it up from the water, continuing the circular motion and punctuating it with small jerks in and out of the water that washed out lighter sand *(right)*, and left only gold-carrying residue.

THE CRADLE

The cradle was an oblong wooden box about three feet in length and mounted on rockers. Bars called riffles were nailed along the bottom of its open lower end; and an apron made of canvas stretched over a frame was placed at a slant inside its upper end. A hopper with a perforated base and a side handle fitted over this end. Rocking the cradle with the handle, the miner poured water over gravel in the hopper *(above, right)*. Strained through the hopper and deflected by the apron, the water ran out of the rocker's lower end, leaving gold-bearing sediment behind each riffle.

THE LONG TOM

The long tom consisted of two parts: an inclined, 12-foot-long trough that ended in an uptilted, perforated iron sheet called a riddle; and the riffle box the trough rested on. Loads of gravel were washed through the riddle to the riffle box, where heavier gold particles were caught by the bars.

THE SLUICE

An improved form of the long tom, the sluice consisted of a series of riffle boxes fitted together. A continuous flow of water ran through the sluice, while miners shoveled in dirt along its sides. Because of its length, the sluice could process more gold-bearing dirt than could the long tom.

THE THREE BASIC TYPES OF RAW GOLD

Nuggets   Dust   Flakes

Once it had been separated from all surrounding material, gold appeared in one of the three forms shown here. Though the relative purity of the different samples causes the piles to vary in size, each weighs about one ounce—worth $16 to a miner in San Francisco in 1849.

An 1852 miner's map of Vallecito shows some worthless holes and a heavy sprinkling of good ones winding along a deposit of gold-rich soil. As the map notes, one pit just south of town yielded $2,366.35.

Joseph Pownall, who came from Louisiana by wagon in 1849, told of arriving at Mariposa early in September, "rather the worse for wear." On the second night there, his mules were stolen and "I had the pleasant reflection of finding myself homeless, friendless, penniless & confoundedly ragged and besides considerably in debt." As for his luck in the diggings: "I must candidly say not quite as well as expected. My calculations were somewhat up in the big figures. That there is gold here and in abundance & scattered all over the Country no one who has ever been here will deny. To get it must needs require not only very hard work but a fair proportion of good luck also, the latter I consider quite essential, for one man may sink a hole & without much trouble take out 1, 2, 3, 4 or more ounces of dust daily, while his nearest neighbor, off only a few feet, equally well accounted with all the necessary implements & withal quite as well raised, educated & good looking must content himself as well as he can with little or next to nothing."

Luck was part of the prospector's gamble; only the naïve thought that anything impressive could be done without it. Few forty-niners, however, were prepared for the incredibly hard work. Working 50 pans of dirt in a 10-hour day was regarded as a reasonable goal. But digging the dirt to fill those pans, sorting it out, panning the more promising material with the whirling motion that would let water carry away the lighter, useless sand and separating the gold (if any) from the remaining heavy sand—all came to far more work than most of the gold seekers had anticipated. Buffum, the ex-soldier, said that gold digging combined "the various arts of canal-digging, ditching, laying stone walls, ploughing, and hoeing potatoes—and adding to this a life in the wilds of the mountains, living upon poor provisions, continually exposed to the burning rays of the sun or the heavy dews of night, and the occupation becomes anything but a pleasant one. But to a man endowed with a constitution to endure hardship, with hands accustomed to labour, and with a heart which suffers not to be sorrowed with disappointment, there was never a better opportunity in the world to make a fortune."

Few forty-niners were so equipped. William McCollum, a physician from Lockport, New York, was in his early forties, much older than most of the forty-niners. At Jacksonville, where he dug with a friend, he noted that some miners were making an ounce ($16) a day. But: "We could not by tasking ourselves beyond the bounds of prudence earn half that amount. Panning is exceedingly laborious and taxes the entire muscles of the frame. In its effect it is more like swinging a scythe than any work I ever attempted. The abundance of gold in California has not been as much overrated as the labor of procuring it has been underrated."

Bayard Taylor, the reporter for the *New York Tribune* who toured the California gold fields in 1849, wrote: "Those who, retaining their health, return home disappointed say that they have been humbugged about the gold, when in fact they have humbugged themselves about the *work*." And the *Calaveras Chronicle,* an early gold-district newspaper, observed that gold mining was "the only occupation in which men appear to engage without the least preparation or forethought."

Despite their lack of preparation and forethought the forty-niners adapted quickly, if they adapted at all. They learned the simple, improvised claim laws that governed whatever camp they were in. The size of a claim, determined mainly by the richness of the diggings in the area, was standard in each camp; in very rich camps it might be as little as a hundred square feet. Each miner was allowed one claim, and he proved possession by the presence of his tools and his continued work on the site. Disputes were settled by juries of other miners in the area. It was a primitive sort of arrangement but, in the early stages at least, it worked well. Still, from the beginning, most newcomers complained that it was difficult to find unclaimed land—a feeling that was later reflected in a popular gold-camp song:

> *When I got there the mining ground*
> *Was staked and claimed for miles around.*

Miners soon learned the rudiments of elementary geology and mineralogy. They came to know that reddish earth is usually more promising than other kinds, and that iron pyrites blink, shatter under pressure and feel gritty between the teeth, while true gold shines evenly, mashes flat under pressure and feels smooth to the teeth. And they were constantly reminded that gold is heavier than the other materials among which it is found—the key to all methods of separating out placer gold.

They got rid of the foppish clothes they had brought with them from the East—the white boiled shirts, frock coats, vests, kid gloves and fancy boots. (Successful miners often bought the clothes, cheap and only slightly used, to go on a spree in San Francisco.) Wardrobes were reduced to a couple of wool shirts, a couple of pairs of heavy trousers, stout boots, a wide-brimmed hat and—a single, harmless touch of the dude—a bright silk sash to wear around the waist. Hair and whiskers went unshorn, uncombed and, usually, unwashed.

Also abandoned was the peculiar mining equipment that many Argonauts had innocently invested in—long earth augers; various patented arrangements of sheet iron and lumber, such as the Great Centrifugal Hydropital Gold Washer; and a number of contraptions that resembled butter churns. Instead they paid dearly for such homely implements as shovels, picks, pry bars and pans. If pans were not available they might make do with a Mexican batea, or wooden bowl, or a tightly woven Indian basket. As soon as they could, most of them equipped themselves with a cradle or rocker, a device used in Europe for at least three centuries.

The gold cradle the forty-niners used—probably after a design brought to California by someone who had seen one in the Georgia gold fields a decade or two earlier—looked much like a tilted infant's cradle mounted on rockers *(pages 74-75)*. It dramatically increased the amount of gold-bearing dirt or gravel that could be processed in a day. It also changed the basic social unit of the diggings. The first Argonauts into the field usually paired off in twos—one to dig and one to pan—and still the man with the pan could not keep pace with his partner. However, efficient use of a cradle required a team of four men—two to dig out the pay dirt, one to shovel it into the hopper and follow it with a bucket or two of water and one man to rock the machine steadily back and forth. The team then split the profits four ways.

A cradle could be built in a few hours at a cost of about two dollars, if the materials for it were available. The materials being scarce, cradles cost as much as $100 in the gold fields. Unable to afford one, Enos Christman and a companion slapped together a makeshift substitute without proper tools or sawed lumber. "Who would have thought," Christman lamented, "that old bachelors like ourselves would be caught making a cradle for our own use? McGowan and myself worked steadily at it all day and yet it is not finished. It will require at least another day's work. In making it, about six feet of boards are requisite and this we had to hew out of the solid timber. I find it the hardest work ever I was engaged in." On top of that, the perforated iron sheet cost them half an ounce of gold dust.

As gold became harder to find, more and more sophisticated equipment was needed. At the outset a jackknife or a spoon had been enough. Then the pan. Then the cradle. Then the long tom, or simply the tom—a larger, longer, more efficient version of the cradle. And as placer gold became scarce, miners looked for ways of recovering gold from solid quartz. One of the simplest was the arrastra, first used by Mexican and Chilean miners in the gold fields (Americans soon shortened the word to raster).

A typical arrastra resembled a crude gristmill built upon a circular pavement of flagstones. In the center stood a post, supporting a long axle and one or more heavy, abrasive stones. A mule or horse hitched to the end of the axle was driven round and round the pave-

Forty-niners in the American River Basin take time out to pose for a group photograph. Smartly dressed townsfolk (*foreground*) visited the diggings now and then to exchange news and gossip with miner friends; and itinerant photographers would preserve the occasion for friends back East.

ment, and the stones crushed gold-bearing fragments of quartz. When the quartz was reduced to powder the miners would rub a pinch of it against an ear lobe to make certain it was completely smooth and fine. The gold could then be extracted either by simple washing or by combining it with mercury; the mercury-gold amalgam could then be separated either by squeezing through a chamois bag or by vaporizing it in a retort.

The end result of all the mining methods was pure gold, but gold varied in quality and size. Although the forty-niners generally referred to all gold as dust, true dust, or fine gold, was gold in the very smallest particles and resembled fine yellow sand. Coarse gold varied in shape and ranged in size from wheat kernels to melon seeds. Lump gold in nugget form was the best of all.

In one form or another, as much as $1,000 in gold could be washed from a single pan. Few forty-niners ever had that exhilarating experience. From a half ounce to an ounce ($8 to $16) of gold a day was generally recognized as the minimum required to keep a miner at work, paying inflated prices for food and supplies and putting a little aside to get him back to his hometown some day. Curiously, most of the miners who left records of their California experience in journals, diaries or letters seemed to have fallen short of that minimum; their day's take usually ranged from a few cents to a few dollars. But those who were more successful tended to be secretive about it, not wanting others to crowd in on their discovery. Newcomers who asked for advice on where to start digging were usually directed to locations that had been thoroughly worked over.

Still, news of rich strikes could not be kept secret. The slightest rumor, based on fact or imagination, would race through a mining camp like wildfire. "It had confidingly come to our ears," wrote D. R. Leeper of his life as an Argonaut near Old Dry Diggings, "that someone had affirmed that he had seen a man who had heard another man say that he knew a fellow who was dead sure that he knew another fellow who, he was certain, belonged to a party that was shoveling up the big chunks." Of all the diseases afflicting the forty-niners, none was more widespread than so-called lump fever, caused by news, no matter how unreliable, of a big strike some place other than where a miner was working.

The alacrity with which miners abandoned one claim to go in search of a better-paying one elsewhere was one of the principal reasons that few forty-niners really struck it rich. They recognized this failing themselves and liked to tell a story about it: a prospector went to heaven (this statement invariably got a laugh) and was turned back at the Pearly Gates by St. Peter because "we have too many prospectors in Heaven already" (this got a bigger laugh). "If I get rid of them for you, will you let me in?" asked the prospector. St. Peter did let him in—provisionally. The prospector then circulated among his own kind, saying that there was a big gold strike in Hell. His listeners streamed back to the Pearly Gates, demanding to be let out. Suddenly alone, the prospector became uneasy. He returned to St. Peter and asked if he too could leave. "Because," he said, "while I started that story about the gold strike in Hell myself, there just *might* be something to it."

Had the forty-niners not been goaded by their eternal itch to move on, many of the richest strikes might have gone undiscovered for decades. As it was, within a year or two of the discovery at Sutter's Mill, prospectors had sampled dirt in nearly every nook and cranny of the Sierra's western watershed. One of the most diligent of these pioneer miners was William Downie, a sturdy little Scotsman with amiable manners.

Downie himself told of how he had been smitten with gold fever while living in Buffalo, New York. From Buffalo he made his way to New Orleans, where he signed on as a seaman aboard the clipper *Architect* to work his way around the Horn. He landed in San Francisco late in June 1849 and worked as a laborer for a few days to fatten his purse. At night he slept under the stars in "Hide Park," a clearing where baled hides were stored for shipment.

A week or so later at Sacramento, Downie joined forces briefly with John Rose, another Scot, who had

A RICH LODE OF REMINISCENCES
"Every heart beat high," exulted John Hovey of Lynn, Massachusetts, in his diary for January 1849, as he joined a group of friends sailing from New York to the gold fields of California. Once ashore, however, the men fell to squabbling and Hovey set off for the fields alone. During the next two years he tramped over the Sierra, but never hit a lucky claim. Finally, in 1851, he walked away from the diggings with no fortune and no further illusions. But his diary of pungent entries, illustrated with his own watercolors, encompassed a fascinating account of a prospector's life.

Cannon Bar, Calaveras River, June 3rd, 1850

Turned out about day light, by the sound of the pick and Crow bar, and tumbling of rocks, and got our breakfast, and with our Pan whent to work and commenced bailing out the water which is full every morning, and when bailed out it keeps one man all the time to keep it free Return'd to our camp from the labours of the Day, about five O'clok makeing thirty Doll — there is about thirty miners at work on this bar and average about twelve Dollars a day, to a man and have to work hard for that I suppose the most of the people in the States would think a man was a makeing his fourtune right of, and so he might if he had no expences especially if they was as high as they are here every thing one Doll per pound, and if he could work every Day; but a miner cannot work more then two thirds of his time, his Claime will either give out so he will have to spend two or three Days or a week and perhaps a fortnight, before he finds a place and then again if he is in the Dry Digings he sinks a hole perhaps from twenty to forty foot which takes two men two to three weeks before he gits Down to the ledge, and then its like a lottery he may be fourtunate and he may not be, and if not all his labour is lost it is supposed to be the hardest work that ever was done on the face of the Globe

Hovey illustrated his entry for June 3, 1850 — a day of disillusionment — with two miners sifting dust in a cradle.

Red Bluff, Tuolumne River, Sept 30, 1850.

This Day the Sheriff and about a dozen of Mexicans made there appearance in Search of Hall for murder, but he got Scent of them and hid in the chaparall untill the next morning, when he made his escape to Stockton from thence to the States it is Supposed, it is the opinon of the Citizens of this place that he is a big villian and that this is not the first bloody Deed that he has Committed in California. We have amongst us all kinds of Gambling from the Card Table to a foot Race. every Saturday afternoon they have a foot Race and a great amount of money is Staked. Last Saturday, one Came of between Mr Reigns of Bath Me. and an English man, Reigns Coming of victor in running twice there were from six to ten thousand Doll Staked

Camp on Red Bluff Bar

A deceptively placid camp scene accompanied diarist Hovey's account of a manhunt and a race for high stakes.

struck gold in 1848 at a spot afterward known as Rose's Bar. From Rose's Bar, Downie went to Bullards Bar where he bought a rocker and mined with little success through August and September.

The very smell of Bullards Bar was oppressive to him: "The perfumes of pork and slapjacks arising from a hundred frying pans," he said, "could only be compared with all the soap factories in Ohio frying out at full blast." But the smells were incidental; Downie was most concerned with the problem of finding gold. He noticed that one group of the miners who visited the store at Bullards Bar consistently paid for their provisions with large lumps of gold and he found that they came from farther up the Yuba River. Immediately, he decided to prospect in that direction.

To get up the Yuba, Downie assumed leadership of a group made up of a white man, a white boy and seven blacks. (At least some of the latter may have been fugitive slaves.) A little later they were joined by an Indian and a Hawaiian Islander named Jim Crow. The enlarged group moved north to Cuteye Foster's Bar. Foster confirmed Downie's guess that there was a lot of gold farther up the Yuba, but warned him that it was too late in the season to travel in that rough country. Downie and his men decided to go anyway. Instead of following the river valley they struck across the mountains on what Downie hoped would be a shorter route. Travel was slow and difficult in the wilderness of the Sierra foothills. The white man had already dropped out; he was a hypochondriac who, Downie said, ate pills "like a chicken eating dough." The rest of the company thought of turning back, too, but Downie persuaded them to stick it out for a bit.

"Had those men prevailed upon me," Downie later wrote, "who can tell what would have been my lot in life? It was traversing those few hundred yards that decided so much afterward and gave me, for years to come, friends, influence, even renown." The "few hundred yards" took them over the mountain crest and down to the forks of the Yuba. Here they camped and Jim Crow killed a 14-pound salmon. The men boiled it in their cookpot—and afterward found specks of gold in the bottom of the pot.

Next morning the oddly assorted company began washing dirt and digging gold out of the crevices in the rocks. After the usual tentative tries and false starts, their luck turned good and got better and better: 17 ounces one day, 24 the next, 29 the next, and 40 ounces—including 14 ounces (about $225) in a single pan —on the fourth day. Clearly, this was a digging that would hold up for a while. The men prepared to settle in for the winter, and part of the company went back for enough provisions to see them through. Downie and the men who remained with him built a cabin of logs, shingles and rawhide at the forks in December 1849. They almost starved to death before they got their provisions—for which Downie paid $3,900, at a flat rate of two dollars a pound for everything. At one point Downie said that their shrinking sack of flour seemed more valuable than their bulging sack of gold. Nevertheless, they continued to mine the gold; Downie himself seldom took less than a pound of gold a day and often as much as 20 to 30 ounces.

So rich a find could not be kept secret long. Before the winter ended hundreds of miners came to the forks of the Yuba and soon Downieville, as the camp came to be known, was a settlement of several thousand.

William Downie was a rich man now, but his essentially generous and tolerant nature did not change and he was often victimized by others. When Cuteye Foster's storekeeper, William Slater, became ill Downie nursed him back to health. Soon afterward, Slater told Downie and other Yuba miners that he knew a way to get $22 an ounce for gold instead of the prevailing $16. He offered to carry a cargo of Yuba gold down to Sacramento and dispose of it at this premium price. Agreeing that Slater should keep two dollars an ounce for negotiating the transaction, the miners entrusted him with $25,000 worth of gold. Downie even made up a special package of specimen nuggets for Slater to take as a gift for Mrs. Slater. Slater was never seen in the diggings again—but Downie heard about him indirectly. A latecomer at the Yuba diggings said he had met Slater in Panama; the ex-storekeeper had recommended that when the miner arrived on the Yuba he look up Downie, "one of the best fellows in the world, ready to do all in his power to assist a stranger."

Downie was not always taken in, however. He had grave doubts about a certain Thomas Robertson Stoddart, whom he found to be "possessed of a gentlemanly bearing and of more than ordinary education, and undoubtedly belonged to a good family. But my impression is that he was not mentally well balanced." Stoddart was, in fact, one of the strangest of the strange characters who found their way to the gold camps. Only one thing about him was indisputable: he had a scar on one leg. On some occasions he said it was from a wound he suffered in an 1840 bombardment of Acre, in Palestine, while serving in the British Navy aboard H.M.S. *Asia.* (Others said he got it from a fall in Philadelphia while living as a remittance man.)

Stoddart claimed that, in addition to his military service, he had worked as a journalist and a schoolteacher, and he also acted as an agent for a dubious mining machine called the Gold and Gem Separator. He had crossed the Plains in 1849; in the winter of 1849-1850 he had shown up, exhausted and near starvation, in the Yuba camps. And he had a parcel of gold.

The scar on his leg was an important part of the story he had to tell—but this time he had a completely different explanation for it. Stoddart said that he and a companion had become lost in the mountains. They came upon a lake surrounded by three high peaks, threw themselves down to drink the cold, clear water, and found that the shores and bottom of the lake were studded with lumps of gold. It was too late in the year to set up camp, so they took some gold and started for the mining camps on the Yuba, only to be ambushed by Indians. Stoddart's companion disappeared and was presumably dead; Stoddart claimed that he had been wounded in one leg—hence the scar—but escaped.

Stoddart's story was regarded with considerable skepticism. For one thing, the wound was remarkably well healed. Some thought him mad, crazed by his experience in the wilderness. Some thought him a plain liar, an embroiderer of current tales about gold-rich lakes marked by a bald mountain or a lone tree or other imprecise landmarks. Still, his tale furnished much conversational fodder around stoves and campfires that winter. And since forty-niners were eager to believe almost anything about the location of gold, a company of two dozen men was formed to follow Stoddart back to his "Gold Lake" in the spring. When warmer weather came they took off, followed at a discreet distance by hundreds of noncompany members.

Stoddart led them this way and that, forging ahead, retracing his steps, taking contrary directions, studying the configuration of peaks and the shadows cast by the sun. Finally the members of the company lost patience and threatened to hang Stoddart if he did not find the treasure lake within 24 hours. Stoddart either fled during the night—accounts differ—or marched back to the forks of the Yuba with the disgruntled miners, who later referred to the venture as the Goose Lake Hunt.

But the futile search for Gold Lake was not without consequences. Three Germans in the expedition headed back for Downieville by a roundabout way, prospecting as they went, in territory farther north and east than anyone had worked before. They had only moderate luck until one of them, carrying water to their campsite on the east branch of the north fork of the Feather, discovered some rocks whose every crack was packed with gold. It was not necessary to pan dirt at that campsite. The Germans pried gold out with their knives—and in four days they had $36,000 worth.

Word of the big strike spread through all the camps. By July prospectors were swarming in, first by the hundreds, then by the thousands. There was unanimous consent on a name for the place: it was simply called Rich Bar (not to be confused with Big Rich Bar and Little Rich Bar on the Yuba). And other bars turned up nearby—Smith's, Indian, Poverty, Peasoup, Missouri, Taylors, Browns, Muggins.

In this rich field, the miners happily agreed to limit their claims to 10-foot squares along the river and 40-foot squares in the dry diggings on the slopes. Early arrivals who held the river claims did astonishingly well. Single pans frequently yielded as much as $2,000; one miner found $2,900 in his pan. A party of Georgians was said to have cleared $50,000 in one day's work. And the gold was not limited to the river. A latecomer named Enoch Judson went so high on a hillside to stake his claim that the other miners laughed at him as a greenhorn and a fool. They were still laughing when he staggered down the hill with his first sack of dirt to wash on the riverbank. That sack yielded $750—enough to send the others scurrying into the hills.

As more and more men crowded into Rich Bar difficulties over claims inevitably arose. A group of Americans disputed one particular claim with a party of Frenchmen. After much argument it was decided to settle matters in a fist fight between one American and one Frenchman. The chosen gladiators slugged it out for three solid hours; by that time the Frenchman could

A neatly symmetrical log cabin houses the Coyote and Deer Creek Water Company, which was one of the first firms to bring water to miners.

Rustic masters of hanky-panky at the gold-camp waterworks

Water was vital to the forty-niners. Each improvement in their tools, from pans to cradles to long toms to high-pressure hoses, demanded water, and miners often staked claims far from streams. Getting water to such claims meant ditchdigging and flume-building on a scale far beyond any one miner's physical or financial means. Therefore, companies were formed to bring in water — at a price.

In 1850 one pioneering company brought water a mile and a half from Mosquito Creek to the Coyote Hill diggings — a tremendous triumph. Before the end of the 1850s some 730 companies had built almost 6,000 miles of ditches, canals and flumes at a cost of $13,575,400. One company ran a 1,500-foot-long flume 206 feet above ground. Another blasted away 80 feet of stony overburden to cut a mile of ditch, then drove a 3,100-foot tunnel through mostly solid rock. But the rewards were rich as a mother lode: most companies charged the first user of their water half his yield; the second user, 40 per cent; and each subsequent user, 30 per cent.

To protect such profits, the water companies were not above an occasional bit of skulduggery. One firm brought water to a small mining town at high rates, promising to reduce the rates as its investment was amortized. But the rates stayed high, and the town finally formed its own company. After months of labor, the townspeople celebrated the great day when water was supposed to flow from a reservoir into a flume and on to the diggings. With a flourish, the mayor opened a valve. Nothing happened. It seemed that during the flume's construction, someone had raised each of the survey stakes — just enough to prove that water will not flow uphill.

no longer get to his feet, and the claim went to the Americans. The Frenchmen obediently moved out, looking for another prospect. They soon found a promising ravine—which turned out to be French Gulch, the richest of the diggings around Rich Bar.

Wherever they found pay dirt, the men settled down to long workdays and rough housekeeping. In advance camps, whether the forty-niners made pennies or hundreds of dollars a day, the food they ate was routinely bad. Sometimes venison and other game might be available, but miners who tended to business had little time for hunting. Occasionally a Mexican would drive in a cow from Southern California or from a nearby ranch, and that meant fresh beef. But in the main it was pork, pork, pork, either pickled or cured, and almost always fried. "I've lived on swine till I grunt and squeal," ran a miners' song. And one diarist noted: "The pork I bought last night is the stinkenest salt junk ever brought around the Horn. It is a hardship that we can't get any better hog meat. We fry it for breakfast and supper, boil it with our beans, sop our bread in the grease."

Most miners became adept at making sourdough bread and flapjacks, and beans could usually be had. But fresh fruits and vegetables were almost totally lacking. Those who had survived cholera and various agues and fevers on the trip west had little chance to recuperate on such a regime. And many who were perfectly healthy on arrival came down with land scurvy.

Edward Buffum, one of the victims, described the symptoms in his journal: "Swelling and bleeding of the gums, followed by a swelling of both legs below the knee, which rendered me unable to walk. For three weeks I was obliged to feed upon the very articles that had caused the disease, and growing daily weaker, enduring the most intense suffering from pain in my limbs which were now becoming more swollen and turning black." Fortunately someone had spilled a sack of beans on the mountainside; they had germinated and one of Buffum's companions gathered the sprouts. For several days Buffum lived on fresh boiled greens supplemented by an infusion of spruce bark. Soon afterward he acquired some potatoes—at three dollars a pound—and the vegetable diet put him back on his feet.

Though the problems of housekeeping were the same everywhere in the diggings, the men who faced those problems varied widely. In fact, though they all came to live and look more or less alike, there was no such thing as a typical forty-niner. Walter Colton, a U.S. Navy chaplain with a passion for alliteration, found the miners "a mixed and motley crowd—a restless, roving, rummaging, ragged multitude never before reared in the rookeries of man."

As the tide of Argonauts grew the newcomers became ever more mixed and more motley. Along with a scattering of experienced miners from the United States, Mexico, South America and Europe, there was a great number of men who barely knew how to pick up a shovel. The greenhorns included doctors, lawyers, preachers, bookkeepers and other white-collar workers, few of them prepared for the hard life of mining.

Hinton Helper described one sad case. He had stopped for the night at a camp near Sonora, had a supper of pork and beans and stretched himself on a rented bunk. "Toward midnight in came a wild, blustering lunatic yelling and screaming as if a legion of fiends were after him. He was bare-footed, bare-headed and bare-legged, having no clothes upon his person except a shirt. He had been roaming about the place four or five days and nights in this condition." The lunatic had been a successful lawyer and a member of the Maine legislature. Having failed to find gold he had "resigned himself to the bottle," and now, Helper observed, "we find him a raving maniac, a poor miserable, crazy vagabond."

Many who were physically or temperamentally unsuited to gold digging resisted the temptation of the bottle and turned to other lines of work. A Yale professor became a freight handler. A New York lawyer became a mule-team driver at $125 a month, explaining that "the whole business of a lawyer is to know how to manage mules and asses so as to make them pay." Other lawyers tried to resume their practice in a country that had gotten along reasonably well without them. "We needed no law," one old pioneer said, "until the lawyers came." But there was plenty of illness to be treated by doctors who had given up gold mining. Their fees were high, and could not always be collected. A doctor who had prospected at Angels Camp before returning to medicine ran a notice in a weekly newspaper: "All persons knowing themselves indebted to the undersigned will please call & settle at least a portion of their indebtedness, as I am much in need of money. William A. Kelly, M.D."

At least Dr. Kelly's patients trusted him well enough to let him treat them. But trust and tolerance were often conspicuously absent around the diggings. During the early days of the gold rush, when placers were rich and pickings easy, a fraternal camaraderie did prevail among the miners. But as gold became harder to find and more and more men tried to find it, envy, covetousness, sharp practice and prejudice became common.

To begin with, suspicion and dislike sprang up between men from different parts of the country. Franklin Buck of Bucksport, Maine, wrote home: "I feel at home with a Yankee. This talk about free-hearted Western men and Southern hospitality is a good deal like Southern chivalry: a humbug. I shall always be a Yankee." But William Perkins, a Canadian who became a storekeeper at Sonora and took a detached view of the Americans' regional peculiarities, observed that Yankees "are little liked for their stinginess and egotism, and their insolent contempt for the rights of others. The cool impudence of a Yankee, joined generally to skin-flint habits, and a sharpness or 'cuteness' of dealing, which verges at times rather palpably onto something very like roguery, have made him disliked by other people, and by none so much as by his own countrymen from the Southern states and Texas. As a friend, a companion, the Southerner is preferable. He is more of a gentleman in his habits and language; more honorable in his dealings; but he is more quarrelsome; too often intemperate; given to gambling, and too ready with his pistol or bowie knife. He is generally indolent."

While Yankees were disliked and distrusted, the so-called Pikes were the subject of almost universal derision. Originally, the term applied to men who came from Pike County, Missouri, but it came to stand for anyone from Missouri or Arkansas, and then for anyone of rustic appearance and limited education. To make the label even vaguer, there were men in the gold fields who did not care to reveal their origin or past history; to the question "Where you from, stranger?" they would abruptly answer "Pike" and move on.

A British artist named J. D. Borthwick, who roamed the gold fields in the early 1850s, described a typical Pike's clothes as "exceedingly old and greasy looking." They were the same clothes, Borthwick thought, that the Pike had worn while crossing the Plains, and would probably be the clothes he returned in. "Their shirts," Borthwick continued, "had, perhaps, in days gone by, been red, but now were a sort of purple; their pantaloons were generally snuffy-brown. Suspended at their back from a narrow strap buckled around the waist they carried a wooden-handled bowie knife in a leathern sheath; and over their shoulders they wore strips of cotton or cloth as suspenders — mechanical contrivances never thought of by any other men in the mines. Their coats, a garment not frequently seen in the mines for at least six months of the year, were extraordinary things — exceedingly tight, short-waisted, long-skirted surtouts of a greyish-blue color."

Then Borthwick turned to the miners who wore that garb. "They were mostly long, gaunt, narrow-chested, round-shouldered men, with long, straight, light-colored, dried-up looking hair, small, thin, sallow faces, with rather scanty beard and moustache, and small, grey, sunken eyes, which seemed to be keenly perceptive of everything around them. In their movements the men were slow and awkward, and in the towns especially they betrayed a childish astonishment at the strange sights occasioned by the presence of divers nations of the earth. Till they came to California many of them had never seen two houses together, and in any little village in the mines they witnessed more wonders of civilization than ever they had dreamed of."

But Borthwick wound up with a grudging respect for the frontiersmen. The Pikes, he said, could "use an ax or a rifle with any man. Two of them would chop down a few trees and build a cabin in a day and a half, and with their long, five-foot barrel rifles they could draw a bead on a deer, a squirrel or the white of an Indian's eye with equal coolness and certainty of killing."

However much they scorned each other, Americans reserved their real hatred for foreigners. At best, they tolerated Anglo-Saxons from abroad, but they heaped discrimination and abuse on all others. Paradoxically, those who suffered most were not foreign at all. They were the California Indians, whom the forty-niners treated with no more compassion than they did wild animals. It was no crime to shoot Indians, and thousands were so dispatched. But some miners found better uses for the Indians than casual target practice.

Indians were a key to many mining fortunes, either as laborers on starvation wages or — with gold they dug on their own—as easily gulled customers in the mining camp stores. At Jamestown, or Jimtown, named for a Colonel George James who had found a 75-pound nugget in nearby Woods Creek, there was a sharp trader named Savage. Savage had Indians doing his digging for him. He also supplied them, demanding—and getting —a pound of gold for a pound of raisins, three pounds of gold for a three-pound blanket. The Murphy boys, John and Daniel, also had Indians working for them at Murphys Camp—and the two young brothers were said to be among the richest men in California.

Of the true foreigners, the Chinese were held in the greatest contempt. At the end of 1848, when miners and would-be miners were flocking into California, only seven Chinese were known to be living there. A few years later at least 20,000 Chinese were scattered throughout the gold country—a country they called Gum Shan (Golden Mountain). Most of them found their way to the diggings; and all, whether miners or not, were victims of prejudice. Sometimes the prejudice took the form of cruel horseplay; it was proposed, for example, that every Chinese man be forced to cut off his queue, or pigtail, to qualify for residence in California. Sometimes the act was brutal, as when a brigand called Three-Fingered Jack was said to have hung up six Chinese by their queues and cut their throats.

The low-stake gambling games of the Chinese and their preference for opium over alcohol were viewed with suspicion by hard-gambling, hard-drinking whites. But most suspicious of all was their frugality and industry. They would work abandoned claims and tailings for specks of gold white men considered unworthy of the effort. The worst possible digging was described as one that "even the Chinese passed by." And on the rare occasions when Chinese miners turned up a promising prospect, they were driven off by the white men.

Spanish Americans stood higher than the Chinese in the bigoted pecking order of the mines for a number of reasons. For one thing, some of them were native Californians and to a reasonable man this fact cast some doubt on whether they were foreign at all. Many were magnificent horsemen and skilled handlers of mules and cattle. They were known as graceful and colorfully costumed dancers, and their balls and dances, at which outsiders were usually welcome, became notable social events in the mining camps. Some were tireless and reckless gamblers, playing with a dash and verve that the more cautious Anglo-Saxons envied. Their women would have been alluring even if women had not been so scarce in the mining camps.

Nevertheless, the U.S. miners detested the "greasers," the term they applied to all Mexicans and other Spanish Americans. One of the causes of friction was the fact that a number of Spanish American miners knew far more about finding gold than the average American forty-niner. Also, there were so many of them, especially in the beginning. Besides the original population, from October 1848 to the end of March 1849, according to statistics compiled by the collector of the port of San Francisco, 454 Mexicans, 270 Chileans and 90 Peruvians arrived at that port by sea—as compared with 340 Americans. In addition there were 178 Frenchmen (called "keskydees" because of their frequent question, *qu'est-ce qu'il dit?*), 162 from the British Isles and 100 Germans. And 5,000 or more Mexicans had come to California overland.

A Scotsman, Hugo Reid, who ranched in California and married a Mexican woman, summed up the forty-niner's attitude toward the Spanish Americans and anyone else different than himself. Warning a friend against coming to the mines, Reid said they "are loaded to the muzzle with vagabonds from every quarter of the globe, scoundrels from nowhere, rascals from Oregon, pickpockets from New York, accomplished gentlemen from Europe, interlopers from Lima and Chile, Mexican thieves, gamblers of no particular spot, and assassins manufactured in hell for the purpose of converting highways and byways into theaters of blood."

Yet for all their differences the forty-niners—Yankees and Southerners, Anglo-Saxons and Latins, even the Chinese—shared certain emotions that drew them together. Perhaps the strongest was homesickness.

Nothing provoked it more than the arrival of mail from home. Miners would cluster around a stagecoach, clutching bottles and sacks of gold dust, eager to pay anything from an eighth to a full half ounce of gold for the delivery of a letter. Enos Christman described one such scene in Sonora: "A huge fellow stepped up. A beard almost covered his face, and a large, heavy revolver in his belt gave him the appearance of a ruffian without a tender spot in his composition. A handsomely enveloped letter was handed to him. After weighing

Clad in picturesque mining costumes — high boots, flannel shirts and battered hats — four anonymous forty-niners show off the tools of their trade: picks, pans, a shovel and a wooden rocker for washing out the gold.

out his two dollars for it he stepped aside, broke open the seals and commenced reading it. In a few minutes this same burly, stern-looking man was in tears. He had heard from loved ones and memory carried him back to happier scenes." Meanwhile another man, pale and youthful, "was told that no letter had come for him. He raised his voice in blasphemy and swore his friends had forgotten him and cared nothing about him."

Christman was no stranger to homesickness himself. When he wrote those words, he had given up his hopes of making a fortune in gold. Instead, he was working as a printer, serving as deputy recorder for Tuolumne county — and saving every penny he could to go home to Pennsylvania and marry Ellen Apple. In January 1852 Christman went out to Cherokee Camp to visit an old friend, Clint Atkins. Atkins had been ill most of the time since his arrival in California (not long afterward, he would die there) but he went on looking for gold.

Christman stayed in the camp with Atkins overnight.

"We were quietly stretched out on our blankets around the fire swapping yarns with some gentlemen whose tents were close by. Suddenly we heard footsteps, as of some person stealthily approaching. As it was dark and therefore impossible to espy the intruders each one of us quickly drew his revolver, being always on guard against marauders. But, before we could fire, two colorfully dressed senoritas tripped out of the darkness into camp. They proceeded to sing many merry songs, accompanying their fine voices with music picked from their guitars."

Then Christman added, "The merry music changed and the senoritas played softly the strains of 'Home, Sweet Home.' A sob was heard, followed by another and another, and tears flowed freely down the cheeks of the gold diggers. And pieces of gold were generously tossed into the tambourine held out to receive them."

Mining that moved mountains and ravaged valleys

By the mid-1850s, large-scale mechanized mining companies had replaced many of the individual prospectors in the gold fields. Machines tore up the California landscape with the force of a combined flood and earthquake, as these pictures show. To expose stream beds for mining, entire river courses were moved by systems of dams and flumes: in 1851, virtually all of the 30-mile American River was temporarily diverted out of its original channel. To get at ore buried in quartz deposits deep in the earth, shafts were driven down as far as 700 feet along the 10-mile length of Amador County's motherlode country. And mammoth hoisting wheels, like the one on this page, raised whole hillocks of dirt to the surface. Of the new techniques, however, the most earth-wrenching was hydraulic mining. At the Malakoff mine *(pages 112-113)*, for example, streams of water daily tore off 50,000 tons of gravel from the towering Nevada County mountains—and left a 550-foot-deep canyon as a memento of their power.

Two miners admire a local marvel, a hoisting wheel that has spewed gravel mounds over the California landscape.

Pushing their wheelbarrows up narrow catwalks, company miners carry raw dirt to rotating screened drums *(background)* called trommels that separate out the gold-bearing sand and sift it down to a flume below. Belt-driven shafts powered by the running water of a creek turn the trommels.

Jet streams of water powerful enough to kill a man blast a mile-long gulch out of the cliffs at a mine in North Bloomfield. To create this liquid barrage, miners first built a 45-mile canal to bring in water, then attacked the cliff with 60 million gallons a day shot through eight-inch nozzles.

4 | The sprouting shantytowns

However unique their names (Ben Hur, Grizzly Flats, Cool) most California mining towns followed the same pattern of rapid growth — and usually, of decline. A potential town was born when a prospector squatting at a wilderness stream washed out a panful of gold-bearing dirt. Hearing of his good fortune, other miners swarmed to the area like ants. A full-fledged community of gold-hungry campers soon appeared; and a store quickly opened.

Major William Downie, who found gold in the winter of 1849 at the juncture of the Yuba River and its north fork, described the sequence of events that followed. During the spring after his strike "people began to build small houses, cabins or shanties." Then "men began to organize matters; to build only in certain positions, and to leave space for future streets."

At a camp meeting someone pointed out that those present "had been arguing about the width of streets, and yet they had not even named the town they were about to found." The name Downieville was immediately adopted — though for some time afterward, according to Downie, "the place continued to be called simply the 'Forks.'" Not until the local justice of the peace saw fit to date his writs from Downieville did the name stick.

Downieville, like Sierraville (below) and scores of similar towns, took shape according to the needs and tastes of the people who lived there. Within a year or less, blacksmiths and pharmacists opened their shops, a bank was built, the spire of a church rose above the skyline. Mail addressed to the town began to find its way there, and so did circuses and troupes of itinerant minstrels. Women, rare sights in the gold camps, appeared in the streets. But if the gold ran out and news reached the townsfolk of a rich strike somewhere else, all the bustle would subside in little more time than it took to pack a mule.

The citizens of Sierraville, as of 1852, include drinkers, card players, women, children and shaggy dogs.

A jumble of log-and-board buildings, the typical mining town of Placerville sprawls along the winding course of an old pack-mule trail. The community had such a reputation for wicked deeds that it earned the nickname of Hangtown.

Merchants and their customers fill the board-paved main street of Grass Valley, deep in the Sierra. Unlike boomtowns dependent on placer gold, which soon ran out, Grass Valley kept on booming; rich veins of gold-bearing quartz sustained the town's prosperity for many decades.

CLOUGH & KIMM[...]
BOOKS & [...]
STATIONERY WHOLESALE & RETAIL [...]
INTELIGENCE OFFICE.
LAW OFFICE

Townsfolk gather in their Sunday best on the main street of Sonora, center of the southern mines. Water buckets line the cornice of the stationery store (doubling as a miner's "inteligence" center) and the *botica*—Spanish for drugstore.

GOOD NEWS
FOR
MINERS.

NEW GOODS,
PROVISIONS, TOOLS,
CLOTHING, &c. &c.

GREAT BARGAINS!

JUST RECEIVED BY THE SUBSCRIBERS, AT THE LARGE TENT ON THE HILL,

A superior Lot of New, Valuable and most DESIRABLE GOODS for Miners and for residents also. Among them are the following:

STAPLE PROVISIONS AND STORES.

Pork, Flour, Bread, Beef, Hams, Mackerel, Sugar, Molasses, Coffee, Teas, Butter & Cheese, Pickles, Beans, Peas, Rice, Chocolate, Spices, Salt, Soap, Vinegar, &c.

EXTRA PROVISIONS AND STORES.

Every variety of Preserved Meats and Vegetables and Fruits, [more than eighty different kinds.] Tongues and Sounds; Smoked Halibut; Dry Cod Fish; Eggs fresh and fine; Figs, Raisins, Almonds and Nuts; China Preserves; China Bread and Cakes; Butter Crackers, Boston Crackers, and many other very desirable and *choice bits*.

DESIRABLE GOODS FOR COMFORT AND HEALTH.

Patent Cot Bedsteads, Mattresses and Pillows, Blankets and Comforters. Also, in Clothing—Overcoats, Jackets, Miner's heavy Velvet Coats and Pantaloons, Woolen Pants, Guernsey Frocks, Flannel Shirts and Drawers, Stockings and Socks, Boots, Shoes; Rubber Waders, Coats, Blankets, &c.

MINING TOOLS, &c.; BUILDING MATERIALS, &c.

Cradles, Shovels, Spades, Hoes, Picks, Axes, Hatchets, Hammers; every variety of Workman's Tools, Nails, Screws, Brads, &c.

SUPERIOR GOLD SCALES.   MEDICINE CHESTS, &c.

Superior Medicine Chests, well assorted, together with the principal Important Medicines for Dysentery, Fever and Fever and Ague, Scurvy, &c.

N.B.—Important Express Arrangement for Miners.

The Subscribers will run an EXPRESS to and from every Steamer, carrying and returning Letters for the Post Office and Expresses to the States. Also, conveying "GOLD DUST" or Parcels, to and from the Mines to the Banking Houses, or the several Expresses for the States, insuring their safety.———The various NEWSPAPERS, from the Eastern, Western and Southern States, will also be found on sale at our stores, together with a large stock of BOOKS and PAMPHLETS constantly on hand.

Excelsior Tent, Mormon Island,
January 1, 1850.

ALTA CALIFORNIA PRESS.

WARREN & CO.

Boisterous habitats that blossomed at the diggings

When young Howard Gardiner and his companions from Sag Harbor, Long Island, came to Sullivan's Creek in the fall of 1849, they were dead broke. Yet, like all fresh arrivals at a new gold field, they went straight to the camp store—in this case, a cramped, canvas-covered shack right in the middle of the diggings. There they learned the local rules governing the size of claims and picked up some clues as to where the best prospects were to be found. The storekeeper—in his memoirs Gardiner called him Bruce F., and noted with glee that he also hailed from Sag Harbor—lent them a tent until they could put up their own living quarters, and extended them credit for food, to be repaid when they found gold. Later that day Gardiner and his partners dropped into the store to settle a dispute over a stray horse they had found and "borrowed" on their way to Sullivan's; they eventually agreed to pay the owners of the horse $40 for their use of the animal. The storekeeper acted as arbiter in the controversy, then lent the young men from Sag Harbor the $40. Afterward, drinks were taken all around.

Gardiner and his friends were making use of the first real institution in a mining camp. If the camp survived, the store formed the nucleus of a future town. And the character of a mining town, its quality of life, could often be traced to the disposition and idiosyncrasies of

---

A poster for a tent store at Mormon Island, near Sacramento, advertises every kind of supply that a miner would need. Some miners found the list incomplete; the Mormon religion forbade tobacco or liquor.

STEAMER UNION.

BOLD VILLAIN.—From the Mountain Messenger we learn that the American House, in Gibsonville, was broken into on Saturday night last and robbed of a revolver, a breast-pin worth $40 or $50. On the succeeding night the Diamond Spring House was entered and a revolver taken. The villain's next descent was upon the Buckeye Ranch, where he took $60 from the bar-drawer and a watch worth $25. An English stuttering Sydneyite who had been loafing about the neighborhood is suspected of being the burglar. He claimed to have lived in Hansonville.

---

the man who ran the original store.

The actual structure that housed this all-important institution was, at least in its beginnings, a humble affair. A typical store consisted, at first, of nothing more than a tent, a frame-and-canvas hut or a log cabin, in which an entrepreneur like Bruce F. sold food, clothing, tools, blankets and the like. But at a successful digging the store would rapidly expand in function and capacity. The storekeeper, usually a man who had done a bit of gold mining himself, knew what fortyniners wanted as well as what they merely needed. He dispensed liquor by the bottle or the drink. He might serve beans and pork and flapjacks to transients or to newcomers who had not yet set up camp. He might rent out a wooden shelf or a space on the floor where a man could unroll his blankets and sleep overnight.

The food was usually dreadful, the liquor vile, the sleeping accommodations uncomfortable in the extreme. The three-card-monte dealer—if there was one in the store, and there usually was—often made more in a night than a moderately lucky miner made in a week. But the owner himself was an important and respected member of the community. He extended liberal credit to miners, unless they proved to be hopeless risks. The store scales measured an individual's accumulation of gold dust. The storekeeper was a repository of information and anecdotes and often, like Bruce F., an adjudicator of disputes. In some stores a cat-o'-nine-tails hung from the center post as a symbol and, on occasion, as an implement of the proprietor's authority.

The store was a social center, too. Miners congregated there in the evening and, standing at the bar or lounging about on the ground outside, talked of the

On a mining-town Saturday night, a gambler starts a game of monte at a table set up for the evening. The scene was depicted by J. D. Borthwick, an Englishman who panned for gold at Weaver Creek in 1851.

day's experiences. They placed greater emphasis on disappointments and mishaps rather than on their successes; a miner who made a lucky strike tried to keep it to himself. But rumors and speculations would be traded on rich diggings elsewhere and men would debate the advisability of moving on. In other moods, the forty-niners would speak of the wonders of the country, from the fierce grizzly bears that stalked the mountainsides to the mysterious origins of gold. They cursed the fleas and lice (which they called quicks and slows) that invariably infested their clothes and blankets. They read aloud their letters from home; or, lacking letters, they sentimentally reviewed memories of pretty girls, easy living, huge meals and feather beds. They relived their adventures at sea or in the deserts and mountains on their journey to California.

The men spoke a vocabulary laced with Spanish words, and used a roughhewn profanity enriched by slang from all quarters of the compass. To be smart or spruce was to be ripsniptious, and a few of them were. To be in a nervous state was to have the peedoodles. A row or a fuss was a conbobberation. A tiny piece of gold was a *chispa,* or spark. What you found if you really hit it rich was a *bonanza*—and the opposite of that was *borrasca.* The Mexicans talked of a *veta madre,* or mother vein, from which the placer deposits had been eroded, and the miners translated this into mother lode—the great, thick depository of gold that everyone thought must still exist somewhere.

Sometimes a fiddle or a flute or a concertina would strike up, and the lonely men would sing songs like "Old Dan Tucker," "Dearest Mae," "Uncle Ned," "I'm Sad and Lonely Here" and "The Old Oaken Bucket." And there were newer songs that dealt with the forty-niners' recent travels and present condition: "Crossing the Plains," "Coming Around the Horn," "Sweet Betsy from Pike," "On the Banks of the Sacramento," "There's a Good Pile Coming, Boys" and, particularly, the spicy one about the young ladies from a camp so tough it was nicknamed Hangtown—

Hangtown gals are plump and rosy,
Hair in ringlets, mighty cozy,
Painted cheeks and jossy bonnets—
Touch 'em and they'll sting like hornets!

Liquor helped with the singing, whether it was a bottle

of genuine New England rum (at $20 a bottle), cheap whiskey or brandy (both of which might come from the same barrel), or home-brewed Tanglelegs or Tarantula juice. And then there were the semilegendary Forty Rod and Sixty Rod, the smell of which would fell a man at those distances, even around a corner. Bar measures frequently dictated the value of gold dust. A pinch of gold, which would buy a drink or two, was reckoned at one dollar. A teaspoonful of gold was worth $16; a wineglassful, $100; and a tumbler, $1,000.

The drinking often got out of hand. In his journal John Doble told of an evening when he returned to Angiers' store on Alabama Gulch so tired after a day's prospecting that he did not even want to eat. "The Store was crowded when we returned & about dark a good many were tolerable tight or in other words 1/2 drunk & after dark they got to singing sailor songs & playing games &c and got us all up & Tom Baldwin played the fiddle for them & they danced and sung till near morning not letting us sleep any. Angiers has his wife here with him & she was greatly disturbed by the noise and obscene Language. Such is California."

Miners in luck liked to indulge themselves with fancy food. Camp stores carried certain exotic items, even in remote regions where staples such as flour and beans might be in short supply. One miner, known only as Buckshot, was said to have panned between $30,000 and $40,000 and to have spent it all on sardines, tongue, turtle soup, lobsters, oysters and French champagne. A miner in Hangtown, wanting to celebrate a streak of good luck, instructed a cook to fry up a mixture of eggs, bacon and tinned oysters—the origin of the celebrated Hangtown Fry.

But if a camp prospered, victuals improved even for those who had not struck it rich. Traffic hammered wilderness trails into a semblance of roads, and supplies came in with more certainty and regularity. Other stores would open. And on Sundays, when most miners laid down their tools—in some cases out of religious conviction, but more frequently because of simple weariness and the need to recuperate—the little camps began to resemble populated towns.

A forty-niner named Charles B. Gillespie described a Sunday in Coloma, where the gold rush had begun. "The principal street," he said, "was alive with crowds of moving men, passing and repassing, laughing, talking." Among them he noted Negroes from the Southern states, mulattoes from Jamaica, Kanakas from Hawaii, Peruvians, Chileans, Mexicans, Frenchmen, Germans, Italians, plus one Irishman and one ragged Australian. "Thimble-riggers, French monte dealers or string-game tricksters were shouting aloud at every corner: 'Six ounces, gentlemen, no one can tell where the little joker is!' or 'Bet on the jack, the jack's the winning card! Three ounces no man can turn up the jack!' or 'Here's the place to git your money back!'"

Now Gillespie caught a glimpse of the business of the place as opposed to its pleasure. Perched on a large box in front of a small canvas booth sat an auctioneer from Maine, "disposing of the various articles in the shebang behind him, 'all at a bargain.' What a ragged, dirty, unshaven, goodnatured assemblage!—swallowing the stale jests of the 'crier' with the greatest guffaws, bidding with all the recklessness of half-tipsy brains and with all the confidence of capacious, well-stuffed gold bags. 'Here's a splendid pair of brand-new boots! Cowhide, double-soled, triple-pegged, waterproof boots! The very thing for you sir, fit your road-smashers exactly; just made for your mud-splashers alone; going for only four ounces and a half—four and a half and gone! Walk up here and weigh out your dust.'"

Farther up the street Gillespie found a crowd gathered in and around an unfinished house. Inside was a preacher, "as ragged and hairy as myself, holding forth to an attentive audience. He spoke well and to the purpose and warmed every one with his fine and impassioned delivery. He closed with a benediction, but prefaced it by saying 'There will be divine service in this house next Sabbath—if, in the meantime, I hear of no new diggin's!'"

Of all the new diggings that became brawling, busy camps almost overnight, one of the most exciting was the aptly named Rich Bar, on the east branch of the north fork of the Feather River. The strike was made when a group of German prospectors, exhausted and bitter after days of futile gold hunting, were headed back to camp. Refilling their canteens, they stumbled into an area with so much gold on the surface that the men could gouge it out of rocks with their jackknives. Before it played out, Rich Bar produced between $14 million and $23 million in gold (like all production figures of the period, the limits vary widely). Its inhabitants, more prosperous than most miners, were addicted to two- and three-day binges. The story was told of a traveler who arrived at Rich Bar at 3 o'clock one morning and went to the grocery-saloon-hotel to seek lodging. The frame-and-canvas building was crammed full of drunken men, cursing, laughing and singing.

"Your customers are up rather late tonight," the traveler said to the proprietor.

"Oh no," said the proprietor. "The boys of Rich Bar generally keep going for 48 hours. It's a little late in the morning for the night before last, but for last night, why bless you, it's only just the shank of the evening."

Like many other boom-and-bust camps, Rich Bar lapsed back into the wilderness after a few years of exuberance. It might have become one dim memory among many, except for the writings of "Dame Shirley," the pen name of Louise Amelia Knapp Smith Clappe. A native of New Jersey, Mrs. Clappe once described herself as a "shivering, frail, home-loving little thistle." She came to California with her husband, Dr. Fayette Clappe, in 1849, and the couple lived for a while in San Francisco, but the city's dampness and fog did not agree with Dr. Clappe. Seeking a better climate in which to take up his practice, he and Mrs. Clappe moved to Rich Bar in the summer of 1851, a little more than a year after the opening up of those fabulous diggings. Dame Shirley's "Letters from the California Mines," originally addressed to a sister back East, were subsequently published in the form of a column in a California magazine. In them, she provided a vivid account of the California mining camps.

"Rich Bar was charmingly fresh and original," she wrote. "Imagine a tiny valley, about eight hundred yards in length and, perhaps, thirty in width, apparently hemmed in by lofty hills, almost perpendicular, draperied to their very summits with beautiful fir trees; the blue-bosomed Feather River undulating along their base." She described the buildings lining Rich Bar's only street: "round tents, square tents, plank hovels, log cabins &c, varying in elegance from the palatial splendor of 'The Empire' down to a 'local habitation' formed of pine boughs and covered with old calico shirts."

The Empire, which made its existence known by a huge red and blue sign painted across its canvas façade, was the only two-story building in town. In Dame Shirley's words, it "absolutely has a live 'upstairs.' You

Lonely miners with cheroot-chomping partners dance at a gold-camp wingding. The men who took the women's parts usually so signified by tying a bandanna around one arm; but a miner who could squeeze into an old crinoline became the belle of the ball.

His clothes torn from his back—and his backside—a miner belabors an antagonist's head in an 1856 engraving by California artist Charles Nahl. The tensions of a chaotic all-male community made such brawls commonplace in many of the mining camps.

first enter a large apartment, level with the street, part of which is fitted up as a bar-room. A really elegant mirror is set off by a back-ground of decanters, cigar vases and jars of brandied fruit, and there is a table covered with a green cloth—upon which lies a pack of monte cards, a backgammon board and a sickening pile of 'yallow kivered' literature. The remainder of the room does as a shop where velveteen and leather, flannel shirts and calico ditto—the latter starched to an appalling state of stiffness—lie cheek by jowl with hams, preserved meats, oysters and other groceries in hopeless confusion." From the barroom four steps led up to the hotel parlor, carpeted in straw matting and draped with purple calico. Four more steps took boarders to the upper story, containing four 8-by-10-foot bedrooms.

Despite these grandeurs, and even allowing for the fact that the building boasted three "glass-paned windows"—the only glass windows in town—Dame Shirley was not greatly impressed by the Empire. "It is,"

she wrote, "just such a piece of carpentering as a child two years old, gifted with the strength of a man, would produce if it wanted to play at making grown-up houses. And yet this impertinent apology for a house cost its original owners more than eight thousand dollars."

When Dame Shirley reached Rich Bar in 1851 four other white women were already living there. One, the first to have arrived after the discovery, was a powerful creature known as The Indiana Girl. (Her father ran a hotel called the Indiana.) She was large and brawny and had a voice to match, wore miner's boots and cleaned dirty dishes on her apron. Once, when the snow was five feet deep, The Indiana Girl trudged into camp carrying a 50-pound sack of flour on her back.

Another woman at Rich Bar was a certain Mrs. R who weighed only 68 pounds but was a hard worker. Shirley quoted a miner on Mrs. R's qualities: "Magnificent woman that, a wife of the right sort, she is. Why, she earnt her old man $900 in nine weeks, clear of all

On Sundays most miners rode into town to sell their gold dust and observe the Sabbath in their own style. Here, Nahl depicted two Sunday celebrants crashing into a store, their horses almost out of control but their whiskey glasses firmly in hand.

expenses by taking in washing. Such women ain't common, I tell *you;* if they were a man might marry and make money by the operation." But not all Rich Bar women were so hardy. A few days after Shirley first met her, a tiny, energetic woman called Mrs. Bailey died of peritonitis. Shirley attended the funeral in a dark, foreboding mood. "The death of one out of a community of four women," she brooded, "might well alarm the remainder."

It was equally alarming, of course, to the men of the community, for the presence of women often spelled the difference between an ephemeral mining camp and an established town. In 1850 just under 8 per cent of California's population was female. In the mining camps, where upward of 50,000 lonely men were working, the percentage was usually much lower, and the arrival of the first woman was an important event. Mrs. James Galloway, for example, was the first female resident of Downieville. When news of her approach reached the camp, the excited miners rushed out to meet her on the mountain trail. There, they picked up Mrs. Galloway and her mule, and carried both of them into camp.

The extreme preponderance of men in the camps was commonly blamed for the recklessness and lawlessness of life at the diggings, and early in 1849 Mrs. Eliza W. Farnham, a former matron at Sing Sing prison and the widow of a pioneer on the Oregon Trail, set out to remedy the situation somewhat. She published an open letter in New York newspapers soliciting 100 to 130 "intelligent, virtuous and efficient" women to accompany her to California, "believing that the presence of women would be one of the surest checks upon many of the evils that are apprehended there." Applicants had to bring testimonials from their clergymen as to their characters, plus $250 to cover the cost of the sea voyage and of getting settled in the Golden State.

The strong-minded Mrs. Farnham received many inquiries in response to her appeal, but only three women

THE MINERS' TEN COMMANDMENTS.

A man spake these words, and said: I am a miner, who wandered "from away down east," and came to sojourn in a strange land, and "see the elephant." And behold I saw him, and bear witness, that from the key of his trunk to the end of his tail, his whole body has passed before me; and I followed him until his huge feet stood still before a clapboard shanty; then with his trunk extended, he pointed to a candle-card tacked upon a shingle, as though he would say Read, and I read the

MINERS' TEN COMMANDMENTS.

I.
Thou shalt have no other claim than one.

II.
Thou shalt not make unto thyself any false claim, nor any likeness to a mean man, by jumping one; whatever thou findest on the top above or on the rock beneath, or in a crevice underneath the rock;—or I will visit the miners around to invite them on my sides; and when they decide against thee, thou shalt take thy pick and thy pan, thy shovel and thy blankets, with all that thou hast, and "go prospecting" to seek good diggings; but thou shalt find none. Then, when thou hast returned, in sorrow shalt thou fin t that thine old claim is worked o t, and yet no pile made thee to hide in the ground, or in an old boot beneath thy bunk, or in buckskin or bottle underneath thy cabin; but best paid all that was in thy purse away, worn out thy boots and thy garments, so that there is nothing good about them but the pockets, and thy patience is likened unto thy garments; and at last thou shalt hire thy body out to make thy board and save thy bacon.

III.
Thou shalt not go prospecting before thy claim gives out. Neither shalt thou take thy money, nor thy gold dust, nor thy good name, to the gaming table in vain; for monte, twenty-one, roulette, faro, lansquenet and poker, will prove to thee that the more thou puttest down the less thou shalt take up; and when thou thinkest of thy wife and children, thou shalt not hold thyself guiltless—but in sane.

IV.
Thou shalt not remember what thy friends do at home on the Sabbath day, lest the remembrance may not compare favorably with what thou doest here.—Six days thou mayest dig or pick all that thy body can stand under; but the other day is Sunday; yet thou washest all thy dirty shirts, darnest all thy stockings, tap thy boots, mend thy clothing, chop thy whole week's firewood, make up and bake thy bread, and boil thy pork and beans, that thou wait not when thou returnest from thy long-tom weary. For in six days' labor only thou canst not work enough to wear out thy body in two years; but if thou workest hard on Sunday also, thou canst do it in six months; and thou, and thy son, and thy daughter, thy male friend and thy female friend, thy morals and thy conscience, be none the better for it; but reproach thee, shouldst thou ever return with thy worn-out body to thy mother's fireside; and thou shalt not strive to justify thyself, because the trader and the blacksmith, the carpenter and the merchant, the tailors, Jews, and buccaneers, defy God and civilization, by keeping not the Sabbath day, nor wish for a day of rest, such as memory, youth and home, made hallowed.

V.
Thou shalt not think more of all thy gold, and how thou canst make it fastest, than how thou wilt enjoy it, after thou hast ridden rough-shod over thy good old parents' precepts and examples, that thou mayest have nothing to reproach and sting thee, when thou art left ALONE in the land where thy father's blessing and thy mother's love hath sent thee.

VI.
Thou shalt not kill thy body by working in the rain, even though thou shalt make enough to buy physic and attendance with. Neither shalt thou k ll thy neighbor's body in a duel; for by "keeping cool," thou canst save his life and thy conscience. Neither shalt thou destroy thyself by getting "tight," nor "slewed," nor "high," nor "corned," nor "half-seas over," nor "three sheets in the wind," by drinking smoothly down—"brandy slings," "gin cocktails," "whisky punches," "rum-toddies," nor "egg nogs." Neither shalt thou suck "mint-juleps," nor "sherry-cobblers," through a straw, nor gurgle from a bottle the "raw material," nor "take it neat" from a decanter; for, while thou art swallowing down thy purse, and thy coat from off thy back, thou art burning the coat from off thy stomach; and, if thou couldst see the houses and lands, and gold dust, and home comforts already lying there—"a huge pile"—thou shouldest feel a choking in thy throat; and when to that thou addest thy crooked walkings and hiccuping talkings, of lodgings in the gutter, of broilings in the sun, of prospect-holes half full of water, and of shafts and ditches, from which thou hast emerged like a drowning rat, thou wilt feel disgusted with thyself, and inquire, "Is thy servant a dog that he doeth these things?" verily I will say, Farewell, old bottle, I will kiss thy gurgling lips no more. And thou, slings, cocktails, punches, smashes, cobblers, nogs, toddies, sangarees, and julips, forever farewell. Thy remembrance shames me; henceforth, "I cut thy acquaintance," and headaches, tremblings, heart burnings, blue devils, and all the unholy catalogue of evils that follow in thy train. My wife's smiles and my children's merry-hearted laugh, shall charm and reward me for having the manly firmness and courage to say NO. I wish thee an eternal farewell.

VII.
Thou shalt not grow discouraged, nor think of going home before thou hast made thy "pile," because thou hast not "struck a lead," nor found a "rich crevice," nor sunk a hole upon a "pocket," lest in going home thou shalt leave four dollars a day, and go to work, ashamed, at fifty cents, and serve thee right; for thou knowest by staying here, thou m ghtst strike a lead and fify dollars a day, and keep thy manly self-respect, and then go home with enough to make thyself and others happy.

VIII.
Thou shalt not steal a pick, or a shovel, or a pan from thy fellow miner; nor take away his tools without his leave; nor borrow those he cannot spare, nor return them broken, nor trouble him to fetch them back again, nor talk with him while his water rent is running on, nor remove his sluice to enlarge thy claim, nor undermine his bank in following a lead, nor pan out gold from his "riffle box," nor wash the "tailings" from his sluice's mouth. Neither shalt thou pick out specimens from the company's pan to put them in thy mouth, or in thy purse; nor cheat thy partner of his share; nor steal from thy cabin-mate his gold dust, to add to thine, for he will be sure to discover what thou hast done, and will straightway call his fellow miners together, and if the law hinder them not, they will hang thee, or give thee fifty lashes, or shave thy head and brand thee, like a horse thief, with "R" upon thy cheek, to be known and read of all men, Californians in particular.

IX.
Thou shalt not tell any false tales about "good diggings in the mountains," to thy neighbor, that thou mayest benefit a friend who hath mules, and provisions, and tools and blankets, he cannot sell,—lest in deceiving thy neighbor, when he returneth through the snow with naught save his rifle, he, present thee with the contents thereof, and if a dog, thou shalt fall down and die.

X.
Thou shalt not commit unsuitable matrimony, nor covet "single blessedness;" nor forget absent maidens: nor neglect thy "first love;"—but thou shalt consider how faithfully and patiently she awaiteth thy return; yea, and covereth each epistle that thou sendest with kisses of kindly welcome—until she hath thyself. Neither shalt thou covet thy neighbor's wife, nor trifle with the affections of his daughter; yet, if thy heart be free, and thou dost love and covet each other, thou shalt "pop the question" like a man, lest another, more manly than thou art, should step in before thee, and thou love her in vain, and in the anguish of thy heart's disappointment, thou shalt quote the language of the great, and say, "sich is life;" and thy future lot be that of a poor, lonely, despised and comfortless bachelor.

A new Commandment give I unto thee —if thou hast a wife and little ones, that thou lovest dearer than thy life,—that thou keep them continually before thee, to cheer and urge thee onward until thou canst say, "I have enough—God bless them—I will return." Then as thou journiest towards thy much loved home, with open arms shall they come forth to welcome thee, and falling upon thy neck weep tears of unutterable joy that thou art come; then in the fullness of thy heart's gratitude, thou shalt kneel together before thy Heavenly Father, to thank Him for thy safe return. AMEN —So mote it be.

FORTY-NINE.

After two profitless years in the diggings, forty-niner J. M. Hutchings struck it rich by printing—initially as a joke—these ten commandments for miners. He quickly sold 100,000 copies and retired from mining.

finally made the voyage around the Horn with her. Nor was this the end of her trouble. En route she had so many quarrels with the ship's captain that the latter forced her to disembark in Valparaiso, Chile, where she waited a month before finding a ship that would take her on to San Francisco.

Somewhat later Miss Sarah Pellet, a temperance lecturer, took up Mrs. Farnham's cause. Temperance was not a popular subject in the mines, but a woman was an attractive curiosity and her lectures drew large crowds. In Downieville the saloons emptied for the occasion and the audience was so impatient to hear the lady that pistol shots were fired in the air to hurry the introductory speaker along. In the ensuing confusion that speaker was killed by a shotgun blast. Miss Pellet fled in great haste and understandable alarm, and business at the saloons immediately picked up again. Like Mrs. Farnham before her, Miss Pellet had conceived a plan to import "5,000 virtuous New England women to the mining camps." But Miss Pellet, too, found few recruits and finally dropped the project.

Mrs. Farnham and Miss Pellet were not the only recruiters of women for California. Several Eastern employment agencies signed up both professional prostitutes and unwary working girls to be shipped West, ostensibly to work as domestics. And large numbers of women from Mexico, South America and France came to California on their own, often to practice the oldest profession and the related trades of dance-hall entertaining and card dealing. Such women were euphemistically known in the mines as soiled doves, the fair and frail, ladies of the line, and sporting women.

Most forty-niners tried to maintain strong barriers between the respectable ladies and the soiled doves. There was the case of Big Annie, keeper of a back-street fandango parlor in Columbia. Annie lurched out of a saloon one day and bumped into the town's prim schoolmistress, forcing her into a dusty road. The teacher delicately raised her skirt to shake off the dust and Annie guffawed and pointed out that the teacher walked on two legs, just like Annie herself and other earthly creatures. This daring observation affronted the town's sense of decency. That night the volunteer fire department wheeled its apparatus up to Annie's shabby establishment and manning the pump with a will spewed forth a powerful stream of water, washing Annie's clients out of the house and Annie out of Columbia.

The few unattached and presumably virtuous women who came to California had easy pickings if they wanted to marry. Similarly, widows rarely stayed widows for long. Peter Decker, the young Ohioan who came overland with the Columbus company in 1849, noted in his diary that on February 6, 1851, in Nevada City, "Mr. Apperson was married to Mrs. Brondurant. He is a widower of about 4 months and she a widow some six weeks." And a newly arrived Canadian told of a Sonora woman who buried her husband one day and married the chief mourner the next afternoon.

Some women did not leave matters to chance but spelled out their intentions and requirements in newspaper notices. One such advertisement read:

A HUSBAND WANTED

"By a lady who can wash, cook, scour, sew, milk, spin, weave, hoe (can't plow), cut wood, make fires, feed the pigs, raise chickens, rock the cradle (gold rocker, I thank you, Sir!), saw a plank, drive nails, etc. These are a few of the solid branches; now for the ornamental. 'Long time ago' she went as far as syntax, read Murray's Geography and through two rules in Pike's Grammar. Could find 6 states on the Atlas, could read, and you see she can write. Can—no *could*—paint roses, butterflies, ships &c, but now she can paint houses, whitewash fences, &c.

Now for her terms.

Her age is none of your business. She is neither handsome nor a fright, yet an *old* man need *not* apply, nor any who have not a little more education than she has, and a great deal more gold, for there must be $20,000 settled on her before she will bind herself to perform all the above."

The hope of finding a suitable wife became a recurrent theme in the forty-niners' correspondence. I. M. Blair, writing from Sutter's Mill to his brother Morris in Yellowsprings, Iowa, quickly brushed over his fair success in the diggings on Weaver Creek and got down to matters that really concerned him: "I want to know what changes have taken place. What of McClures family are married? Who of Johnsons, Wrights, Andersons,

Topped by the curlicues of a fancy pediment, the Miners Hotel lends an air of refinement to the gold town of Mormon Island. When this picture was painted, between 1849 and 1854, the town could support several hotels, for nearby gold was so plentiful that it was measured by the pint.

McMullens, yes, everybody. Who talks most about *me,* for thems the ones I'll save a chunk of gold for."

The few decent women in the camps were the recipients of much attention and polite scrutiny. Franklin Buck, attending a dance in Weaverville, reported that 32 "respectable ladies" had been brought in for the occasion from the surrounding region. One of them, he wrote, was "very lady-like and genteel," but some were "rotten, on the backwoods order." And he noted that a Mrs. Harper "put on more airs than anyone. She waltzes rather better than I would want my wife to."

Women remained comparatively scarce in the mining camps until 1855, when completion of the transisthmian railroad in Panama made the trip west faster and easier. But there were exceptions to the rule, most notably Sonora, in the Tuolumne district of the southern mines. The town had originally been settled by immigrants from the Mexican state of Sonora, and many of the Mexican miners had brought their wives or mistresses with them. When other women, particularly from Peru, Chile and France, arrived in California they were naturally attracted to Sonora because the town already held large numbers of women.

By 1849, when many American and other non-Mexican miners began descending upon Sonora, the little town had an exotic, enchanting air. The Canadian William Perkins described the town as it appeared to him in the spring of 1849: "I had never seen a more beautiful, a wilder or more romantic spot. It was literally embowered with trees. The habitations were of canvas, cotton cloth, or of upright unhewn sticks with green branches and leaves and vines interwoven, and decorated with gaudy hangings of silks, cottons, flags, brilliant goods of every description." Brightly dyed scarves, shawls and many-tinted Mexican blankets he called *zarapes* completed the kaleidoscope of colors.

"On Saturdays and Sundays," Perkins' description continued, "the old camp used to wear, night and day, an almost magic appearance. Numberless lights shone from gaily decorated houses, all of them with their fronts entirely open to the streets, and the streets themselves were strewn with lighted tapers. Where there was an open space, a Mexican would take off his variegated *zarape,* lay it on the ground, put a lighted candle at each corner, and pour into the centre his stock of silver and gold. The *zarape* would soon be surrounded by his countrymen who, seated on the ground, would stake and generally lose their hard-earned weekly wages.

"On either side of the street were ranged gambling tables, generally covered with a scarlet, gold-embroidered cloth. Behind the tables were counters on which were ranged all kinds of liquor. It was not uncommon to see a Mexican call for a bottle of brandy worth an ounce of gold, and, taking a wine glass, deliberately pour the bottle's whole contents into it, spilling all that the glass would not contain. The bottle being empty and the wine-glass full, he would swallow its contents with pride and satisfaction. Elsewhere were tables loaded with sweetmeats of every description, cooling beverages with snow from the *Sierra Nevada* floating in them, cakes and dried fruits, hot meats, pies, everything in the greatest abundance. The noise of drums, guitars, fiddles and the ringing metallic thrum of the little Mexican lute never for a moment ceased from Saturday to Monday."

Perkins was more candid and cosmopolitan than most of his fellow forty-niners in his frank admiration of the foreign women. Both Mexican and French women, he thought, made splendid mistresses. The Mexican woman "will not marry a heretic, but will live with him. Mexican and French women make faithful, happy and contented helpmates, as long as they are well treated, or until they desire a change." And when he met a certain Mrs. Lewis C. Gunn, one of the first American women in Sonora, Perkins confided to his journal: "It is too much to expect from weak male human nature in California that a man should prefer the lean arm of a bonneted, ugly, board-shaped specimen of a descendant of the Puritans, to the rosy cheeked, full-formed, sprightly, and elegant Spaniard or Frenchwoman, even with the full knowledge that the austerity of virtue accompanies the one, while the dangerous fascination of Vice lies hid under the exterior of the other."

Such fine distinctions — and, more important, the leisure to make them — marked a civilizing trend in the California boom. In 1848, during the first furious excitement over gold, the men in the diggings had been preoccupied with making their fortunes just as soon as possible. Rock crevices were picked over and promising dirt dug and washed during every waking moment. The Reverend Walter Colton, the U.S. Navy chaplain and newly appointed alcalde of Monterey, noticed this absorption during a visit to the mines: "Nothing is a

This cartoon illustrated a poem, "We Miss Thee, Ladies," published in San Francisco by some miners. Desperate for female companionship, the men ended their lament with an offer to marry any willing women.

novelty here for more than a minute; were a man to cast his skin or lose his head, no one would stop to inquire if he had recovered either."

But by 1849 some men had accumulated so much gold that they relaxed their search a little. Others had concluded, sadly perhaps, that not everyone was going to get rich, and there was really no great hurry. In either case more time was spent seeking distraction and amusement, no matter how improvident, irrational or trivial.

"If a terrier catches a rat," wrote chronicler Hinton Helper about one of the gold towns, "or if a big turnip is brought to market, the people cluster together and scramble for a sight with eagerness and impetuosity." A fist fight or a comical drunk was considered an attraction of a somewhat higher order.

As opposed to such impromptu entertainments, organized public diversions were hard to find. One of the most notable was the bull-and-bear fight. Mexican immigrants had brought with them the tradition of matching men and bulls in the ring. In California miners hit upon the idea of pitting fighting bulls against the 1,000- to 1,500-pound grizzly bears that roamed the woods and mountains. The bear would be captured in a pitfall, transferred to an iron-reinforced mobile cage and held until a sufficiently large and fearless bull could be found. Then the date was set and the forty-niners had one more occasion to risk a few ounces of gold in bets.

J.D. Borthwick, the British artist, saw this poster advertising a bull-and-bear contest:

War! War!! War!!!
The celebrated Bull-killing Bear
GENERAL SCOTT
will fight a Bull on Sunday the 15th inst. at 2 P.M.
at Moquelumne Hill

The Bear will be chained with a twenty-foot chain in the middle of the arena. The Bull will be perfectly wild, young, of the Spanish breed, and the best that can be found in the country. The Bull's horns will be of their natural length, and *"not sawed off to prevent accidents."* The Bull will be quite free in the arena and not hampered in any way whatever.

Borthwick attended the fight. A 40-foot arena was sep-

A lithograph of a pretty girl's arrival in a mining camp shows the population's glee. In the camps of the early 1850s where men outnumbered women by more than 12 to 1, miners would welcome a female with gifts of gold dust worth up to $100.

arated by a five-barred wooden fence from the surrounding tiers of seats. Two fiddlers played "appropriate airs" while the spectators, who had paid $3.00 apiece for admission, took their seats.

As Borthwick described it, the audience was unforgettable. He saw "bronze and bearded faces under hats of every hue; revolvers and silver-handled bowie knives glanced in the bright sunshine, and among the crowd were numbers of gay Mexican blankets and red and blue French bonnets, while here and there the fair sex was represented by a few Mexican women in snowy-white dresses, puffing their cigaritas."

The bear, tethered by his chain, prepared for battle by scooping a hole several inches deep, in which he lay down. He would fight from a sitting or prone position, trying to pull his antagonist down to his level, while the bull, with his horns and powerful neck and shoulders, would try to hook the grizzly and toss him up into the air. (The animals' tactics were to provide Wall Street and other financial centers with some basic jargon: a bull market goes up; a bear market, down.)

The bull facing General Scott paused, pawed the ground and charged, striking the bear heavily in the side but apparently doing no great damage. Immediately, the bear grabbed the bull by the nose with his powerful jaws and locked his forelegs around the bull's neck, while the bull beat a tattoo on the bear's body with his hoofs. The animals separated and the bull, his nose in tatters, paused, then charged again—only to be locked again by the bear's jaws and hug. Sensing impatience in the audience, the impresario announced that for $200 he would supply another bull. A hat was passed, the money raised and a second bull was let into the ring. Attacked by two bulls at once, General Scott was sorely tried. But he swatted and bit so savagely that the bulls were finally adjudged the losers and shot on the spot to put them out of their pain.

Though the audience was apparently well satisfied, Borthwick felt that he "would rather have prevented than witnessed" the spectacle. And he noted that the valiant General Scott was killed in his next fight when a bull drove its horns into his rib cage.

Orthodox bullfights—human against bull—were also held in the mining camps, from time to time, but their authenticity was shaky at best. Sensing that the strict rules and traditional pageantry of the Mexican *fiesta brava* might be lost on an audience that cared more for excitement than for elegance, the impresario on one particular afternoon fraudulently announced that the bull would be dispatched by a lady bullfighter. This device proved a profitable fiction—even when wigs and flouncing gowns failed to conceal the beard, large feet and manly gait of the matador. The very idea of a woman, even a spurious one, was a lure.

Such oddities, however, soon gave way to more conventional entertainment. Itinerant performers and minstrels had been making the rounds of the mining camps almost from the beginning of the gold rush. One of the earliest was a rotund, ruddy little Englishman named Stephen C. Massett, who billed himself as Jeems Pipes of Pipesville. A wanderer and a Jack-of-all-trades, sometimes an auctioneer, sometimes a newspaper correspondent, Massett had the kind of gift for the absurd that was later to make Mark Twain famous. He sang songs of his own composition, the romantic ones in a fine baritone and the ridiculous ones in falsetto; and he had a particular talent for mimicry and burlesque. One of the most popular acts he performed in the mining camps was the portrayal of a New England town meeting in which he played seven different roles.

Another pioneer was John A. Stone, known on stage as Old Put. Like Stephen Massett, Stone was both a composer and singer, though on a somewhat lower professional level. His songs, which included "Hangtown Gals," "Joaquin the Horse Thief" and "The Shady Old Camp," were immensely popular among the miners, and booklets of their words were brisk sellers; but Old Put himself was little more than a barroom singer who managed to live well, if erratically, on the sale of these songbooks and gifts of food, drink and money. He did a little mining, too, and one day in Tuolumne County he dug up a chunk of quartz that yielded $15,000 in gold. Characteristically, he headed for San Francisco and soon squandered the money. Afterward he drifted back to the mining camps and saloon singing, but his life had lost too much of its zest and Old Put finally ended his days as a suicide.

The miners' tastes in entertainment were remarkably catholic. They liked romantic and nostalgic songs, and loved comedy acts. Broad satire, even when they themselves formed its targets, was invariably a hit. Dr. David "Yankee" Robinson, who came out in 1849, had great

The mining country's riches attracted gold diggers of both sexes. In this cartoon printed in an Eastern magazine a voluptuous "girl of New York" clutches a bag of gold and urges her weary miner to dig faster.

success in the camps with a satirical revue called "Seeing the Elephant" and with songs and skits loaded with good-natured ridicule of miners and mining life. They even showed a sentimental enthusiasm for the most stilted kinds of stage tragedies — perhaps as a relief from the real tragedy in the everyday life around them. Actresses, no matter what their specialty or vehicle, were always applauded heartily; male actors, particularly if they overacted, were sometimes pelted with vegetables. When the hammy protagonist in a Nevada City presentation handed an actress his sword and bared his chest there was a roar from the audience: "God damn him, kill him!"

The great Booth family — Junius Brutus Booth; his son, also named Junius Brutus; and his younger son Edwin — formed part of the rich theatrical stew available to the miners. Edwin had acted a few roles before coming to California, but he got his seasoning on the boards out West, playing Hamlet, blackface comedy roles, and between acts, the banjo. On one of his tours through the mining camps each of five consecutive appearances was, by unlucky coincidence, followed by a major fire. When his troupe reached Downieville he was refused permission to perform and asked to leave town as soon as possible. And forever afterward, Edwin Booth was known in California as The Fiery Star.

The nickname was actually a play on words, for the latest rage in the mining camps had been a variety of talented child performers collectively known as the Fairy Stars. The greatest of them, unquestionably, was Lotta Crabtree, whose beginnings as a performer were strangely linked with the career of one of the most talked-about women of her time, a woman famous in Europe as well as America. This was the notorious Lola Montez *(pages 148-150)*. Born Eliza Gilbert in Limerick, Ireland, she came to California in 1853, at the age of

35. By then, Lola had already run through three marriages, a trial for bigamy and internationally scandalous liaisons with several European bigwigs. (She persisted in calling herself the Countess of Landsfeldt, a meaningless title that one of her titled lovers had bestowed upon her.) In San Francisco, Lola was soon married again, this time to Patrick Purdy Hull, a newspaperman. Acting and dancing were her public talents and she appeared for three weeks in San Francisco, performing, among other things, her famous Spider Dance, in which spiders made of cork, rubber and whalebone were shaken out of her skirt.

Lola's affected acting and inept dancing provided rich ammunition for the comic performers of the day, who burlesqued her mercilessly. At the mining towns audiences were plainly bored with her; she threatened one unfriendly newspaper editor with a horsewhipping and challenged another to a duel. (In Sacramento she also dumped her current husband by pitching him down the hotel stairs and tossing his baggage out a window.) Then, uncharacteristically, she settled down for a couple of years in a little house in Grass Valley west of Lake Tahoe. There she gardened, kept a bear cub as a pet and maintained a salon for visiting theatrical people.

The women of Grass Valley were mostly unfriendly to Lola. Not so Mrs. Mary Ann Crabtree, keeper of a boardinghouse and wife of a luckless prospector. Mrs. Crabtree was as straitlaced as any of the other Grass Valley women, but she was fascinated by the theater and had ambitions for her red-haired, black-eyed, six-year-old daughter, Lotta. Soon Lola was teaching Lotta songs and dance routines and having her perform in her house for visiting actors, who were invariably enthusiastic about the child's talent.

In 1855 Lola left Grass Valley looking for other worlds to conquer. Meanwhile, the Crabtrees had moved to Rabbit Creek, where the luckless John Crabtree hoped he would at last strike gold (he never did). Once again, Mrs. Crabtree ran a boardinghouse, and Lotta took singing and dancing lessons from a part-time cobbler, part-time entertainer, part-time saloonkeeper named Mart Taylor.

When a Fairy Star named Sue Robinson came to Rabbit Creek, her manager attempted to obtain the use of a small log building that Taylor sometimes rented to visiting performers for their shows. But Lotta's mentor refused; he had chosen the occasion for Lotta to make her debut on his own stage, and Sue Robinson was forced to appear in another building across the street.

At least half the foreign-born mining population of Rabbit Creek was Irish. Mrs. Crabtree had hastily put together a long green coat, green knee breeches and a tall green hat. Taylor had cobbled a tiny pair of Irish brogues and whittled a miniature shillelagh. And the sprightly Lotta, facing a familiar audience, went through a furious set of jigs and reels, grinning and laughing all the way, to the delight of the miners. For a finale she appeared in a white dress and sang such sentimental ballads as "How Can I Leave Thee?" By that time, the rival show across the road was deserted; everyone had come over to see the sensational Lotta, who was then barely eight years old and looked even younger.

When she finished, the smoky room was full of shouting, cheering miners, and a makeshift stage was showered with dollars, Mexican pesos, a scattering of nuggets and sacks of gold dust, and one octagonal $50 gold slug. It was more money than Lotta's father had made in the mines in four years. It was also the beginning of one of the century's most spectacular careers — a career that took Lotta from crude stages in Rabbit Creek, Quincy, City of 76, Port Wine, Rich Bar, Gibsonville and Bidwell's Bar to the great theaters of San Francisco, New York, Washington, London and Paris.

The availability of entertainment in the mining camps, some of it of a high order of excellence, was only one of many signs of increasing civilization in the gold region during the 1850s. Isolation was diminishing. While travel would remain hazardous for a long time to come, stagecoaches began serving the larger mining towns on fixed schedules, bringing passengers, supplies, mail and news of the outside world, and taking out the miners' mail and gold. The forty-niner who had once gone for months without hearing from family, friends or sweetheart might now hear from them with some regularity. The temptation to seek solace in alcohol began to lessen. Daguerreotype shops opened in the larger mining towns and the men sent their portraits to the folks at home (a daguerreotyper usually kept a stock of prop jewelry for the portrait sitter to wear with an air of bogus prosperity). And with stage service and banks available, a successful miner

The oom-pah-pah of a German band celebrates May Day in Weaverville. The scene reflects the ethnic diversity of the town, whose citizens also knew the sound of Spanish fandangos and Chinese dirges.

could have his new wealth sent home rather than risk it recklessly at the gambling tables.

Preachers began to turn up at the mining camps in greater numbers. Their services were often held in saloons in which liquor sales were piously suspended and the nude paintings turned to the wall for a few hours. While both saloons and gambling rooms continued to thrive it was apparent that sobriety was making gains. Many forty-niners took the pledge. On August 15, 1851, for example, James E. Doss, accompanied by two witnesses, appeared before the county judge in Sonora to swear that he would not touch liquor for eight years: "Whereas I have been in the habit of drinking strong drink, yea, even unto drunkenness and disgrace, seeing as I see, that unless I abandon this my drunken habit, I am forever lost unto my dear family, myself, my God and My Country and to decency, and that I may better reform this brutal habit, I pray that My God will give me the fortitude to abstain."

Smartly drilled and uniformed military units and volunteer fire companies (most towns in the mining region were destroyed by fire at least once) provided both communal activity and social distinction. So did various lodges — the Masons, the Odd Fellows and the strange E Clampus Vitus, a secret lodge set up to burlesque secret lodges. The head of each chapter of E Clampus Vitus — and there was a chapter in almost every mining camp — was called the Noble Grand Humbug; meetings were held in the Hall of Comparative Ovations. One of the order's announced aims was comforting widows and orphans, particularly the former. But in its lapses from buffoonery the order frequently — and quietly — performed such useful functions as providing food for the unfortunate and educating deserving youngsters.

As the forty-niners married or brought their families West, schools were built but the towns frequently had difficulty in securing teachers. Prentice Mulford, who had poor luck finding gold, applied for the position of teacher at a Tuolumne county school in 1858. He was examined by the school board, composed of a doctor, a saloonkeeper and a miner. To test his competence he was asked to spell "cat," "hat," "rat," and "mat." After doing this correctly he was told by the doctor, "Young man, you'll do for our camp. I wouldn't teach that school for $5,000 a year; and there are two boys you'll have that I advise you to kill if possible the first week. Let's all go over and have a drink."

In some camps — Hawkins' Bar was an example — miners helped found free libraries equipped with encyclopedias, books of science, philosophy, fiction and poetry, and the most recent periodicals. *Harper's Magazine* was a favorite — and, oddly enough, so was a magazine for women called *Godey's Lady's Book*.

Most mining camps on the verge of becoming permanent towns had a newspaper, and sometimes several of them; but the presses and other equipment were often as nomadic as the miners themselves. Thus, the *Sonora Herald,* which began publication on July 4, 1850, used an antique Ramage press that had been hauled across the continent in 1832 and had seen service in Monterey, San Francisco, Sacramento and Stockton before coming to Sonora. The same press was to see service on still another paper, the Columbia *Star,* before finally being destroyed by fire.

Civilizing trends there surely were, but there was also a shocking—and in some places, an increasing —amount of crime and bloodshed. Most of the forty-niners had taken too literally the stories of quick and easy wealth in California. When it became apparent that fortune came neither quickly, easily, nor, above all, with any certainty, many men expressed their frustration in irrational behavior. The easiest way was to drown disappointment and loneliness in alcohol. Great numbers drank themselves into quarrels, incoherence and even death. Thievery, almost unknown in the diggings at the outset, increased year by year, and tempers grew shorter. The absence of jails in all but the most stable towns restricted the available punishments to banishment, whipping (a common judgment was "40 stripes save one") and death.

The miners took it all in stride. At a time when the theft of anything worth $100 (and frequently of things worth much less) was supposed to justify immediate execution, hangings came to be taken as a matter of course. Indeed, they were often regarded with remarkable calm by the victim as well as the executioner. One young man wrote this letter from Murphys Camp:

Dear Friend:
I take this opportunity of writing these few lines to you hoping to find you in good health me and Charley is sentenced to be hung today at 5 o'clock for a robbery good by give my best to Frank and Sam and Church.
John Bucroft.

As early as January 1849, only a few weeks after a flood of miners from outside California began to arrive at the diggings, lynch law was practiced at the mines. At Old Dry Diggings, in what was to become Eldorado County, five men were caught while trying to rob a local gambler. Edward Gould Buffum, the former Army lieutenant, was trying his hand at mining in the area at the time; he not only saw what happened afterward but also tried to prevent it.

The five would-be thieves were tried by an informally chosen jury and sentenced to 39 lashes apiece for their attempted crime. When the whippings had been administered, additional charges were raised against three of the men for an alleged attempt at robbery and murder the previous year on the Stanislaus River. The accused men were too weak to attend the utterly illegal trial that followed, and they would not have understood the proceedings anyway, since they spoke no English (two were French and one Chilean). Nevertheless, a crowd of approximately 200 miners constituted itself as a jury, decided the men were guilty and sentenced them to hang, all in the space of a half hour.

"I mounted a stump," Buffum said, "and in the name of God, humanity, and law protested against such a course of proceeding; but the crowd, by this time excited by frequent and deep potations of liquor from a neighboring groggery, would listen to nothing contrary to their brutal desires, and even threatened to hang me if I did not immediately desist from any further remarks." The condemned men asked for an interpreter, but were shouted down by the crowd. They were placed on a wagon bed, nooses were tightened around their necks and the ropes were tied to the limb of a tree. Then the wagon was driven away. Thus Old Dry Diggings acquired its notorious nickname—Hangtown. Later, out of civic pride, the town fathers decided to pick a new name. They thought of Ravine City and then finally settled for the more euphonious Placerville.

Foreigners like the three men at Hangtown were the most frequent victims of mining-camp violence. Many American forty-niners expressed animosity toward foreigners even before arriving in California. Early in the gold rush all Spanish Americans, including a number of native Californians, were expelled from the camps on the American River with only three hours' notice. Sometimes the causes of friction were trivial. Three drunken Americans were said to have hanged a Mexican who asked them to moderate their language in the presence of his wife. More often the Americans complained that the foreigners only wanted to get rich quick in California and then return home to enjoy themselves, doing nothing to build up the country. (The same complaint, of course, could have been made against most of the American forty-niners.)

Perhaps the most durable relic of the wave of anti-foreigner sentiment was the legend—or legends—of a bandit called Joaquin Murieta. There is some doubt that the man ever existed. On the other hand, there may have been as many as five Joaquins: some Mexicans and native Californians became outlaws, and one or more of them may have been named Joaquin. But in a time of high feeling and haphazard communication all mysterious crimes committed by Spanish Americans tended to be ascribed to Joaquin Murieta. Joaquin's motives, if he had any, were equally mysterious; his admirers spoke of a public whipping, the rape of his wife by drunken Americans, the murder of a brother, the jumping of his gold claim or the rustling of his cattle. In retaliation—and in the tradition of folk heroes—Joaquin was said to steal from the rich to give to the poor.

Whatever the truth, the California legislature authorized a ranger named Harry Love to form a company of 20 men and, within three months, to capture "the five Joaquins." Love and his men used up two of their three

The short, unhappy war of the Weaverville tongs

Among the miscellany of men scrambling for gold in the diggings of California were thousands of Chinese who had fled from a series of famines in their homeland during the 1840s. Most of the Orientals clung stubbornly to the habits and traditions that they brought over with them — including floppy shirts, wide straw hats, a language the other miners found wholly impenetrable, and a propensity for gathering into clannish fraternal organizations called tongs.

Virtually every gold camp seemed to have its own tong, or two or more, depending on the size of the Oriental quarter. Basically these tongs served as congenial refuges where a lonely man could find a friend or perhaps help in getting work or lodging. Sometimes, however, they hardened into reservoirs of old-country prejudice, where old hatreds were nurtured and old feuds flared anew.

In the summer of 1854, for example, denizens of the normally placid Chinatown in Weaverville, California, suddenly began ordering medieval weapons, custom-made by the local blacksmiths: 15-foot pikes, five-foot swords, giant pronged spears. The smiths flashed the word to the white community: Weaverville's two tongs were going to war, why, no one could say. But a fight — and it would be a big one — was surely coming.

On July 15, carrying spears and swords at shoulder arms, the two forces marched to a large field, followed by 2,000 cheering townspeople. The 150 men of one tong wore red hats; their opponents, 400 strong, carried a banner inscribed "Canton City Company." To the clang of gongs and the bang of drums, red hats and Cantons charged ferociously at one another, stopped dead, ran off — and then went through the whole menacing drill all over again. Finally an exasperated young Swede fired his pistol into the ranks. That touched off 10 minutes of frenzied fighting *(below)* that ended, to everyone's astonishment, in the pell-mell retreat of the numerically superior Cantons.

After the dust had settled and the casualties were carried off, the townspeople discovered the inspired strategy by which the red-hats' puny force managed to win the day. It seemed that their leader, a natural military genius known only as Charlie, had secretly engaged some of the spectators to cover his troops' exposed rear once they had broken the Canton front. The plan worked: split by a red-hat charge and blocked by the whites from closing ranks, the Cantons fled, leaving eight dead and six wounded on the field. (Also found there, to no one's particular regret, was the body of the battle-hungry Swede, shot in the head by an unknown party.) Next day the Chinese buried their dead. The tongs did not reveal what had caused the dispute. But whatever it was had apparently been settled, for the two sides never fought again.

Equipped like ancient Oriental foot soldiers, with plaited-straw shields, pikes and spears, the two armies have at each other in Weaverville's tong war.

Scowling indomitably and slashing the air with a knife, the Mexican-American bandit Joaquin Murieta clatters over the sheer cliffs of an unlikely looking mountain trail in Charles Nahl's 1859 watercolor portrait.

months before encountering a supposed bandit band in the Panoche Pass in Tulare Valley. They killed and decapitated the leader, whom they identified as Joaquin Murieta, and placed his head in a jar of spirits. They did the same with the deformed hand of one of the other members of the band; this, said the rangers, was the hand of the infamous Three-Fingered Jack, the cutthroat who had murdered a half-dozen Orientals. Thereupon, the rangers shared a reward of $1,000, and Harry Love received a bonus of $5,000.

There was, however, some question as to just who it was the rangers had killed. The *Alta California* reported that the supposed bandit gang was actually a group of seven native Californians and Mexicans who had been rounding up wild mustangs; the rangers had attacked them without provocation, killed four of the seven and cut the head from the body of one of them —but they had never found Joaquin Murieta. Nevertheless, the pickled head and hand were advertised (*opposite*) and exhibited widely as reminders of California's liveliest and most lawless days.

An even grimmer example of mining-camp justice occurred in Downieville in 1851. It was grimmer because the victim was a woman—and the incident took place on a national holiday, the Fourth of July, in a mining town that had been proud of its gallantry. The observation of Independence Day was a great occasion in all the camps. Drinking usually started early in the day, with storekeepers simply knocking the necks off bottles instead of drawing the corks, because service at the bar went faster that way.

On this particular Independence Day in Downieville, the celebration was especially elaborate, with lots of bunting, lots of flags, a platform for the orators and a patriotic speech by Colonel John D. Weller, a candidate for the United States Senate. A correspondent for the *Pacific Star* saw "a multitude of people, each fired with patriotism in commemorating the anniversary of our nation's birth and re-baptizing by immersion the memory of our glorious ancestors."

One of the well-soaked celebrants was a convivial miner named Cannon (his given name is less clear; it was either John or Fred or Frederick Alexander Augustus). That evening Cannon and two companions, staggering along the road arm in arm, came to a cabin occupied by a Mexican dance-hall girl named Josefa and her lover, José; because of his nationality, José was prohibited from working as a miner and made his living as a card dealer in Craycroft's saloon. Cannon lurched against the door of their cabin, snapped its leather hinges and stumbled into the room. He extricated himself and with his friends' help he put the door back in place. They then left, laughing tipsily.

The next morning José accosted Cannon in the road near his cabin and demanded payment for the broken door. While they argued, Josefa emerged from the cabin. When Cannon raised a fist as if to strike José the woman pushed herself between the two men. Cannon, who spoke Spanish, called her a *puta,* or whore. Josefa dared him to come inside the cabin and repeat the insult. Cannon followed her, and as he stood in the broken doorway she stabbed him with a large bowie knife. Cannon died shortly afterward.

A mob seized the Mexican couple and proposed hanging them immediately. Cooler heads insisted on a

A grisly trophy drew crowds for years after the capture of Murieta and his henchman. Despite the guarantees at the foot of this poster, a lady who said she was Joaquin's sister insisted the head surely was not his.

WILL BE EXHIBITED
FOR ONE DAY ONLY!

AT THE STOCKTON HOUSE!
THIS DAY, AUG. 12, FROM 9 A. M., UNTIL 6, P. M.

THE HEAD
Of the renowned Bandit!

JOAQUIN!
AND THE
HAND OF THREE FINGERED JACK!
THE NOTORIOUS ROBBER AND MURDERER.

"JOAQUIN" and "THREE-FINGERED JACK" were captured by the *State Rangers*, under the command of Capt. Harry Love, at the Arroya Cantina, July 24th. No reasonable doubt can be entertained in regard to the identification of the head now on exhibition, as being that of the notorious robber, *Joaquin Murietta*, as it has been recognized by hundreds of persons who have formerly seen him.

The lynching of Rafael Escobar typified the lawlessness and violence of mining towns. Accused of murder, Escobar was hanged without a trial, becoming the tenth victim to be strung up on the same tree.

trial. It began at once on a bunting-draped speakers' platform, the scene of yesterday's patriotic oratory. At first there were about 600 men in attendance; but in a little while the crowd grew to 2,000. The saloons were doing a brisk business. Cannon's body, with his red flannel shirt pulled back to reveal the fatal chest wound, was on exhibition in a tent nearby. Emotions became increasingly steamy and some men began to shout "Hang them! Hang them!"

The judge, a rancher named John Rose, managed to restore order and Josefa was allowed to speak in her own behalf. She admitted the knifing, but insisted that it was done in self-defense. Cannon had previously molested her with evil intentions, she said, and she kept the knife at hand to protect herself from him. A physician, Dr. Cyrus D. Aiken, bravely spoke for Josefa, saying that if she was hanged two lives would be taken, for she was three months pregnant. Now the mob demanded that Dr. Aiken be hanged too. Three other doctors took Josefa to a tent and examined her. They gave it as their opinion that she was not pregnant.

The case was given to the jury. Its deliberations lasted only a few minutes. Verdict: guilty. Sentence: "That she suffer death in two hours." José was found not guilty but was nevertheless ordered to get out of town within 24 hours. Colonel Weller, the orator of the day before and a future governor of California, was present for the proceedings but refrained from interfering.

A little after 4:00 in the afternoon Josefa was hanged from the bridge that crossed the Yuba from Jersey Flat to Durgan Flat. She climbed to the scaffold unassisted, placed the noose around her neck with her own hands, saw to it that her skirts were tied down for modesty's sake, and bade the crowd a polite *"adios, señores."* The saloon business was good that evening.

The Daily Placer Times and Transcript editorialized that "the violent proceedings of an excited mob are a blot upon the history of the state. The perpetrators have shamed themselves and their race." But with a more personal note Franklin Buck, the Yankee storekeeper from Bucksport, Maine, later recalled the grisly event in a letter: "I always think of the Spanish girl standing on the plank of the bridge, tossing her hat to a friend and putting the rope around her neck, folding her hands and facing death with a bravery that shamed us men. And girls were so scarce in those days, too."

147

A cargo of dreams for the lonely forty-niners

When the voluptuous dancer Lola Montez sailed away from Europe in 1851, she left behind a slew of sorrowing lovers, among them Emperor Ludwig I of Bavaria, and a recently shed husband (her third). Lovely Lola had become bored by her Continental conquests and was heading off for fresh game in California.

The woman-starved forty-niners did, indeed, represent a bonanza to a pretty performer intrepid enough to tour the mining circuit. Burlesque comics like Mabel Santley and Helen Western were literally showered with sacks of gold dust. Even child actresses like the Bateman sisters, Kate and Ellen *(page 152)*, were lustily cheered through their appalling performances: in 1854, nine-year-old Ellen's Hamlet drew a eulogy from a California paper: "A masterpiece of art," thrilled the reviewer, "the child vanished on assuming, Minerva-like, the panoply of the Jove of Avon, and became a prince."

But when Lola opened in Sacramento, her posturing dances brought guffaws from the miners. Fiery Lola flared, tongue-lashed her audience and stalked offstage. After a few weeks, still smarting, she retired to the town of Grass Valley, "shorn of glory," wrote a critic, and "trailing clouds of wickedness." There she amused herself by teaching a neighbor's child named Lotta Crabtree *(page 151)* stage arts—so successfully that Lotta eventually became a great star. Then Lola sailed away from California (and from yet one more former husband), this time bound for Australia—where another gold rush was on.

A cartoon in 1852 showed Lola Montez blowing a last kiss to her sad European admirers as she embarked for the U.S. An equally flattering San Francisco newspaper called her "the very *comet* of her sex."

149

In a sentimental drama, *Yelva*, Lola Montez *(left)* played a deaf-mute opposite the talented Sophie Judah in 1853. Since Lola did not speak, she could hide the fact that her acting — like her dancing — was terrible.

Lola's greatest contribution to American theater was to coach Lotta Crabtree, a miner's daughter who began as a child star *(below, left)* in a mining camp. She grew up to become America's top comedienne.

SACRAMENTO THEATRE

Dress Circle and Parquette...$2 00.   Pit...............$1 00.
Box Office open from 10, A. M., to 2, P. M., when seats may be secured.
Doors open at 7½—Performance to commence at 8 o'clock.

FAREWELL NIGHT
OF THE RENOWNED
BATEMAN CHILDREN!
BENEFIT
—OF MISS—
KATE BATEMAN!
LITTLE ELLEN
In her Great Character of "WILL, THE NEWSBOY," in which she will sing the popular Song entitled "YOUNG AMERICA."

POSITIVELY THEIR LAST APPEARANCE
GRAND GALA NIGHT!
Sacramento Engine Co. No. 3,
Will visit the Theatre This Evening, in full uniform.

Saturday Evening, May 20th,
The performances will commence with the successful Drama of
Young America!
Or, The New York News Boy!

Will,	Two fatherless children,	Miss Ellen Bateman
Susan,		Miss Kate Bateman

Mr. Everington (a Wealthy Planter)......Mr. J. THOMAN
Mr. Plausible (a Real Estate Agent)......WOODARD
Dr. Anthem (a Fashionable Preacher)......PEARSON
Tim Doolin (an Irish Waiter)......C. A. KING
Cato (a Negro, Servant to Mr. Everington)......GEO. SPEAR
Johnson (an Editor)......HANKS
Bolt (a Jailor)......HARROLD
Waiter (at the St. Nicholas)......WILLIAMS
Citizens, &c., &c.
Widow Melvitte (a destitute Needlewoman, Mother of Will and Susan)......Miss DEMING
Mrs. Jones (a Friendly Neighbor)......Miss S. EDWIN
Miss Jerusha Plausible (a Strong-minded Woman, Sister of Plausible)......Mrs. CAMPBELL
Sally Soapsuds (a Yankee Chambermaid)......Miss RIVERS
Ladies, Servants, &c.

Synopsis of Scenery, Incidents, &c.
Act 1—SCENE 1st—A room in Mr. Plausible's House. An Irish Courtship. Yankee Independence. A Bloomer Spinster. The Reform Movement. SCENE 2—Parlor in the St. Nicholas. A young Southerner and an old Northerner. Caution vs. Credulity. The Boy's warm heart not to be overcome by worldly Prudence. Cato's speculations on his future state—his views of Abolition and the land of Free Niggerdom—he resolves not to try "dat Jordan." SCENE 3—The Widow's Attic. A sketch from a Picture of real life. Penury and Want. The Mother and the Child.

*If there be a tear
From human drops refined and clear'd,
A tear so limpid and so meek
It would not stain an angel's cheek,
'Tis that which pious parents shed
Upon a dutious daughter's head."*

A grasping Landlord. Right is Right. The little Champion—"No you don't." A hasty Toilet and a Declaration of Independence. Hostilities suspended. A kind Neighbor and a welcome Breakfast. Privation and poverty brings to light many a good phase in weak Human Nature. The suggestions of work. "Only tell me what I can do to help mother." A brilliant thought—"I'LL BE A NEWSBOY!" A Lad's first essay in this busy world. A mother's blessing.
Act 2—SCENE 1—Broadway..."Here's the Sun, Tribune, Herald and Daily Times."...Song, "FOUR AND TWENTY NEWSBOYS."...A Customer....A Temptation bravely resisted....The glow of conscious rectitude above all price. SCENE 2—Parlor in Plausible House....The Southerner and his antipodes....Cato gives his experience....The Abolitionist bluffed off....A little Petitioner....The wants of the Starving forgotten in the woes of the Esquimaux...."The Greeks are at your door, Madam,"...Erin go Bragh!...The blessing of a gentle heart upon the Green Isle....Song, "THERE IS AN ISLE OF GREEN." SCENE 3—Outside of Broadway Theatre....Omnibuses, Apple Stands and Loafers....Little Industry off his feet....Forty Winks....The box discovered....Malice Triumphant...."We were all so happy!"—Mother, Sister, what will you think has become of me?"....The anguish of despair.
Act 3—SCENE 1—The Tombs....The little one alone....The chances for liberty. The honest pride of the Newsboy....The Betrayer baffled....Paddy again on the side of the helpless....The deep trust confirmed. SCENE 2—Street at daybreak....The Reveller and the Beggar....Benevolence leads to many unlooked-for blessings....The contrast afforded by a great city. SCENE 3—The Widow's Attic....The last throes of a broken heart....The prayer is heard....Succor comes in time....An unexpected meeting....The sins of the father visited upon the children....The mother's joy is turned to anguish...."My child! my child!" SCENE LAST—Corner of Hague street....A crushed building....The promise of a bright future withered....The Mother's agony....A Sister's love and self-control....A brave Boy's unselfish death-struggle....A pure and true spirit passeth away. TABLEAU.

An Original Firemen's Address!
Written expressly for this occasion, and dedicated to the SACRAMENTO FIREMEN, will be spoken by Miss ELLEN BATEMAN, in the character of
Little Mose!
To conclude with the First Act of the celebrated Nautical Drama of
BLACK-EYED SUSAN.

Jacob Twig	Miss Ellen Bateman
Dolly Mayflower	Miss Kate Bateman
William	Mr. Bateman
Capt. Crosstree — Folland	Blue Peter — Sam
Raker — Harrold	Seaweed — Woodward
Hatchet — E. D. Campbell	Quid — Hanks
Doggrass — Pearson	
Gnatbrain — Daniels	Black-Eyed Susan, Miss Edwin

A Magnificent Entertainment Sunday Night!

UNION STEAM PRESSES

The precocious Bateman girls could handle both soapy melodrama *(left)* and Shakespeare. Ellen rendered Richard III with a suitably evil sneer *(below)*, while Kate posed manfully as his adversary, Richmond.

152

A veteran of the English music halls, Mabel Santley toured the camps with her Blonde Burlesques, a troupe of comely females who delighted miners with an upbeat repertoire of comic skits and risqué dances.

Brawny Helen Western appeared toward the end of the gold rush in *The French Spy,* disguised as an Arab. She wore fake whiskers and a scanty costume that, as one critic panted, "men pay any price to see."

5 | Boomtown on the Bay

Though there were moments following the first pell-mell exodus of miners when San Francisco appeared almost as placid as depicted here, during most of the 1850s it was the most exciting city on earth. Fed on a diet of gold from the Sierra mines, each day San Francisco spawned an average of 30 new houses, two murders and one fire.

Its young, heavily armed and largely male populace drank at more than 500 bars and gambled at 1,000 dens.

Nothing but life was cheap in this city, where eggs went for six dollars a dozen and landlords collected a mother lode of rentals for canvas shanties, abandoned ships' hulls and rooms in tinderbox houses. Gambling halls raked in hundreds of thousands in gold each day; one prostitute retired with $50,000 after a year's work. Recalling his days in the bustling gold-mine terminus, innkeeper John Henry Brown wrote later: "I feel almost ashamed to put in print some of the things that happened in those early days, as they seem almost incredible, and still it is the truth."

San Francisco's boom had barely begun in this lithographed view of a ship-jammed harbor by artist Frank Marryat.

155

San Francisco vigilantes use a cargo derrick to string up an ex-convict named English Jim Stuart after he had confessed to a long series of crimes. Stuart was but one of eight malefactors lynched by the vigilantes, who summarily deported dozens of other criminals, flogged one and generally frightened the city's roisterers into more acceptable behavior.

San Francisco had more ships ashore than were anchored in most other harbors. Abandoned vessels were run aground and leased as stores and hotels for $3,000 a month—more than they ever earned afloat. As this 1850 lithograph shows, subsequent landfills left ships like the cargo vessel *Niantic* far inland, nestled among conventional buildings.

Fires, often set by loot-hungry arsonists, razed San Francisco six times in 18 months with losses of $25 million and hundreds of lives. During a holocaust such as this one in 1851, wooden shanties blazed like tinder and even supposedly fireproof iron buildings literally melted. But after each disaster the city rose once more, bigger and better.

161
The Oakland Museum

A bawdy paradise, built on forty-niners' gold

At 7:45 on the evening of November 15, 1855, in San Francisco's American Theatre the celebrated Ravel family troupe of pantomimists was preparing to open in the world première of *Nicodemus; or the Unfortunate Fisherman*. All San Francisco — or to be more precise, some 2,000 of its burgeoning population of 55,000 — had turned out for the occasion, packing the American to the top of its glittering oval dome. The crescent of the first balcony and boxes revealed a goodly number of the city's most elegant and notable people, the well-groomed gentlemen in tailored vests of richly colored satins and velvets and frock coats, the ladies showing off the latest fashions from Paris.

The pit and the rear balconies held the common throng, including a fair sprinkling of gallused miners down from the diggings for a spree — though not so high a proportion as might have been at a big show a few years earlier when San Francisco was first aswarm with the forty-niners upon whose gold the city had been built in a breakneck half decade. The American Theatre itself, though its foundation had been laid as recently as 1851, was one of the oldest major buildings in town. Most of the others had been destroyed and rebuilt several times over, due largely to the scores of devastating fires that had kept the tinderbox city in a constant state of renewal — and of dizzying change —

since the beginning of the gold rush.

A number of those more sensitive theater patrons in the town's fast-thickening upper crust thought the American could use a good fire, too, if only to get rid of its hideous curtain, adorned with a dyspeptic-looking George Washington draped in an American flag against a lurid background of San Francisco Bay and the Golden Gate. On this particular Thursday evening, however, even before the offending curtain was raised, the American Theatre was to present the opening act of a real-life drama far more intriguing than the stage show, whose players languished behind the melancholy image of the nation's founding father. By the time it had run its course this unscheduled melodrama would reflect or embrace the entire booming, comic, gaudy, rich, deadly, boisterous, illicit and wholly fascinating phenomenon that was the city of San Francisco during the 1850s.

In the first balcony a pair of angry voices had erupted. One was that of General William H. Richardson, Southern gentleman, officer of the state militia and duly sworn federal marshal. The other voice belonged to a man named Charles Cora who, with his voluptuous wife Belle, sat directly behind the Richardsons. The Coras, General Richardson loudly insisted, must move to other seats immediately. Richardson actually was relaying the demands of his straight-backed wife, a lady who, according to later news reports of the event, was in a "delicate situation." The close presence of such disreputable people as the Coras had apparently upset her beyond endurance.

And indeed the Coras were quite a pair. Charles Cora, born in Genoa, Italy, educated in the bordellos of New Orleans, coal black of hair and the possessor of a magnificent, full mustache, counted himself among the

The scruffy forty-niner as observed in San Francisco — beady-eyed at the assayer, amorous with the ladies, thirsty and pugnacious on the town — became a stock figure in humor following the publication of caricatures like these by itinerant artists.

Bottle in hand, detective Isaiah Lees hardly looked "astute and energetic" as the press called him. But in 1852 he brought in San Francisco's first murderer to be legally executed since the beginning of the gold rush.

city's best professional gamblers. His wife (or as it was whispered, the woman who *called* herself his wife), a brunette beauty with alabaster skin and hazel eyes, was the proprietress of the city's most lavish and notorious bordello. Too bad for squeamish Mrs. Richardson and her antiquated Southern social distinctions. The Coras had arrived in San Francisco way back in '49, and they considered themselves one of the city's oldest families — worthy members of the establishment, major contributors to the economy.

They refused to budge. The general thereupon descended to the foyer to put his case to the manager. Again he spoke loudly and in heat, his words eagerly savored by the multitude. But the manager merely shrugged his shoulders, and in the end it was the Richardsons who left the theater.

The following day the reviews of *Nicodemus* were raves, but the real talk of the town was the spat between the Richardsons and the deliciously wicked Coras. However, the Cora-Richardson extravaganza had only begun. Two evenings later, while relaxing at the Blue Wing Saloon on Montgomery Street, Charles Cora was called outside by General Richardson, who appeared quite drunk. The two men then walked off together for a short distance. Suddenly they scuffled and Cora shot Richardson with a derringer — a weapon that was standard equipment for gamblers of the day — killing the general instantly. Richardson's own loaded and cocked pistol was found lying beside his body.

Cora was swiftly indicted for murder. And when asked if he wished to appear with counsel, he answered that since he had shot Richardson in self-defense he actually did "not wish to appear at all." But appear Cora did—handsomely defended by Colonel E. D. Baker, the most celebrated trial lawyer west of the Mississippi. The story went around that Colonel Baker, at first reluctant to accept so unpopular a case as that of a gambler who had shot a prominent federal law officer, had set what he considered the prohibitively high fee of $30,000. Belle, seated in her parlor, accepted without quibble, counting out $15,000 as a cash advance.

True to his reputation, and despite a bungled attempt by Belle to bribe a witness to testify that Richardson had drawn his pistol before Cora, Baker produced a spellbinding summation in defense of his client. The jury announced itself deadlocked, and Cora was remanded to the county jail to await a retrial.

Richardson's friends and the city's reformers were scandalized by such indecision. "Rejoice, ye gamblers and harlots! Rejoice with exceeding gladness!" boomed the *Evening Bulletin*. But the public clamor over the shooting quickly abated. It was generally conceded that when the last act of the thriller that had begun at the American Theatre was finally played, Cora would be set free in a brief retrial.

Meanwhile San Francisco would have plenty to keep busy on. So much was always happening around this bursting new city. So much already had happened in the past half-dozen years on the sandy, windswept tip of the peninsula that commanded the Golden Gate—so many murders, so many fortunes made and lost in business and at the gaming tables, so many rampant fires, so many wicked women loved and lost or forgotten, so much building and tearing down and building up again. Like the Cora trial, nothing ever seemed to be settled. And nothing could be counted on to last. Men who had seen San Francisco on their way to the gold fields and then returned only a few months later found an entirely new town.

Every ship that crowded into the harbor brought in more gold seekers, all needing food, lodging, supplies, services and agreeable diversions and distractions. The ships also brought supporting forces of merchants, traders, speculators, money men, gamblers and prostitutes. Separated from the rest of the world by a wide continent on one side and a wider ocean on the other, San Francisco represented a new sort of society come into being. Old values, old social and occupational distinctions of the sort General Richardson and his lady had sought to maintain, were cast aside. So, to a large extent, were mid-19th Century restraint and the inhibitions that had earlier governed most forty-niners.

One shipmaster, on coming ashore in 1850, tossed his valise to a ship's porter and said "Carry that valise to the hotel, my boy," pitching him 50 cents. The boy let the 50-cent piece fall to the ground, stared haughtily and pulled two half dollars out of his pocket, turned his head and said, "Carry it yourself." John Henry Brown, an Englishman who had arrived in San Francisco before the rush began and remained to become one of the city's leading tavern keepers, told of a drunk who announced that he was going to ride his horse through the big window of Brown's saloon. Brown warned the man that it would be the most expensive ride he had ever taken.

"How much?" was the reply.

Brown said it would be $500. The drunk tossed him a sack of gold, told Brown to take out $500 worth and enough more for a basket of wine, and rode through the window.

Gold was the very foundation of San Francisco —gold from diggings well beyond sight of the town to the east. For ship-borne forty-niners, San Francisco became the portal to the gilded pilgrimage. And for all men working in the gold fields it was the ultimate place for a lively, even riotous, time when they had dug enough gold to afford it. From the original strike in 1848 until the mid-1850s, when the initial boom subsided, $345 million worth of pay dirt arrived in San Francisco. A lot of the money stayed there, some in legitimate investments; but most of it went whirling away on the winds of celebration and wild chance. As the compilers of *The Annals of San Francisco* wrote in 1854, "Dust was plentier than pleasure, pleasure more enticing than virtue."

Some successful miners even considered it bad luck to head back to the mines after a roistering visit to San Francisco if they had not spent every ounce they had brought with them.

One such celebrant, remembered only as Flaxhead, had arrived in town with 20 pounds of gold dust, worth

San Francisco burgeoned into a major seaport within one year of the discovery of gold in the Sierra. This 1850 photograph — the earliest live visual record of the city — shows the bay thick with vessels behind a waterfront of multistory brick buildings where, as recently as 1847, cows had grazed and farmers and a modest handful of sea traders had dozed.

San Francisco's streets, rumored to be paved with gold, were in fact not paved at all. In the rainy season, or even at high tide, the mud forced pedestrians to don hip boots or to hop from plank to plank.

about $5,000 if he got a fair rate of exchange—which he probably did not. But even with discounted gold, exorbitant prices for food, lodging and drink; even with losses at the gaming tables and generous tips to bar girls and lady dealers in the gambling halls, Flaxhead still had gold dust when the time came for him to head back for the mines. He paid his hotel bill, bought camp supplies and a boat ticket for the trip back up the Sacramento River to the diggings. Then he poured the balance of the dust into a boot, slung the boot over his shoulder and made his way to the bar of the city's foremost hotel, the Parker House on Portsmouth Square. Here Flaxhead drank and bought rounds for everybody until the boot was empty. When someone cautioned him about his spendthrift ways, Flaxhead replied: "There's plenty more at the mines."

The unflagging confidence in plenty more, along with the happy accident of its geography, was perhaps the key to San Francisco's unique character. And indeed the "plenty" of gold streaming down from the mountains turned San Francisco into the rip-roaringest and liveliest boomtown of its day.

There had been a good deal of turning to do, in order to transform the sleepy Mexican port of Yerba Buena, which originally occupied the site, into the phenomenon calling itself San Francisco. The population of the port during the summer of 1847, before James Marshall's gold discovery, had been reckoned at 459, including 228 native-born United States citizens, and lesser numbers of Indians, Hawaiians, Mexicans, Canadians, Chileans, Britishers, Frenchmen, Germans and Swiss (a few years later someone noticed in the cemetery on Russian Hill that the headstones bore inscriptions in 13 different languages). It was also predominantly a male population; only 138 of the 459 were women. There were 26 carpenters, 20 laborers, 13 clerks, 11 merchants, 11 farmers and a fair representation of bakers, blacksmiths, navigators, doctors and

168

San Francisco's indoor amusements rivaled many European cities'. In saloons like this one, Spaniards, Chinese and Americans drank at ornate bars whose fixtures had been shipped from halfway round the world.

lawyers—and only one miner, whose identity and subsequent fortunes were somehow lost to history.

About the only excitement before Sam Brannan ran through the streets shouting about "gold on the American River" had been generated by Commander John B. Montgomery, skipper of the U.S. Navy's sloop of war *Portsmouth*. It was Montgomery who raised the American flag on July 9, 1846, in the town's plaza (subsequently named Portsmouth Square) in response to news of the war with Mexico. And it was Montgomery's shore detail of U.S. Marines that gave the town its first reputation for roistering buffoonery.

Each night the *Portsmouth*'s top Marine, a Captain Watson, used to sneak a visit with the innkeeper John Henry Brown to have his flask filled with an extra dollop of whiskey to supplement his regular ration. He would tap on Brown's shutter and give the password: "The Spaniards are in the brush"—a satirical reference to the scattered and apathetic remnants of the Mexican garrison. One night Brown was sleeping more soundly than usual, and Watson's taps on the shutter failed to awaken him. Whereupon Watson fired his pistol in the air and roared out the password about the Spaniards in the brush. The gunshot aroused the Marines and the shout persuaded them that they were under attack. They stumbled into formation and spent the rest of the night shooting at scrub oaks that were swaying in the wind in a menacing manner.

Shortly thereafter, another fusillade erupted, this one triggered by a brand-new pressure coffeepot Brown had bought for his kitchen. An inexperienced kitchen hand screwed the lid on too tight and a steam explosion followed, blowing the poor man out of the kitchen. Once more the Marines went into action to save the town from the treacherous Spaniards.

That was just about the full measure of thrills until April 1848 when the rush to the mines began in earnest. Immediately San Francisco's population jumped

A flood of new buildings covers the flanks of Telegraph Hill in the spring of 1851. Many of these dwellings were prefabricated in the East, then shipped around Cape Horn and slapped together in San Francisco. The three-story Oriental Hotel looms over its neighbors in the left background.

GROCERIES.

Sam Brannan, dean of San Francisco's entrepreneurs, dressed the part in 1855. A street orator of proven power, Brannan exhorted the citizenry to practice lynch law when other measures failed to curb crime.

to about 850—by which time the embryo boomtown acquired the more elegant name of San Francisco from a Spanish settlement that had once existed nearby. By the beginning of 1849 it had grown to 2,000; and before the end of that momentous year the number of residents soared to between 20,000 and 25,000. Nearly twice that number disembarked at the port during 1849, staying a few days before going on to the mines. (Among them, on December 28, were Charles and Belle Cora, carrying a stake of $40,000 which they fattened considerably before returning from the mining towns to settle and prosper in what was already the biggest city in the Far West.)

Real-estate values zoomed even faster than the population. A 50-vara lot—roughly 150 feet square—traded in 1846 for a keg of whiskey or a sore-back mule would soon be sold for thousands of dollars. Bought in 1847 for $16.50, a lot facing Portsmouth Square went for $6,000 in the spring of 1848, and was resold six months later for $45,000. Rental space became proportionately dear. For example, the canny Mormon emigrant Sam Brannan managed to convert some of his gold-camp profits into San Francisco rental properties that netted him $160,000 in 1849 alone. Another of Sam's coups was cornering the market in carpet tacks, which he sold for $16 a package to free-wheeling building contractors.

Other prices shot up apace. The cost of lumber went from four cents a board foot to a dollar or more, and still the need so far outstripped the supply that available bolts of canvas and calico were shaped into tents or stretched over wooden frames to make so-called rag houses. With two men in every three heading off for the diggings, the demand for labor sent wages soaring from one dollar a day to $10, $20—even $30 a day, and many jobs still went unfilled.

For who wanted to sweat as a day laborer when he could so easily make a fortune with a miner's pick—or better yet, by his wits? One merchant bought 1,500 dozen eggs off a coastal schooner; he quickly sold them at 37½ cents a dozen and, minutes later, saw them offered for resale at four dollars a dozen. He bought all of them back, took them to Sacramento on the river steamer and sold them for six dollars a dozen. An equally energetic young Frenchman did a brisk trade selling suspenders for six times and toothbrushes for 10 times their original cost. His stock ran so low that finally he had nothing left but 248 small packs of toothpicks —the kind that were given away in restaurants in France (and that he had brought out for his own use). A customer willingly paid him two dollars for four packs, each containing two dozen toothpicks. That night the Frenchman split each remaining pack into demipacks of 12 each, and sold all of those at 50 cents each.

Perhaps the pinnacle of this kind of merchandising was achieved by a ship captain who, aware of the prevalence of rats in San Francisco, brought in a shipload of stray cats and sold them for $10 apiece.

Because storage space was scarce, importers frequently auctioned off ships' cargoes at wharfside or in the street—with a brass band to attract a crowd. Not infrequently, tradesmen and speculators found themselves forced to buy the entire cargo of a ship in order to get the one part they wanted. Even so they would come out ahead. One hotel owner bought an entire shipload to get the cases of gin and baskets of champagne that were aboard. He found himself in possession of vast quantities of men's boots, clothing and other dry goods for which he had no use. On the way back to his hotel he met a merchant who took the goods off his hands for a sum which not only paid for the liquor but also gave the hotel man a profit of $10,000.

Occasionally, however, the market for some items would be too glutted even for San Francisco. One storekeeper, stuck with a cargo of washing pans that he was having trouble peddling, hit upon an ingenious solution based upon a forty-niner canard that gold lay about on the city streets. First he surreptitiously sprinkled several ounces of gold dust outside his store. Then, he re-entered the store and, with much ostentation, reappeared holding a shovel and pan, with which he scooped up a panful of dirt. This drew a crowd. When he started to wash it the crowd was even larger. Finally he had washed out all the dirt and there at the bottom, sure enough, was about two ounces of gold. The bystanders rushed into his store to buy wash pans for themselves. He sold them out at two dollars apiece instead of the 10 cents or so they normally would have brought.

Other merchants, less ingenious, simply dumped their unwanted goods in the street. Though profitless, the practice provided a public service of sorts. The city's dirt streets were a chronic problem, being anywhere from ankle to eyeball deep in mud during the wet winter months. Live horses and mules and—so claimed a chronicler—three drunken men fell and suffocated in the worst of the mudholes. Over one such deadly bog a sign appeared: "Head of navigation; no bottom." A sign at another morass warned: "This street is impassable, not even jackassable."

Into these mud pits went the unsalable goods—cast-iron stoves, chamber pots, kegs of nails, casks of tobacco, sacks of flour—to become the foundations of some of San Francisco's major thoroughfares.

But this kind of informal land filling was barely noticed in a city that was busily dumping every available cubic yard of sand or dirt into the bay itself to create more of San Francisco's scarcest of all commodities: real estate. So fast did the shoreline march seaward that within a year wharves that in 1849 had extended far out over the tidal flats turned into extensions of city streets. Beached ships like the bluff-bowed cargo vessel *Niantic (page 159)* became located farther and farther inland. A theater thrown up on one patch of unsettled fill sank several inches under the weight of its first full house; thereafter occasional flood tides entered the aisles to lap around the boots of the audience.

What had once been, in fact, the high-tide line became Montgomery Street, where a hive of jerry-built banks and brokerage houses quickly sprouted into one of the world's busiest and most thoroughly venal financial centers. Banking hours were from 6 a.m. to 10 p.m. Interest on loans ranged from 3 to 14 per cent per month (at nearby gambling establishments loans were made to losers at 10 per cent interest per hour, a rate that, on an annual basis, amounted to 87,600 per cent).

Located a block inland from Montgomery Street on a slope above the bay, was Portsmouth Square—the onetime potato patch of Yerba Buena, but by late 1849 the hub of a dizzying whirl of living. Ranged around the square, on Dupont, Clay, Kearny and Washington streets stood San Francisco's finest hotels, the best restaurants, plushest saloons, most glittering gambling rooms and billiard halls—sometimes all under one roof. (Urbanization had been so sudden that even by 1856 local livestock had not yet adjusted to all the changes; the Board of Supervisors was still debating how best to keep the square's central mall free of "any itinerant mule or donkey that may select it as a pasture ground.")

House flags like those of clipper *Flying Cloud* (*bottom, center*) or the Pacific Mail (*top, second from right*) identified arriving ships.

From a house atop Telegraph Hill, San Francisco's highest point, a semaphore reports ship arrivals, drawing mail-starved crowds.

Bright flags to signal mail for homesick Californians

Nowhere but in the California of the gold rush days were so many 19th Century Americans so isolated from the rest of the U.S., and so wholly dependent on ships to bring them everything they wanted and needed. Overland transport by foot or wagon was hopelessly rough and risky.

The forty-niners, particularly around San Francisco, waited eagerly for the arrival of the score or more of ships that hove to in the harbor each week to unload their cherished cargoes. These vessels came from nearly every port in the world, each raising to its masthead an identifying flag called a private signal (*left*) as she came within sight of the Golden Gate.

For San Franciscans the incoming vessels were barely less exciting than hangings, fires or new gold strikes. Virtually everyone in town knew by heart the code signals to describe each vessel that were relayed inland by semaphore from Telegraph Hill. At a San Francisco theater one night an actor threw wide his arms while delivering the line: "What means this, my lord?" Replied a boisterous voice from the gallery: "Sidewheel steamer!"

Before a vessel had even docked, small boats swarmed out to meet her in the bay. There she was boarded by customs and quarantine men, citizens seeking relatives and friends, merchants avid for goods that could be sold at two to 20 times purchase price. Most eagerly awaited of all, however, were the relays of Pacific Mail steamers that arrived every two weeks with sacks full of what forty-niners craved more than anything else—mail from back home (*overleaf*).

175

The semimonthly visits of Pacific Mail steamers generated a convivial excitement that San Franciscans came to celebrate. Steamer Day remained a local institution some 30 years after the railroads arrived.

As soon as a mail ship docked, crowds of 500 or so lined up at San Francisco's post office, even though clerks might need 12 to 20 hours to sort the mail before the lines could start inching forward—at a rate of about 40 feet an hour. An observer noted that by evening the lines were "but little shortened, and the rush sometimes continues for three days." But what were a few more hours to a homesick émigré who had already waited months for a letter?

"I am more anxious to hear from you than I ever was to have any thing in this world," wrote Henry Page to his wife back in Illinois. His fellow miner William Miller complained to a correspondent: "I have looked for letters until I got tired of asking the postmasters. This is the 15th letter that I have rote to you since I left home and receive 4 letter." And a contemporary chronicler describes one "rough looking customer" wetting his beard with tears of joy over a letter from home while mail-less companions "go sullenly back to work, unfitted by disappointment for social intercourse the rest of the day."

Waiting for letters was vexatious enough in San Francisco, port of arrival for most California mail. Worse yet was the situation at the few, tiny, inland post offices struggling hopelessly to get tons of mail up from the coast by wagon or pack mule, and then dealing with the miners' own avalanche of 50,000 fortnightly letters home.

Recognizing a demand, profiteering private mail carriers began bringing letters direct to miners from San Francisco, initially charging as much as $16 a letter. These messenger services grew into powerful express companies that challenged the government mail monopoly. In California they roused public support for turning over to private enterprise the whole U.S. postal system. The issue died only as a result of the sharp drop that occurred in mail traffic as the gold rush petered out in the late 1850s, and the completion of the first transcontinental rail link a decade later.

Eager forty-niners queue up outside San Francisco's post office, to wait for mail or to sell their places for $25 to letter-starved latecomers. Clerks inside worked around the clock, catnapping on the wooden floors.

Portsmouth Square was the real core of the city, where the forty-niner down from the hills came with his pockets full of pay dirt and his head full of big ideas for a blowout. Once he had hired himself a room (prices ranged from $37.50 a week for a single room at the St. Francis Hotel to six dollars a week for a flop in a 50-man dormitory), the gold miner, just like the trail-driving cowhand come to town, got himself spruced up. First he headed for one of the city's public baths, widely advertised as "a grand antidote for the dust that abounds in the city."

Next he got a haircut, probably a shave but often no new clothes, since most forty-niners felt they must maintain the panache of rough fellows just in from the diggings. Then he set out to stuff his stomach with something better than the beans and salt pork on which he had been existing for weeks or months. A chaplain with simple tastes, Walter Colton, ordered ham and eggs, which cost him six dollars. But despite exorbitant prices, few heavy-pocketed celebrants wanted to settle for such prosaic fare. Much better was available.

Restaurants served food in French, German, American, Mexican and Chinese style. And the raw materials, especially the meats, were rich and varied: beef, mutton, grizzly bear, elk, deer, antelope, turtle, hare, partridge, quail, wild goose, brant, curlew, snipe, plover, duck, salmon, trout and oysters. A lawyer named John Felton, who not surprisingly suffered from gout, went every noon to the plush bar of the Bank Exchange on Washington Street and consumed three dozen oysters and a quart of champagne.

This kind of gorging became a San Francisco institution. One eating group included Dave Scannell, the fire chief and sheriff; Sam Hall, a hotelkeeper; and several judges and lawyers. These men had a round table permanently reserved at the Occidental Restaurant, where they would gather every day. If court was not in session they assembled at 10 a.m. and breakfasted until early afternoon. Then, court or no court, they convened again at around 5:00 to commence a feast that would last until 9:00 or 10:00 at night with copious drinks before, during and after the meal. Scannell and Hall scouted the markets for the greatest delicacies, choicest cuts of wild game, cockscombs, sweetbreads and very small shad. A special favorite was canvasback duck, roasted exactly 13 minutes and served with blood oozing from it and accompanied by a special punch made of equal parts of red wine, white wine, sparkling burgundy, champagne and cognac.

Cheek by jowl with the restaurants, and sometimes inside them, were the gambling halls. These operated mostly on a nonstop basis and paid the biggest rents in the city — $60,000 a year at the Parker House alone. Poker was regarded as too slow and complicated a way to win or lose money. Forty-niners preferred craps, faro or the French card games of *vingt-et-un* or *lansquenet*. But the favorite, whether at the Parker House, the El Dorado, the Verandah or the Aquila de Oro, was the Mexican card game, monte. In one of several variations of the game a miner would select two of four cards laid face up on the table and bet on one to be matched before the other as the rest of the cards from the deck were dealt one by one. Usually the bets ranged from 50 cents to five dollars but occasionally they ran as high as $20,000.

In the larger establishments a bettor in from the mines with a sackful of gold dust to spend was asked to change it for coin, usually at scalper's rates, before stepping up to the table. But in the smaller operations a miner might plunk down an unopened bag of dust on a card and announce what portion of it he meant to bet. If he won, the dealer paid him without ever seeing the color of the miner's gold. If he lost, he could continue to play until he quit or until the dealer judged that the total amount of the bag was exhausted. In either case, play would stop while the dealer pulled out his scales, weighed the gold and settled up. And woe to the miner who took strong exception to the settlement, or was found to be fattening his bag with brass filings. For Charles Cora was not the only gambler who kept a derringer at hand.

The gambling halls proved so profitable that owners laid on every inducement to attract customers: free food and liquor, thick carpets, huge mirrors, paintings of women in various stages of undress, crystal chandeliers and music either from soloists or string ensembles. By the early '50s, the halls were further decorated by women dealers and barmaids of great allure. These were especially welcome in a town where women had for a long time been so scarce. Jessie Frémont, wife of the explorer John Frémont, had noted in the spring of 1849 that at a party given for a bride recently arrived from

New York, "the whole force of San Francisco society came out, the ladies sixteen in number."

Alas for propriety, not all of San Francisco's ladies remained ladies — at least not in the strictly moral sense. "While there are very many beautiful, modest and virtuous women," wrote the authors of *The Annals of San Francisco* in 1853, "numbers of the sex have fallen very readily into the evil ways of the place. Perhaps the more lovely they were the more readily they stooped to folly. It is difficult for any woman, however pure," the *Annals* explained gallantly, "to preserve an unblemished reputation where there is so great a majority of men, and where so many are unprincipled in mind and debauchees by inclination."

Foreign women, be they French, Mexican, Chilean or Chinese, exercised a special attraction for the Argonauts. These exotic charmers charged an ounce of gold (or about $16) to sit at the bar with a lonely miner. To spend the night with him they might demand 25 to 35 times as much.

Albert Benard de Russailh, a sharp-witted young Frenchman who arrived in San Francisco in 1851, counted 10 or 12 of his countrywomen already working in the city. He noted in his keenly perceptive diary that the men "much preferred the French women. Americans were irresistibly attracted by their graceful walk, their supple but easy bearing and charming freedom of manner, qualities, after all, only to be found in France. If the poor fellows had known what these women had been in Paris, how one could pick them up on the boulevards and have them for almost nothing, they might not have been so free with their offers of $500 or $600 a night. Some of the first in the field made enough in a month to go home to France and live on their income. There are also some honest women in San Francisco, but not very many."

Despite such formidable competition a 20-year-old Cantonese woman named Ah Toy became one of San Francisco's busiest prostitutes. At her place of business off Clay Street she prospered despite various brushes with the law, including one deportation action instituted by a man in Hong Kong claiming to be her legal husband. However, in this case the judge, after hearing from Ah Toy that she had come to San Francisco to "better her condition" and wished to stay, decided she could. On at least one occasion she went to court as a plaintiff, complaining that certain of her customers, like those of the smalltime gambling halls, had tried to dupe her by paying in brass filings.

One of the first of the really high-class bordellos, the so-called parlor houses, was opened by one Irene McCready. Mrs. McCready arrived in San Francisco with her lover, a gambler named James McCabe in April 1849 (they had an eight-month head start over the similar team of Charles and Belle Cora). McCabe became co-owner of the lavish and successful El Dorado on the Kearny and Washington sides of Portsmouth Square. On the opposite, Clay Street side, Mrs. McCready opened her house in a one-story frame building. She had been in business only a few months when her establishment and about a million dollars' worth of other buildings, including McCabe's El Dorado, were completely destroyed in a terrible fire that swept through Portsmouth Square on Christmas Eve, 1849. However, Mrs. McCready's cash position was so strong that she was able to rebuild almost immediately along more luxurious lines — only to be wiped out again by another fire a few months later.

In 1850, once more rebuilt and back in business, McCabe and Mrs. McCready, who had indulged in a number of public scraps, parted company after the gambler thrashed his lady. The action came in response to one of her many jealous tantrums, which, however justly motivated by McCabe's wandering eye, had become vexatious to him. But Mrs. McCready got in the last lick. Sweet-talking her ex-lover back for an evening of fun and frolic, she slipped him a drugged glass of wine and while the gambler was unconscious she shaved his head "as Delilah of old did with Samson," an acquaintance reported. The same man added that for some time afterwards the thoroughly humiliated McCabe "did not appear in his usual haunts."

All these grand diversions for the forty-niners — dalliance, gambling, eating, fighting — were accompanied by drinking on a heroic scale. Gin cocktails were favored as an early morning restorative. Hot drinks made of brandy, syrup and nutmeg were popular in inclement weather, as was a mixture of whiskey and apple cider called a stone fence. Imported wine, champagne cocktails and Queen Charlottes (a mixture of claret and raspberry syrup) were called for when there appeared to be a premium on sobriety, which was not often. And

On June 22, 1851, San Francisco's sixth conflagration since Christmas Eve of 1849 roared through the sprawl of jerry-built wood houses. Exploding kegs of miners' blasting powder and bands of looters added to the terror of the blaze that destroyed some three million dollars' worth of property.

181

straight whiskey and brandy were consumed at all hours in all seasons. A survey in 1853 showed 537 places in San Francisco where liquor was sold, including 144 "tavern restaurants," 46 gambling houses and 48 places "kept by bawds."

With all that booze and gay companionship available, it did not take much of an excuse to get a party going in San Francisco. Nor did it take much more to turn a spontaneous party into a regular holiday. One such was Steamer Day, the semimonthly celebration built around the regular arrivals *(pages 174-177)* and departures of the mail ships that plied between San Francisco and the crossing points on the Central American Isthmus. By Steamer Day, the 1st and 15th of each month, merchants and importers had been busily collecting money due them to meet their own debts before ordering more goods. Letters home were written and posted. Miners leaving for the states shopped for souvenirs—often including a heroic snootful of liquor—to take home with them. Then, long before the hour of sailing, passengers boarded ship while their friends swarmed the wharves, joking, reminiscing, giving advice and bidding sentimental farewells.

One happy celebrant, who typically had no dockside mission save diversion, described the holiday mood. "Passengers crowded to the side," he reported, "to exchange farewell salutations. 'Good bye, Jones,' 'Good bye, Brown,' 'God bless you old fellow, take care of yourself,' they shouted. Not seeing anyone that I knew and fearing the passengers might think I had no friends, I shouted 'Good bye, Muggins,' and had the satisfaction of having a shabby man, much inebriated, reply as he swung his rimless hat, 'Good bye, my brother.' Not particularly elated at this recognition, I tried again, with 'Good bye, Colonel,' whereat thirty-four respectable gentlemen took off their hats."

Other kinds of outdoor entertainment flourished in San Francisco. In 1850 a stock company sponsored the building of a planked toll road (25 cents for a horseman, 75 cents for a two-horse wagon) from the center of town out to the Mission Dolores—a favorite place for outings but one that had been all but inaccessible over the sandy roads. Soon two race tracks were operating there, the Union and the Pioneer. And nearby, two amusement parks, Russ Gardens and The Willows, offered havens where weary miners could stroll among the trees and flowers, drink beer, eat and listen to band concerts.

As early as October 1849, a circus visited the city (by 1850 it would have three). Clowns, acrobats and trick riders performed for customers sitting on hard benches at characteristically high prices—as much as $55 for a private stall.

Even with this giddy round of other diversions, San Franciscans, like their neighbors in the mining camps, seemed to have a special fondness for all kinds of theatricals *(pages 148-153)*. The city's first important theater, the Dramatic Museum, opened smashingly on July 4, 1850 (15 months ahead of the swiftly successful American), under the direction of the talented impresario-writer-performer Dr. David "Yankee" Robinson. His burlesque farce *Seeing the Elephant,* which had delighted audiences on its out-of-town tour through the diggings, was an enormous hit with the San Franciscans. However, the first formal entertainment of any kind occurred as early as June 22, 1849, put on by a roly-poly, curly-haired little Englishman, Stephen C. Massett, a part-time lawyer, part-time journalist and full-time composer, singer and monologuist.

For his première, Massett rented the schoolhouse on Portsmouth Square, borrowed a piano—one of a few in the city—from E. Harrison, the collector of the port, and paid $16 to have it hauled across the square from the customhouse to the schoolhouse. He packed the room at three dollars a head and cleared $500 from a foot-stomping audience. Massett sang his own songs, such as "List While I Sing" and "When the Moon on the Lake Is Beaming" and did multiple impersonations. One newspaper later noted with pleasure that "four ladies were present." Two and a half years later Massett presented a farewell performance before leaving for a tour of the East. This time he performed in a large and formal concert hall, accompanied in the same, good old songs by a full orchestra, before an audience as glitteringly dressed as only a collection of new sophisticates can be.

Most persistent of all San Francisco's impresarios during this period was Tom Maguire, best remembered for his presentation of Adah Isaacs Menken in the title role of *Mazeppa,* in which she wore flesh-colored tights that made her appear to be nude. A onetime New York City hack driver, Maguire opened the first of

Where gold dust was made into eagles – that sometimes flew away

Amid all the hurly-burly of construction in San Francisco, one of the most important buildings in the city was a dark, little 60-foot-square United States branch mint. To this building came the wiser forty-niners, down from their diggings and carrying their sacks of gold dust. There the dust was weighed and the miners paid off at the official rate of $16 per ounce — instead of at the fluctuating open-market prices that, in the gold-glutted city, could sink to eight dollars.

Then mint workers promptly began an elaborate work sequence in which, a reporter observed, "every man is more or less in the other's way." The gold dust was melted, refined and cast into strips that were punched into blank coins. Finally the coins were fed into a press and stamped into legal tender with Liberty heads on the face and eagles or wreaths on the back. The coins were generally called eagles, double eagles, etc. *(below),* according to denominations.

During its first year, 1854, the mint produced four million dollars in gold coins; by 1856, the figure was up to nearly $24 million and included silver as well. But as production boomed, so, alas, did embezzlement. One of the better-known cases was that of a cashier named Macy, who had devised a simple but effective technique to skim loot. He tore off the identifying tag reading $120,000 from a sack of freshly minted coins, and then sent a message to the coiner that he had lost the tag from a $100,000 sack. Given a new tag, Macy attached it to the sack — after having first removed $20,000. By the time his thefts were discovered, Macy had fled with $39,000.

Another scandal involved an assayer who, when questioned about shortages that kept occurring, said they were caused by gold drifting up the chimney. The claim was partly substantiated when a check of the roof led to the recovery of several thousand dollars' worth of dust that actually had been sucked up by the chimney draft. But since the losses were even greater than this amount, the assayer was forced to resign.

And a janitor, much praised for ridding the premises of rats, was finally found to be sewing $20 gold pieces inside each dead rat before throwing it on the trash heap. Returning to the heap after hours, he collected the rats, slit them open, retrieved the money, and then set out to have himself all the fun his double eagles could buy.

A mint worker stamps out coins.

$20 Double Eagle $10 Eagle $5 Half Eagle $3 Gold Piece $2.50 Quarter Eagle

The bursting new city loved festivities of any kind, especially a Fourth of July like this one of 1851. Townspeople cheered a parade of militia, complete with fife-and-drum corps, cannon and flag-decked floats.

three Jenny Lind theaters on the floor above his saloon, in October 1850. It went up in the flames that swept the center of the city on May 4, 1851. He immediately built a second Jenny Lind and opened it June 13, 1851. Nine days later it too was destroyed by fire. Undaunted, Maguire built again, this time a handsome and more durable building of brick — the third Jenny Lind. It survived, though Maguire, pressed by mounting debts, was forced to sell the building to the city for $200,000 for use as a city hall.

The fires which helped drive Tom Maguire into bankruptcy were the curse of all San Francisco throughout the decade of the gold rush. In fact the town burned down with such terrifying regularity that the conflagrations became a kind of grim joke with the inhabitants. "You have heard of our fires," wrote lawyer Joseph Glover Baldwin. "They throw light on our character. We burn down a city in a night and build it in a day. Contracts for new buildings are signed by the light of the fire that is consuming the old."

The first major fire broke out on Christmas Eve, 1849, in Dennison's Exchange, a popular saloon and gambling hall on the east side of the Plaza. Like all of San Francisco's major blazes, there are conflicting accounts of its origins. The most probable version had its roots in 19th Century racism. It was the custom at the time in the more expensive saloons to discourage what was known as the Negro trade. Blacks ordinarily would be served one drink on the house, but that would be all. When, on this particular holy eve, one black man was bold enough to put down his coin and ask for a second round, he was stabbed by the bartender. In falling, the victim knocked over a lantern and the cotton-cloth ceiling of the Exchange caught fire.

Within minutes the blaze had spread to the adjoining buildings. Then someone yelled "Stored powder!" which was not true, but led spectators and fire fighters alike to flee the area, leaving the flames to sweep on unchecked. The fire was not brought under control until later when volunteers blasted firebreaks with gunpowder and plastered other buildings with fire-resistant mud scooped out of the streets.

The burned area was quickly restored, only to be leveled again on May 4 by another rampaging fire, almost in the same location. This one wiped out three entire city blocks at a cost of about $3 million. The following month it happened once again, this time on the south side of the Plaza.

George Coffin, master of the ship *Alhambra,* then anchored in San Francisco Bay, witnessed the June fire. He had gone ashore in his ship's boat to post some letters when he saw the flames and smoke on the east side of the Plaza. Realizing that it threatened the rooms of a friend living in that section of town, he raced to the scene just in time to help his friend carry out a chest containing $30,000 in gold (nearly 120 pounds). They lugged the chest down to Howison's pier where, if necessary, it could be thrown into the shallows of the bay for safety. Coffin then ran through a hail of wind-blown sparks to Long Wharf to see to his boat, which he had left moored there. Suddenly a cart clattered onto the wharf and dumped a large military chest. Coffin looked at it and discovered the label "Gunpowder." With the help of other boatmen he hurriedly pitched it off the wharf and buried it in the bayshore mud.

The Army quartermaster's warehouse was nearby, Captain Coffin noted later. It was "said to contain 5,000 stands of loaded muskets. The constant discharging of these would at any other time have sounded like a military engagement, but amid the roar of this awful conflagration they were not heard. The rapid and constant succession of flashes showed that they were being discharged. Our escape was owing to the fact that these muskets were fitted in perpendicular racks so that the shells were thrown upward."

The English writer and artist Frank Marryat arrived back in the city from a visit to the countryside at the very hour when the flames were at their worst. After they subsided he toured the scene where 400 buildings had been destroyed: "Gun barrels were twisted and knotted like snakes: there were tons of nails welded together standing in the shape of the kegs which had contained them. An iron fire-proof safe had burst. Spoons, knives, forks and crockery were melted up together in heaps; preserved meats had been unable to stand this second cooking and had exploded in every direction. But there was little time wasted in lamentation. Forty-eight hours after the fire the whole district resounded to the din of busy workmen."

Three more disastrous fires swept the city. The worst of them came on May 4, 1851 (the anniversary of an earlier fire). It had special significance because all

Hamming it up for the camera, prospectors down from the mines burlesque San Francisco high life at a liquor store. Their props include ladies' crinolines — items of fascination where ladies themselves were scarce.

Highlights of San Francisco's lowlife were enthusiastically reported by the *California Police Gazette,* the city's favorite scandal sheet, which specialized in racy prose and titillating woodcuts like the ones below.

"Pretty waiter girls," as the *Gazette* sometimes called them, entice big spenders at a local dive.

At Madame Reiter's Bagnio, a patron whose wallet had been lifted settles the score with his hostess.

evidence pointed to its having been set by arsonists. For more than a year the city had been plagued by bands of roving hoodlums. The worst of these were the Sydney Ducks, or as they referred to themselves in their own Cockney slang, coves or birds.

The Ducks were Australians or Englishmen-by-way-of-Australia. England was still using Australia as a dumping ground for convicts. For these exiles, news of California's gold had been irresistible. Though some of the men from Down Under were not convicts, and others had served their time and were free to come, more came on "tickets of leave," i.e., illegally.

A miserable San Francisco slum, with dingy grogshops, gambling rooms and bawdy houses, just south of Telegraph Hill was a favorite haunt for these rough immigrants. Known as Sydney Town, it was recognized as one of the most dangerous sections of the city. From here the Ducks set out to prey on miners, merchants, gamblers or anyone else who might have money; or to set fires in retaliation for arrests and to provide an opportunity for looting.

As the anniversary of the May 1850 fire approached, several notorious Ducks openly boasted of their intention to burn the city down. And on the night of May 3, a few minutes before 11 o'clock, a man was seen running furtively from a paintshop on Portsmouth Square. Moments later the building burst into flames. At almost the same time a half dozen other fires broke out around the business district. A strong wind was blowing from the northeast, helping to fan the flames —and to drive them in the opposite direction from the Ducks's stronghold near Telegraph Hill.

During the fire, bands of Ducks swarmed out of Sydney Town to plunder and loot. Enraged citizens caught and killed several of them, together with one innocent bystander, a sailor, who was shot to death when he picked up a burning brand to light his pipe.

By the time the holocaust was brought under control, 18 blocks had been destroyed, including some 2,000 buildings—many new and supposedly fireproof brick structures with iron doors and shutters. One group of six men who had taken refuge in one of the supposedly fireproof brick buildings was found there the next day roasted to death, as if in an oven.

Water had been short during this blaze as in all others, since the city's few cisterns were speedily exhausted. (One warehouse owner saved his property by dousing it with 80,000 gallons of vinegar.) Had there been adequate water, the city might have been able to defeat the arsonists and avert real disaster, since by 1851 San Francisco boasted a collection of the most vigorous, numerous, proud and gaudy volunteer fire companies of virtually any city in the world. And clearly, no city had shown a greater need.

To fight the Christmas Eve fire of 1849 there had been only two hand-drawn, hand-pumped fire engines available. One, imported from the Hawaiian Islands, was worn out and useless. The other, a pitifully small machine once used by President Van Buren to water his gardens in New York, had been shipped to California to pump water from gold mines. The only suitable solution to this dangerous shortage appeared to be the formation of volunteer fire companies, each providing its own engine.

The first company was formed in early 1850 under the leadership of a former New York fire fighter named David Broderick, who brought his expertise to California in 1849. In his honor the company was called Broderick One. It was soon followed by others: Protection Two, Howard Three, California Four, Knickerbocker Five and so on.

Many of the companies had a regional cast. Knickerbocker Five, for example, was made up largely of former New Yorkers, Crescent Ten by men from New Orleans, Howard Three by Bostonians; Lafayette Hose was French. A competitive spirit—speed in getting to a fire and putting it out—gave the fire companies a special, chauvinistic verve. Regional and national pride intensified these feelings, as did the lively inter-company meets the volunteers periodically staged. At one such event, Monumental Six (or Big Six, as its members preferred to call it) set a record for a hand-pumped stream of water with a majestic squirt that traveled 229 feet and 8 inches.

Whenever a fire broke out the companies were alerted by the clanging of the great city bell, and the location of the blaze was pinpointed by coded strokes of the clapper. Thereupon the volunteers dropped everything, grabbed their helmets and boots and ran to their station (although members of High-Toned Twelve were said to disdain such equipment; instead they ran directly to the fire in patent-leather boots, frock coats and

Coves such as this one, where the variegated armada of abandoned ships that brought the forty-niners was anchored, quickly vanished under the land-fill programs of real-estate promoters. The barren sandy bluff in the foreground overlooks Market Street, San Francisco's principal thoroughfare.

stovepipe hats). The first members to arrive at the station would grasp the front shaft that guided their four-wheeled fire engine; the others—and often numerous enthusiastic friends—would seize ropes to pull the engine at a dead run through San Francisco's dangerous up-and-down streets. At night torch boys would race ahead to light the way.

Charles Robinson recalled his days as a torch boy —and particularly one night at North Beach when his services proved vital: "Three of us were running with the engines. The first boy darted ahead, and suddenly we saw his light disappear. I was next. Down I went into a hole on top of the first boy. When the men with the engine saw two lights disappear, they knew something must have happened. So the third boy steered off in another direction. A big hole had been dug that day right in the middle of the street."

Sailor Eight, a company made up of former seafaring men, introduced the practice of singing sea chanteys while manning the pumps. A more formalized blend of music and fire fighting was embodied in Charles Schultz, a German immigrant, violinist, composer and a long-time orchestra conductor. Schultz was also an enthusiastic member of St. Francis Hook and Ladder, and he composed "The Firemen's March," a popular number which became a standard selection for public occasions. Whenever he played it, Schultz dramatically clapped his fireman's helmet on his head.

In their dazzling dress uniforms (Social Three had gold capes) the volunteers proudly marched in holiday parades, their engines draped with ribbons, banners, bouquets and wreaths supplied by admirers. They held receptions, tea dances, chowder parties, dinners and balls in their headquarters, moving the fire engines outside to make room for dancing. The companies often attended theatrical and musical presentations in uniformed groups. In the case of a particular stage favorite, such as Kate Hayes, who was variously known as the Irish Linnet or the Swan of Erin, they would escort her to and from the concert hall in parade formation with all the solemnity of a palace guard.

Social Three was the most ostentatious of all the companies. It owned a piano, had a glee club and entertained lavishly. Its engine was silver-plated and the foreman's speaking trumpet was gold (most such trumpets were of silver). While all companies had well-stocked bars in their headquarters, Social Three was reputed to have the greatest tipplers. During a fire at the Pacific Warehouse in Front Street, members of Social Three were said to have discovered a cache of champagne and to have poured more down their gullets than they did water on the fire. Social Three later reformed and went on the wagon en masse, forming a temperance group known as the Dashaway Society with a song to fit, sung to the tune of "America":

> *With manly self control*
> *We'll dash away the bowl*
> *That would ensnare the soul*
> *To wine's dark sway.*

Competition between the volunteer companies and a prideful resistance to change finally led to the volunteers' undoing. In other cities, horses, steam engines and telegraphic alarm systems were changing fire-fighting methods. Besides, more and more towns were converting to paid, professional fire departments. The California legislature had considered a bill that would do away with the volunteer companies and replace them with professionals, but many San Franciscans of the old guard resisted the change and the bill had languished for months in endless wrangling. The volunteer companies were politically potent and there was even fear that abolishing them might lead to riots.

Instead, a riot led to their abolition. An alarm at Fourth and Mission set off a heated race, and then a bloody free-for-all between Social Three, Knickerbocker Five and Big Six. While the blaze died of its own accord, firemen bashed at each other with spanners, crowbars, pieces of wood and stones from the street. The ruckus forced the law through the legislature and the era of the volunteers was at an end.

Besides inspiring one of San Francisco's most colorful and boisterous institutions, the fires both great and small that cost so much treasure and anguish contributed to the formation of the city's grim, deadly committees of vigilance. Some precedence for self-appointed citizen committees to enforce law and order had been established on a scattered, short-term basis as early as pre-Revolutionary days. But it was San Francisco, with its fear of arsonists and other rampant criminals, that produced on a grand scale the model for the vigilante groups whose members would take the law into their own

As dramatized in this cartoon, vigilante committees sprang up in San Francisco as the result of anger at unchecked crime (particularly arson in the tinderbox city) and the city's haphazard police and courts.

hands on the Western frontier for decades to come.

The Sydney Ducks were not by a good measure the only lawless element in San Francisco in the early '50s. A corrupt court and a graft-infested police force shamelessly refused to protect the public against the depredation of other robbers, arsonists, looters and even murderers. In an 1851 editorial called "Crime Among Us," *Alta California,* the most moderate of the city's newspapers, thundered: "How many murders have been committed in this city within a year? And who has been hung or punished for the crime? Nobody!" And the paper then went on to suggest that a threat of lynch law was "the only remedy, in case the powers that be do not do something for public relief and protection."

On June 8, 1851, an open letter appeared in the *Alta California* over the signature "Justice." It suggested "a committee of vigilance" whose duty it would be "to hunt out these hardened villains" and give them five days to leave the city. And after that a "war of extermination" would be commenced against them.

Sentiments such as these led to a meeting that afternoon among Sam Brannan; George J. Oakes, a merchant; and James Neall Jr., a lumber dealer. The result: a "Committee of Vigilance for the protection of lives and property of the citizens." The group was pledged to "sustain the laws" and even more significantly, to

193

Fort Gunnybags, stronghold of San Francisco's second vigilance committee, was a converted liquor warehouse ringed with sandbags; also added were the alarm bell and cannon on the roof. The painter of this view embellished it with the vigilante emblem *(above)*, an all-seeing eye.

The shooting that touched off a climactic surge of enforcement by the vigilantes took place on one of the city's busiest corners in May 1855. James Casey, a local politician, gunned down a crusading newspaper editor, James King, who had criticized him.

"aid" in their execution. In emergencies members would be summoned by a series of double strokes on the fire bell in the tower of the City Hall. One hundred and three members were signed up immediately (by invitation) and before the year was out 600 more had volunteered. Incendiary crimes, which had cost the city so much during the past year and a half, were foreseen as the principal target.

Just as the committee was being organized, a different sort of crime occurred that galvanized the vigilantes into their first violent action. A tall, muscular Australian from Sydney named Simpton stole an iron cashbox from the Long Wharf office of a shipping agent. The agent spotted Simpton as he was trying to escape in a rowboat. Simpton was caught by boatmen and turned over to the Committee of Vigilance.

Double taps sounded on the fire bell and 80 of the 103 committee members rushed to committee headquarters where the robber had been taken. Police, feeling decidedly upstaged, pounded at the door, demanding the prisoner. The committee ignored them and proceeded to take testimony and examine evidence. Simpton was swiftly and unanimously judged guilty, the punishment to be hanging.

A large crowd, meanwhile, had gathered outside and Sam Brannan went out to describe in a booming voice the committee's action. The crowd shouted its approval. At 2 a.m. the committee members marched four abreast—with Simpton in their midst—to Portsmouth Square. A group of Simpton's countrymen rushed the marching column in a rescue attempt, but they were thrown back. At 2:10 a.m. Simpton, a noose around his neck, was dragged up to an old adobe house, a relic of Mexican days on Portsmouth Square that miraculously had escaped the city's many fires. Someone tossed the rope over a projecting beam and 20 vigilantes hauled Simpton into the air.

In a little more than five hours a criminal had been caught, tried and executed. It was the sort of speedy and effective disposition of criminal matters everyone had been demanding. When the coroner's jury, in its verdict on Simpton's death, named several of the committee members as having been in the hanging party, the committee issued a public statement bearing 183

As King lay dying, vigilantes besieged the jail where Casey was held. Nearly 2,600 strong, the vigilantes were armed with muskets and a brass six-pounder. San Francisco's sheriff surrendered Casey, together with another prisoner who was accused of murder.

signatures. All signers, said the statement, were "equally responsible for the first act of justice that has been dealt to a criminal in San Francisco since California became a State of our Union."

Shortly, the committee arrested a suspected thief, who turned out to be a notorious rogue named English Jim Stuart. Stuart confessed to some two dozen crimes, including a robbery for which an innocent man, whom the committee had mistaken for Stuart, was presently languishing in jail. Stuart, once he started to sing, told all. He acknowledged other aliases he had used and identified several members of his gang. On July 11 the committee took him to the end of the Market Street wharf and hanged him.

Working on information obtained from Stuart, the committee soon had in custody two other notably vicious Ducks, Sam Whittaker and Robert McKenzie, and strung them up from beam-ends at the committee's headquarters on Battery Street.

After these four executions the committee considered that it had made its point and lapsed into inactivity. Although there had been some criticism both in California and elsewhere of the usurpation of the processes of law and justice, the work of the vigilantes was generally regarded in San Francisco as necessary for peace and order. And San Franciscans did not hesitate to take the same steps again in early 1856.

Two years earlier, the unthinkable had begun to happen—the placer gold on which San Francisco had so confidently built its bumptious growth was becoming scarcer. Flaxhead had been wrong. There was not "plenty more where that came from," at least not plenty more that was easy to reach. And before new, mechanized mining methods were perfected to start the gold flurry again, San Francisco began to sink into its first depression. More than 300 stores closed, jobs became hard to find, people left the city and rents declined.

Matters were made worse by the machinations of a quick-footed character named Henry (Honest Harry) Meiggs. Meiggs was an important property owner in the North Beach section of the city, a patron of music and, after Sam Brannan, one of the richest and most promotion-minded of all Californians. He was also a member of the city council and had added to his fortune by

The two prisoners were standing vigilante trial when word of King's death came. Casey, the politician, took 10 minutes for his last speech. The other prisoner was allowed to marry his mistress. Then the two men were hanged from the roof of Fort Gunnybags.

forging municipal notes that he used as collateral on his real-estate loans. When his gambler's nose suggested that he had bilked his creditors to the limit, Meiggs chartered the brig *America* and, with a fortune in gold, took off for the South Seas.

San Francisco was furious. And the mood of the city darkened further in early 1855, when the collapse of two major and apparently stable banks brought on a brief but serious financial panic.

It was in this climate of depression and discontent that the gambler Charles Cora, provoked or not, made the mistake of shooting General Richardson. Beleaguered San Franciscans immediately seized upon the act as a symbol of all the ills that plagued their city. The mistrial appeared to many San Franciscans as just one more example of the ineffectualness if not downright chicanery of their courts and government. The fact that the city's leading madam had bought the fanciest lawyer in town and then attempted to bribe a witness merely confirmed their suspicions of corruption.

A loud voice in the renewed attack on vice and corruption at this time belonged to the editor of the *Evening Bulletin,* a former banker with the odd name of James King of William (he added the "of William" —his father's name—to distinguish himself from several other James Kings). Among his favorite hates were gambling and prostitution, the very sins the Coras represented. It had been King who, on the day that Charles Cora was remanded to the county jail for retrial, had exhorted the city's gamblers and harlots to "rejoice with exceeding gladness!"

At the same time as the Richardson shooting, King of William was also flogging editorially a powerful politician named James P. Casey. On May 14, 1856, the *Bulletin* pointed out that Casey, an ex-New York ward heeler, was also an alumnus of Sing Sing, and that he had assured his election to the Board of Supervisors by stuffing a ballot box. That very afternoon Casey stormed into the *Bulletin* office and warned that he would go after King if the editor continued to smear his name. King retorted that he would publish what he saw fit, and when he left his office at day's end, Casey was waiting for him. He confronted King near the Pacific Express office on Montgomery Street, told him to defend himself, drew his pistol and shot the popular editor in the left side.

Casey's supporters hurried him to the safety of the county jail to avoid a lynching. As he was being locked into a cell near Cora's, the fire bell sounded the doleful double stroke. "Jim," Cora prophesied, "you've put the noose about the necks of both of us."

As in the days of the first vigilance committee, the bell convened a mass meeting. William T. Coleman, a veteran of the 1851 movement, took over and directed a new committee. He set up a headquarters on Sacramento Street in a building ringed with sandbags *(pages 194-195)* in case of real trouble from the police or some of the less highly motivated members of the political establishment. Within a few days the committee had 2,600 members—armed, organized and drilled in military fashion.

There was some reason to expect trouble. "Word was brought," wrote Coleman later, "that the roughs were organizing in large numbers, arming and threatening with determined energy to defend Casey, Cora and their friends at all hazards, and to lay the city waste if need be." Also, he noted, opposition to the committee included "the mayor and all the militia of the state; they had with them the law, and most of the lawyers and all the law-breakers. We asked nothing but to be understood and judged rightly."

In opposition to the vigilantes, city officials tried to enlist the support of the state militia, as well as the United States Army and Navy. They failed on all counts (many militiamen, it turned out, were also vigilantes). In the heat of the moment Coleman sought out California's Governor J. Neely Johnson and explained the committee's intentions. The latter slapped Coleman on the shoulder and said, "Go to it, old boy," but urged him to act quickly since there was "terrible oppositon and terrible pressure."

The committee did as it was bid, snatching Cora and Casey at cannon point from the county jail. Their trials began the day word reached committee headquarters (dubbed Fort Gunnybags by the public) that King had died. Both men were found guilty; on the day of King's funeral they were conspicuously hanged from the upper windows of the headquarters building.

Coleman later observed that the committee's work, "while outside the law," had been done "under solemn dictates of duty with due and solemn reverence for the law as it should be executed."

With Cora and Casey disposed of, the vigilantes turned their attention to several scores of other lawbreakers; these were gathered in, tried and found guilty. Those whose crimes were on a small scale were merely sentenced to banishment and placed on outward-bound ships at committee expense. Two went the route of Cora and Casey.

Thereupon the members of the San Francisco vigilantes were ready to call it quits. On August 18, they paraded through the streets, then assembled in military formation in front of Fort Gunnybags and turned in their weapons, some of which were adorned with bouquets of flowers.

Three years later Richard Henry Dana Jr., whose *Two Years before the Mast* had by now made him a celebrated author, visited San Francisco again. He recalled how, 24 years before, his ship the *Alert* had quietly entered the Golden Gate, "the vast solitude of the Bay of San Francisco." But this time he arrived aboard a "superb steamship, gay with crowds of passengers, brilliant with lighted saloons and staterooms," bound for "San Francisco, the great centre of world-wide commerce." And he reflected that what had been a solitude was "now the most quiet and well-governed city in the United States."

Dana, who stemmed from staunch New England Puritan stock, considered these to be words of praise. And for the straitlaced, progress-minded Americans of the budding Victorian era, perhaps they were. But not to the real forty-niners. Not to those bold, foolish, tough, optimistic men who had rushed off to the gold fields, stopping on the way in and the way out at the biggest boomtown America would ever see. To them, San Francisco meant noise and adventure, not some stiffnecked notion like law and order. A more fitting eulogy, to their lusty way of thinking, had been provided by a visitor named Hinton Rowan Helper, who wrote, "I have seen purer liquors, better segars, finer tobacco, truer guns and pistols, larger dirks and bowie knives and prettier courtesans than in any other place I have ever visited. California can and does furnish the best bad things that are available in America."

The forty-niners could only agree with Helper—and be mighty glad that they had been there to see it.

In August 1856 the vigilante committee, finally satisfied with the state of law and order in the city, disbanded with a flourish. To the cheers of a grateful populace they paraded through the streets dressed in frock coats, accompanied by 15 artillery pieces, blaring bugles and prancing horses.

The Oakland Museum

"An accurate drawing of the famous hill of gold, which," according to lithographer Nathaniel Currier's caption for this 1849 cartoon, "has been put into a scow by the owner, and attached to a sperm whale towing it around the Horn."

6|Wondrous end of a wild quest

Every tired, hungry Argonaut in the diggings had a vision of his grand homecoming after he had found his own private hill of gold. These improbable visions invited satire, including cartoons such as those shown here and on the following pages.

The hard facts emphasized how unlikely the visions were. Few Argonauts found more than enough gold to keep themselves alive. And in the first seven years of the gold rush, the mother lode yielded a total of no more than $350 million worth of gold—far less than future strikes would turn up in Nevada, Dakota and the Colorado Rockies.

Yet whatever luck the individual gold seekers may have had, their search transformed them, their generation and their country. They turned a distant, alien territory into the vital, rollicking Golden State of California. They helped give impetus to such triumphs of engineering as the transcontinental railroad. They salted the American language with their argot of optimism: *stake a claim, see if it pans out, strike it rich.* And their tales, true or fanciful, provided a rich vein of humor and pathos that would flourish long afterward.

Another lampoon that Currier published before entering into his famous partnership with James Merritt Ives showed the California shoreline aswarm with gold-toting miners vainly begging a ship's master for passage back home at any price.

RETURNING FROM CALIFORNIA
via Cape Horn!

Big winners, big losers and 100,000 also-rans

During the half-dozen furious years following the discovery in 1848 of gold at Sutter's Mill, there seemed never to be a moment when thousands of men were not tearing at the California earth, each of them certain that the next swing of a pick would put him in a mansion on the hill. It seemed that nearly every stream and bank, every gulch and gully from Shasta in the north to Mariposa in the south had felt a prospector's pan. In 1853 alone, an estimated 100,000 Argonauts swarmed over the mountains producing $67 million worth of gold. From Downieville to Hangtown to Sonora to Angels Camp, the lusty mine camps rocked to the clangor of gold-grubbing, of boomtown building, of the forty-niners' crude revels and their raucous and often murderous quarrels. Monotonously their conversation turned on gold and how to find it — or the consequences of having tried. At night they dreamed about gold. And such was the lure and the momentum of this grand adventure, that life in much of California would continue in that pattern for years afterward.

Yet by that very year of 1853, whether or not the Argonauts could sense the change or cared to admit what was happening, the big bonanza was ending. The rich, easy-to-reach placer deposits were all but exhausted. Tailings left by earlier prospectors had been worked over two, three, even four times by hapless latecomers. And impressive though that $67 million boodle of 1853 had seemed, in cold point of fact it amounted to $14 million less than the gold fields had yielded during the peak year of 1852. Nor in future years would the take go anywhere but down.

There was still gold in the hills, but no longer could the little man with his wash pan and his pack mule realistically expect to make his fortune digging it. From now on, sophisticated engineering skills and heavy machinery *(pages 108-113)* would be required to get out the ore. And for that little man the time had come to stand up and look around, to see what he had done, to take stock of his own situation — and if he was smart, to cash in his chips and move on.

One thing he had done, quite by accident but with dizzying speed, was to expand the physical scope of the United States so that it now embraced the entire width of the North American continent. During those half-dozen years the momentum of the gold rush had drawn to California more than a quarter of a million people from every part of the world, in contrast with the mere 14,000 that had settled there before the discovery of gold. No doubt, with or without the discovery of gold along the Pacific, the dynamic young nation would have grown to span the continent and achieve the two-ocean destiny that Americans called manifest. But under the spell of gold the enormous change had taken place with almost magical swiftness, the population hurdling fully half the country so that the intervening high plains and mountains remained nearly empty for years after California had become settled and civilized.

Only two years after Marshall's portentous find, California was admitted as the 31st state in the Union — 62 full years before Arizona came in, 17 years before

New York cartoonist Robert Elton offered a dismaying — though not too inaccurate — view of the return to home and reality of the typical forty-niner who had been certain he would strike it rich in California.

207

Mr. John Smith takes final leave of Mrs. John Smith.

John Smith, being short of Cash, turns porter to the Elephant House.

John Smith having made a pile leaves for Sacramento on a "bust."

John Smith bets his pile on the Jack.

John Smith resolves to reform.

Fortune favors John Smith & he invests his dust in a "Ranch."

A saga of a gold seeker adorned one side of this time-worn stationery sheet for sale to miners in California. Encouragingly, the pictures show the hero recovering from temptation and returning to his faithful wife.

Nebraska, and even nine years before Oregon, the United States' original outpost on the Pacific. Nor did the Golden State, as it proudly proclaimed itself, come in with the usual new-boy posture, hat in hand. Rather it entered the Union as a rich, proud partner whose chief port, San Francisco, had grown overnight from a quiet anchorage for whalers and freighting schooners into a major center of finance and commerce. The names of its most illustrious citizens—such men as Huntington, Hopkins, Brannan, Stanford, Sullivan, Bidwell—would soon snap heads to attention on Wall Street, and California's new-found wealth would excite the interest of the world's other financial centers.

The most envied of these instant capitalists were the men who had made their pile—or at least their first pile—with a pick and shovel right in the diggings. John and Daniel Murphy, for example, who had come overland in the 1840s, were among those who got there first and came away with the most. They arrived in Calaveras County early in 1848, and by the end of that year they had made $1.5 million. John went from mining into politics; Daniel parlayed his dust into holdings of some three million acres of cattle land in California, Nevada and Arizona.

In just three months, onetime ox-team driver John Sullivan took $26,000 out of the gully known as Sullivan's Creek on the Stanislaus, headed for San Francisco and there used his stake as the foundation for building a powerful banking house. William Downie of Downieville panned and sifted his way through the Sierra gravel until, through luck and diligence, he hit gold—which he proceeded to spend just as fast as he found it. An acquaintance said: "We have seen the Major go through two or three pounds of dust on one Sunday, and after emptying the company sack, the party would sober up, disperse and dig more." But, said this same friend, "in 1854 the Major dissolved partnership with Messrs. Barleycorn & Co. and became a rigid and influential Temperance man." After this he dug gold in British Columbia and Panama and became, finally, a prosperous and respected gravel dealer.

John Bidwell, who had guided a party of immigrants across the plains to California in 1841 and later became a trusted friend and lieutenant of John Sutter, began prospecting in early 1848. On July 4 he made one of the richest strikes of the entire gold rush. His version of the discovery was a notably laconic declaration in an age of exuberant, extravagant language: "Dickey, Northgraves and I went to what is now Bidwell's Bar and there found gold and went to mining."

Bidwell stayed at his mining for a very short time, and came away with a great fortune—which he promptly used to buy and cultivate a sprawling fiefdom of farming lands. Over the ensuing decades he became one of the richest and most respected Californians, a Congressman and a candidate for President on a Prohibition ticket. Long after the real excitement over gold had dwindled away, his plantation in the upper Sacramento valley remained a showcase of agrarian prosperity: 20,000 acres of lush, level fields delineated by 60 miles of board fencing, a permanent work crew of 100 men, 2,500 acres in wheat, 700 of barley, nearly the same in oats, 1,500 head of cattle, 3,000 sheep, 2,000 hogs, 300 horses, 300 acres in vineyards (although as an ardent supporter of Prohibition he used the grapes for raisins, not wine), hedges of pomegranates protecting 100 acres planted in figs, English walnuts, cherries, peaches, apricots, almonds and apples.

And so the excitement over gold was slow to dwindle; because always there glimmered that one, slim, seductive chance to make some kind of strike tomorrow, as others had yesterday—like the man named Dye from Monterey, who in two months took out more than $76,000, just for himself. Or the lucky little Davenport boy, hardly more than 12 years old, who scraped up $2,700 in two days.

Even when the visions conjured up by such heady tales gave way to the reality of muscle-tearing work and frustration, the most passionate of the forty-niners tried to convince themselves—and others—that their luck, too, would come. James H. Carson, who set out into the gold fields with the Murphys and soon struck it rich on his own at a spot that came to be called Carson Hill, gave this little pep talk in the early 1850s to some downhearted forty-niners:

"Don't any of you despair; there are yet just as rich diggings as have ever been discovered, and as large 'chunks' beneath the earth as have ever been taken therefrom. It is true you have to work harder now to get it than formerly, yet it is to be had; thousands of square miles are yet lying untouched by the pick, beneath which millions of dollars of hidden treasure lie concealed. Thousands will be making fortunes in the mines of California a hundred years hence."

As if to bear out Carson's confidence, the largest single nugget ever found in the United States—195 pounds—was dug out of Carson Hill three years later.

But Carson was wrong, of course. There had never been more than a relative handful of lucky ones. The gold rush was a lavish gamble that inevitably produced many, many losers who, if they survived the quarrels and the mining accidents, the scurvy and the cholera, gathered in the bars of Sacramento and San Francisco to sing the forty-niners' lament:

*I lives way down in Maine, where I heard about the diggin's,
So I shipped aboard a darned old barque
    commanded by Joe Higgins,
I sold my little farm, and from wife and children parted,
And off to California sailed, and left 'em broken-hearted.
Oh, I'm a used-up man, a perfect used-up man,
And if ever I get home again, I'll stay there if I can.*

One of the most used-up men was James Marshall, the man who started the whole thing. The first piece of gold he picked up in John Sutter's millrace on the morning of January 24, 1848, was worth no more than 50 cents—but it triggered the golden flood that, over the next quarter century, reached about $978 million.

However, none of that lode stuck to Marshall's own hands—not even the first piece. Looking back, Marshall thought that perhaps he had turned the historic nugget over to Mrs. Wimmer, the camp cook, for safekeeping, and that Mrs. Wimmer had spent it for camp supplies. Mrs. Wimmer had a different story. She said Marshall had told her: "Jenny, I will give you this piece of gold. I always intended to have a ring made from it for my mother, but I will give it to you." And Mrs. Wimmer added: "I took it and have had it in my possession from that day to this. Except for the color, it looks like a piece of spruce gum, just out of the mouth of a schoolgirl—full of indentations."

However he may have disposed of that first nugget, it was, Marshall later grumbled, "a discovery that hasn't as yet been of much benefit to me." Nor would it ever be. Marshall's life in the wake of the gold strike was one disappointment after another. The sawmill in which he and John Sutter had been partners—and in whose millrace the gold had turned up — went broke and closed down. In an effort to recoup his losses, he claimed the land around the discovery site for mining purposes. His claim was a solid one, based not only on the generally accepted doctrine of squatters' rights, but also on a perfectly honorable leasing agreement that he and Sutter had originally drawn up with the local Coloma Indians, whose good will they wisely courted.

But the area was aswarm with prospectors. They paid no attention to Marshall's title and instead posted claims of their own. Some of the intruders even threatened to dismantle the sawmill in the hope that there might be gold underneath it. Marshall, a gentle man by nature, was neither hardhanded enough to drive off the claim-jumpers by force, nor clever and influential enough to maintain a long-term legal hold on his property.

Marshall also suffered as a result of the friction that soon broke out between the Indians and the newly arrived squatter-miners. Both Marshall and Sutter had managed to get along well with the Indians, hiring them for work, paying them wages in goods or credit. (The Indians, in turn, let Marshall and Sutter develop the land, refrained from killing the stock that Sutter imported and generally treated the two men as acceptable neighbors.) But the gold seekers observed no such inhibitions. Many were confirmed Indian-haters, particularly the Oregonians, some of them fresh from a bloody and frustrating war with the Cayuse tribe to the north.

In the spring of 1849, seven men from Oregon were camped in a canyon on the middle fork of the American River. One day, some supplies were stolen from the camp and the whites blamed the Indians. A mood of hostility settled over the valley. Shortly thereafter two of the group left to prospect for better diggings while the other five remained on the site—which was to become known as Murderers Bar. When the two returned a few days later, they found their friends missing, the remaining supplies stolen and bloodstains on the ground.

The survivors rode for help into the town of Coloma that had sprung up near Marshall's property. A posse was organized and, although the whites were unable to find the bodies of the missing men, they did come upon an encampment of Indians. The posse killed and scalped four of them, then moved on and found a larger encampment. They killed a score or more Indians, took 40 prisoners and marched them back to Coloma. Seven were selected to be put on trial, whereupon they made a break for freedom. All seven were killed.

The more stable residents of Coloma, Marshall among them, protested the slaughter, thereby incurring considerable enmity. One sympathetic townsman wrote that Marshall was "reasonable" and would have cooperated in bringing the guilty Indians to justice. But: "because he advanced reasons why an indiscriminate massacre of all should not be made, he has become the object of hatred of these men, who not only charge him with taking the part of all the Indians, but say that he has instigated them to murder the whites wherever they could. He considers his life in danger here."

Marshall was indeed in danger, both from the gold-mad whites and now, too, from the Indians, who felt that he had betrayed them. Marshall later commented: "Knowing the false manner that the Indians had been made to believe that I brought the whites into the mountains and had had their chief man murdered, I left until the mob dispersed and the Indians could be made to know the truth." He never had a chance.

While Marshall was gone the mob did not disperse, but instead staked more and more claims on land that Marshall considered his. Several weeks later he returned and, in a typically ineffective gesture, posted notices on trees warning off trespassers. Of course it did no good. "My finding gold," he realized, "was to deprive me of my rights of a settler and an American citizen."

All this happened to Marshall in the span of one short year. And at the end of it, despairing of holding onto his property, Marshall began prospecting for himself. Many of his fellow forty-niners believed Marshall had psychic powers to locate gold and so they followed him wherever he went. Sometimes it was done furtively; but there were occasions when he was angrily confronted by his uninvited followers and ordered to lead them to gold. On at least one such occasion he was threatened with hanging for protesting that he was unable to help them.

Nor, in the quest for gold, was he able to help himself. He never completely abandoned his pan and shovel but, after years of futile prospecting, settled as a blacksmith at Kelsey, a small settlement between Coloma and Placerville. And he was drinking heavily.

From there, Marshall's long and sorrowful slide to oblivion accelerated. For a time he toured as a ragtag

212

The most important by-product of the gold rush was the creation of the State of California and its bustling river-port capital of Sacramento, shown here in an 1849 lithograph. With typical, gold-oriented bravado the motto on the new state's seal *(left)* read *eureka* — Greek for "I have found it!"

lecturer, spieling the story of how he had first found the gold, and selling autographed cards. Meanwhile, any hopes that Marshall may have had about recovering his lost properties were squashed by the powerful, mechanized mining companies that had moved into the diggings in the late 1850s and 1860s, pushing through the law courts their own claims to mining properties —Marshall's included.

By 1872, Marshall, penniless, petitioned the California legislature for a $200-a-month pension "in recognition of his considerable service to the state." The lawmakers consented. But at their very next session they cut the sum in half; and in 1878 the pension was discontinued altogether after Marshall showed up drunk at the assembly chamber in Sacramento, where he had gone to lobby for improvement of his stipend.

His last years were spent in abject poverty. When he died in 1885, he was buried on a hill overlooking the place where, 37 years earlier, he had stooped to change the history of the United States. A month after his funeral a California fraternal group called the Native Sons of the Golden West passed a resolution pledging the "erection of a suitable monument." Their choice was a 10-foot statue of Marshall holding a nugget in one hand and pointing with the other to the site where the first gold was found in California. The memorial cost the organization $25,000, and the caretaker they hired to look after it and 14 acres of surrounding parkland was paid $75 a month.

The decline and fall of John Augustus Sutter was more spectacular because he was, by far, a more high-blown and expansive man than Marshall, the simple millwright. When the gold rush started, Sutter was a man of soaring ambition whose dream was to establish nothing less than a freeman's agricultural kingdom in the new world of California. For a time after he first arrived there, he appeared to be on his way to doing just that. He had secured grants from the Mexican government totaling some 230 square miles: a tract straddling the Central Valley of California embracing lush agricultural lands, navigable portions of the Sacramento, Feather and American rivers, and the principal approaches to what were soon to become the gold fields. These holdings, together with the livestock and crops he began to develop on them, quickly made him one of the most important men in all of the American West.

After the discovery of the first nuggets, Sutter's name became synonymous around the world with California gold. Sutter himself recognized that, with all this, he should have become one of the world's richest men, certainly the richest on the Pacific Coast. Had he been less genial and more calculating, less openhanded and more ruthless, less sybaritic and more self-disciplined, he might have been both.

As it was, Sutter showed himself to be appallingly careless about his debts and his business dealings generally. He had pronounced weaknesses for Indian girls and for the potent *aguardiente* he distilled within the walls of his original compound at Sutter's Fort. As the gold rush swept over him, washing away first his dreams and then his fortune, he spent more and more of his waking hours befuddled by alcohol.

In the spring of 1848, as the rush began, Sutter had watched helplessly as his workers began disappearing to the gold fields. That fall his wheat was rotting in the fields, his stock straying through broken fences or being stolen and killed by hungry miners. Instead of fighting back by recruiting new help at top dollar, Sutter decided to rush off and try digging gold himself. With those of his retainers who had remained with him, he set off on two successive prospecting expeditions:

"I got a number of wagons ready, loaded them with provisions and goods of all kinds, employed a clerk and left with about one hundred Indians and about fifty Kanakas. The first camp was about 10 miles above Mormon Island on the south fork of the American river. In a few weeks we became crowded, and it would no more pay, as my people made too many acquaintances. I broke up the camp and started on the march further south, and located my next camp on Sutter creek, and thought I should be there alone. The work was going on well for a while, until three or four traveling grog shops surrounded me. Then, of course, the gold was taken to these places, for drinking, gambling, etc., and the following day they were sick and unable to work, and became deeper and more indebted to me. I found that it was high time to quit this kind of business and lose no more time and money. I therefore broke up the camp and returned to the fort. This whole expedition proved to be a heavy loss to me."

Sutter had other troubles, too. When he had first set out to build his private empire, he had been forced to borrow capital. Now his creditors were closing in. And to prevent them from attaching his properties, Sutter turned over his biggest holdings to his son, John Jr. The younger Sutter managed to raise money to pay off the worst of his father's debts by selling building lots in a booming new townsite called Sacramento. But the father, in his typical quixotic way, was not happy about that solution. Faced with the reality of the gold boom, he was nonetheless unable to quit his dream of a bucolic kingdom. Old John began to see Sacramento as the symbol of his frustrations. He raged at his son, exacerbating their differences to the level of a family feud. And he took on the notion that he was an entirely innocent victim in a cosmic tragedy.

John Jr. saw it otherwise. Said he of his father, "All this time hardly a day passed in which he himself, and his clerks, partners, Indians, etc. were not on a general frolic, intoxicated, I am sorry to say, more than once." With the elder man in this condition, Fort Sutter—once the principal way station and supply depot between San Francisco and the Sierra—quickly fell into disuse. And before the year 1849 was out, Sutter sold the installation for $40,000 and retreated to the last of his holdings, a 600-acre grain-and-cattle complex called Hock Farm, on the Feather River.

John Jr. turned back to his father the remaining lands on which he had held temporary custody. But the elder Sutter continued to lose money through poor judgment, worse luck and an incapacity for enforcing his rights on property and livestock. (One Sacramento meat company made $60,000 during the winter of 1849-1850 by dealing in nothing but stolen Sutter cattle.) "The country swarmed with lawless men," Sutter remembered. "Talking with them did no good. I was alone and there was no law."

As an antidote to these indignities, Sutter's pride had been soothed somewhat, and his attention further diverted from business, when he was chosen as a delegate to the state constitutional convention that met in Monterey during September of 1849. There he reveled in the debates, hoisted a glass at every toast to the future of the budding new state, and marveled at the militia parades, chirping happily whenever the commoners fired a salute—a ceremony that he adored. As the convention ended, his vanity allowed him to be persuaded by friends to run for the governorship in the first state election. He attracted a total of only 2,201 votes.

On top of this defeat, Sutter found himself in new trouble with squatters in and around his remaining Sacramento properties. Sutter's title rested upon two land grants from the Mexican government, one of which was dated 1841, the other 1845. The squatters, who felt that any and all former Mexican land was up for grabs by right of the U.S. victory in the Mexican War, paid no attention and took whatever they could. Sutter's claim to the property was confirmed by a U.S. Land Commission in 1855 and reconfirmed by a district court. The squatters then appealed to the U.S. Supreme Court, which held in 1858 that the original grant was valid, but that the second was not because it had been granted by Mexican military fiat.

The loss of the second grant was bad enough. However, Sutter was also under obligation to indemnify those who had earlier bought land that had been part of the grant. It was this last financial blow that brought about Sutter's ruin. The last of his servants, retainers, vaqueros and field hands drifted away. The onetime liege lord was a poor man. In 1864, friends in the legislature managed to push through a bill granting him $15,000 in monthly payments of $250—an insignificant sum for a man of Sutter's tastes. And it did not really help. The next winter, floods along the Feather River repeatedly inundated Hock Farm; and then one night the great house itself burned to the ground in a blaze rumored to have been set by an arsonist.

At that, John Sutter gave up. With his wife, he left California for Washington, D.C., to push a claim against the federal government. He asked for $125,000—part of it for what he described as reimbursement of aid given in years past to California-bound emigrants; and the rest for the losses he had suffered in consequence of the discovery of gold which had, as he argued, vastly enriched the United States.

Sutter pleaded his case personally with important congressmen. And although he had not intended to remain long in the East, year followed year until finally, in 1880, it appeared that he was near success. But on June 16 the 77-year-old Sutter learned that Congress had once more adjourned without acting on his relief bill. He took to his hotel bed. When a friendly senator came by to tell him that the bill would certainly be passed in Congress' next session, Sutter was dead. ◉

Master miners of high-grade humor and pathos

Before Sam Clemens came to the Far West he had never been much of a hand at writing—too busy as a journeyman printer, a riverboat pilot and a summer soldier in the Confederate Army. In 1861 he arrived in Carson City, Nevada, with his brother, the secretary of the new Nevada Territory (a land that looked to Sam like "a singed cat, owing to the scarcity of shrubbery"), tried prospecting and lost his only strike to claim-jumpers.

Broke and discouraged, he began covering murders and fires for the *Nevada Territorial Enterprise* as "Mark Twain" (a riverboat leadsman's term meaning two fathoms of water). He was acting editor when he got into a bloodless farce of a duel with a journalistic rival. The man backed out when a friend of Twain's shot the head off a passing bird and gave Mark, who was a terrible shot, the credit. But a new antidueling law forced Twain to light out for San Francisco.

By 1864 he was a reporter on the *Call*, working among budding literati like Ambrose Bierce, Henry George, and San Francisco's best-known writer, Bret Harte. The dandified Harte had roamed California in patent leather shoes as teacher, drugstore clerk, stagecoach guard, compositor and reporter—getting run out of one town for reporting a massacre of peaceful Indians by local whites. Now he held a job in the San Francisco Mint and on the side was star writer and sometime editor of a literary weekly.

Harte hired Twain as a contributor and helped him polish a robust style well suited to San Francisco. When a local lady blew her nose in a Twain masterpiece of society reporting, "its exquisitely modulated tone excited the admiration of all who had the happiness to hear it." Or Twain could picture a victim of police brutality "sleeping with that calm serenity peculiar to men whose heads have been caved in with a club."

Twain soon hit literary pay dirt with a widely reprinted flight of fancy about a frog-jumping match in Calaveras County. Three years later Harte struck it richer still with a tragic tale of Roaring Camp miners who adopted a prostitute's orphaned baby.

Subsequent fame swept both men out of California forever. Yet the gold rush remained the mother lode of Harte's scores of stories, with their miners, bandits and gamblers. Twain, too, relived his days on the frontier in *Roughing It,* before pouring his genius into such masterpieces as *Tom Sawyer* and *Huckleberry Finn.* And in later years Twain would sometimes reach back to his gold rush days for nuggets of humor. As late as 1880, he read a newspaper story about recovering gold from spring water in California. The old master topped it handily with a tale about pumping his uncle full of such water and extracting the gold through his pores. "I have," Twain roundly asserted, "taken more than eleven thousand dollars out of that old man in a day and a half."

Mark Twain in the 1880s

Bret Harte in the 1870s

In this drawing illustrating the climax of Mark Twain's first literary hit, *The Jumping Frog of Calaveras County,* the favorite in a jumping contest has been left at the post, filled to the brim with birdshot by a wily opponent and thus unable to respond to the prodding of his patron.

The raw realism of Bret Harte's short story, *The Luck of Roaring Camp,* upset some critics but won Harte national fame. In the scene below, miners adopt a dying prostitute's newborn son and line up to contribute money to the baby's support. Says one, deeply moved: "He rassled with my finger, the d---d little cuss!"

217

With Sutter's death, the most renowned of all the gold-rush figures passed from the scene. But in a way, though his fall was tragic and his ending pathetic and lonely, John Sutter was really no more than the most visible symbol of the fate suffered by so many of the forty-niners. As far back as 1851, George McKinstry Jr., who had worked for Sutter at the outset and later became an assayer wrote an extraordinary letter to an old friend, Edward Kern of Philadelphia. Kern had been in California with the explorer John Charles Frémont, and for a short time had been second in command at Sutter's Fort. McKinstry gave him an accounting of the gold fields and the forty-niners they had known. It was a lugubrious recital of disaster, sudden death and disappearance:

"Since you left this country a most astonishing change has taken place. The new Yankees would say for the better, but not we old fellows. The Embarcadero is now the large city of Sacramento. The old fort is rapidly going to decay; the last time I was there I rode through, and there was not a living thing to be seen within the walls. Ah, what a fall is there, my fellow! The old Sacramento crowd are much scattered by death and disaster since you left. William Daylor by cholera; Jared Sheldon, shot in a row with miners; Perry McCoan by a fall from his horse; Sebastian Keyser drowned; Little Bill Johnson, who knows?; Captain 'Luce' missing in the mountains; Olimpio, Sutter's Indian messenger, shot by miners; old Thomas Hardy, *rum;* John Sinclair, cholera; William E. Shannon, cholera; old William Knight, *rum* as expected; Charley Heath, *rum* and missing; Bob Ridley, fever, I think.

"Our good friend Captain John Sutter seems to be smashed to flinders; Daylor and Sheldon estates said to be insolvent; our old and particular crony John L. Schwartz God knows how he stands the present pressure; he goes it though, more than ever, on the rum. Old James McDowell was shot down by miners some two years since—his widow is the owner of Washington, the town opposite Sacramento City; many fine buildings there but at present it is no go. Old Kitnor, made a fortune and went bust; William A. Liedesdorff, dead; old Eliab Grimes, dead; Jack Fuller, ditto—also Allen Montgomery. Montgomery's widow married the man who called himself Talbot H. Green. His real name was found to be Paul Geddes some time back, a bank robber from the United States. He departed to clear up his character, which was the last seen of him. Pierson B. Reading is on his farm raising wheat and pumpkins in abundance. He was the Whig Candidate for Governor but could not make it. It was said his friendship with Captain Sutter cost him the Squatter votes. Sam Norris made two or three hundred thousand, but is reputedly hard up and thought to be busted. Sam Brannan ditto. In fact I could fill a foolscap sheet with busted Old Guard, including your humble servant."

Throughout the gold region and the approaches to it, there was even terser testimony to the end of the golden quest. It appeared on makeshift grave markers, made of bits of painted or carved board and, sometimes, of scraps of paper attached to sticks: M. De Morst of Columbus, Ohio, aged 50, died September 16, 1849, "of Camp Fever." John Chancellor of Lexington, Missouri, died September 22, 1849, of typhoid fever. John A. Dawson, of St. Louis died October 1, 1849, "from eating a poisonous root at the spring." Mr. Eastman, first name and provenance apparently unknown, died October 4, 1849, "killed by an Indian arrow"—and the arrow was stuck in the grave. W. Brown of the Rough and Ready Company of Platte County, Missouri, aged 35, died September 19, 1849, "with *skervy.*" Samuel McFarlin of Wright County, Missouri, died September 27, 1849, "of fever. *May he rest peaceably in this savage, unknown country.*"

Another cause of death, though it was discreetly omitted from most grave markers, was drink. Among its victims was Charles W. Churchill of Lawrence County, Ohio. He had arrived in California in August 1849, had mined at Mormon Island, at Cuteye Foster's, at the forks of the Yuba, at Nevada City, Columbia and Mariposa, never getting more than a few dollars ahead. Finally he gave up mining and clerked in a store on Mariposa Creek for $75 a month and, apparently, all the whiskey he could drink. His brother Mendall wrote the man who had sent word of his brother's death: "The news fell like a thunderbolt on me, particularly that part announcing his habits of dissipation. I thought my Brother was proof against that under any circumstances. It is a great consolation to me, my Dear Sir, that he had every attention and comfort in his last hours, and to know that he was attended by one he esteemed as a friend—but it seems very hard to die 6,000

PROSPECTORS WHO PANNED NO GOLD

Most gold-rush fortunes did not blossom from a lucky strike, but were built on brains and hard work. John Studebaker, for example, took work almost as an article of faith—hardly a typical Argonaut. He and his brothers (John is seated at far right) had a modest wagon works in Indiana, with $68 in funds. In 1852, John migrated to Placerville, California, where he took a job making wheelbarrows for miners. By keeping his hand to the forge, abjuring the sins of the gold fields, he saved $8,000 in five years. Then, in 1858, Studebaker returned to Indiana, added his stake to the family works, and helped it grow in little over a decade *(below)* into one of America's largest and most famous carriage makers.

miles from home." Apparently Mendall Churchill's knowledge of geography was as limited as his awareness of the wicked ways of the world.

John S. Hittell, who had been a forty-niner himself and later became a California historian, wrote in 1869 that none of the great battles of the Civil War "broke so many heartstrings and caused such widespread pain as did the California gold migration."

Perhaps the ultimate irony of the gold rush lay not in its tragedies but in the fact that many of its greatest winners — and most spectacular losers — acted out the dramas of their lives without having successfully panned a single nugget or flake of gold. These were the men who saw that the real California bonanza would be found in catering to the needs of the gold seekers. One such opportunist was the icy-handed entrepreneur Collis Huntington. A 27-year-old New Yorker, he had used an enforced three months' stay in Panama to make $1,000 a month trading with future prospectors. He arrived in California in the spring of 1850 with a stock of miners' supplies, barreled whiskey — and a shovel. Like most everyone, he tried his hand at finding gold, but it took him only a day's digging and panning gravel to decide that prospecting was a loser's game. Buying and selling were his line and for three years he made good money as an itinerant merchant. Then, with a partner, Mark Hopkins, he opened a hardware store specializing in miners' supplies on K Street in Sacramento.

At one time or another Huntington and Hopkins cornered the markets in shovels and blasting powder, for which the forty-niners paid dearly. The two partners joined hands with another frustrated Argonaut-turned-shopkeeper, Charles Crocker. Then together with Leland Stanford, who had started with a grocery store in the mining camp of Michigan Bluff, they became the financing partners of a railroad that would surge halfway across the West to join the other half of the transcontinental railroad, the Union Pacific, at Promontory Summit, Utah. Stanford had become Governor of California. And he and his partners, by then renowned as the Big Four, established themselves as the first of the great Western railroad barons, whose fantastic mansions and extravagant tastes became representative of California's new, gold-supported prosperity.

Some of the winners may have been less spectacular, but they were hardly less effective in accumulating rich-

PANTSMAKER TO THE ARGONAUTS

The silk-hatted Bavarian at right was a resolute pragmatist who knew a better thing than gold when he saw it. He sailed from New York in 1850 with a stock of cloth, sold most of it to passengers and arrived in San Francisco with only a single bolt of canvas tenting. On the quay he met a miner, sold him the canvas for a pair of heavy trousers—and Levi Strauss was in the pants business to stay. Then he joined in patenting *(left)* the use of little copper rivets to reinforce seams. Strauss's riveted jeans promptly became the *sine qua non* of Western workaday fashion. And by the end of the 19th Century, Strauss's plant *(below)* in San Francisco employed 500 workers, while the owner grossed around a million dollars a year and became famous selling the pants everyone knew as Levi's.

es by serving the miners' needs. A humble but canny dry-goods dealer named Levi Strauss *(pages 220-221)* designed a pair of heavy canvas pants for a miner he met as soon as he stepped off the boat at San Francisco. Within a year Strauss was the biggest pantsmaker in California—and eventually one of the biggest in all the world. In the mining camps of El Dorado County, a young country butcher named Philip Armour was carving up his first hogs and cattle—in preparation for a spectacularly successful career of carving for himself a large chunk of the entire U.S. market for meat. And in Placerville, John M. Studebaker salted away sufficient capital making wheelbarrows to allow him to go back to Indiana and build up the famous and long-lasting Studebaker wagon works.

Yet even a few of these tough-minded entrepreneurs became so diverted by the pleasures of San Francisco high life—and by the temptation to overreach for empire —that they, like the high-rolling prospectors, came crashing to the ground. For example, during Sam Brannan's first years in California, everything seemed to turn his way. With profits from a mining-equipment store, he bought key properties in the burgeoning port of San Francisco. Selling off the first acquisitions at outrageous profits, he proceeded to gobble up more and more San Francisco acreage until, at one point in 1856, he was said to own one fifth of the entire city and just as big a piece of Sacramento.

An unabashed extrovert, Brannan reveled in his sudden wealth and the prominence it brought. In fact he managed to acquire a vision of Sam Brannan as the leading citizen of all California and basked under the informal title "the first forty-niner"—though he had actually arrived in 1846, well before the gold rush, and in all his years in California had carefully refrained from ever putting his hand to pick or shovel.

Proudly, he organized and served as president of the Society of California Pioneers, and became principal patron of the San Francisco Music Fund. Brannan was also widely noted for his charities, among which was a gift to the Odd Fellows of valuable land for a cemetery. In fact there seemed no act of worthy citizenship that Sam would refuse—and never mind the trouble or expense. In addition to his leadership of the first Committee of Vigilance in San Francisco, Brannan bought, for a fire company he himself founded, the city's most elaborate and beautiful fire engine, built by a Boston firm to his specifications. When this awesome machine finally arrived by clipper ship, one breathless newspaper described it as "the most complete and beautiful pieces of mechanism we have ever seen." And indeed it must have been, judging from the subsequent description:

"Every portion of the steel and iron-work is richly plated with silver. Imposing as the tout ensemble is, yet in detail all is plain and in perfect taste. There are but three colors of paint upon the woodwork: green, gold and the richest shade of carmine. The woodwork of the box is of the finest mahogany. In the rear, on each side of the coupling, is a griffin's head, finely carved and gilded. On the left side of the box is a landscape painting with horses, trees and a lake with a boating party; above it on the same side of the air chamber is an exquisite painting of four female figures in the foreground dancing to the music of Old Father Time. Beyond the dancers is a monument with carved busts upon it wreathed with ivy, and above on a cloud in his golden chariot sits Phoebus. On the right of the box is a beautifully correct view of Niagara Falls on the Canada side; above on the same side is a painting representing three females at bath, one of them dallying with a swan upon the stream. There are four richly painted fire buckets hanging upon the scroll work. The paintings upon them represent the four seasons, beautiful in conception and execution."

The wonderful machine cost Brannan $10,000. To some it seemed to be far too cumbersome and ornate ever to use in dousing a fire. But Sam Brannan had given San Francisco a fine and useful gift, and a rousing party and parade celebrated the engine's initial passage through the city streets.

In other moments the indefatigable Brannan pursued the actress Lola Montez, issued his own paper currency from a bank he founded, served on the city council and in the state senate, politicked in Washington and made several grand tours of Europe. Passionately pro-Union when the Civil War broke out, he got into a widely publicized barroom fight with a ship captain who had been in the slave trade. Later he staged a costly banquet in celebration of the fall of Charleston (which, as it turned out, had not yet fallen). As a climax to the party Brannan had persuaded a local artillery officer to fire a salvo from his garrison battery. The blast shat-

A BUTCHER WHO CARVED A FORTUNE

Beginning with a strong back — and the precept that gold is glitter but beef is basic — Philip D. Armour built one of the fattest American fortunes. At the age of 20 Armour left home, a farm near Stockbridge, New York, and started walking to California. He made it six months later. But despite the seductive tales about instant wealth for lucky prospectors, Armour decided not to dig for gold. He became, instead, a digger of ditches.

At that profession he made $8,000 in five years, enough to open a butcher shop in Placerville (where his friend John Studebaker was accumulating an identical bundle). Armour's meat market prospered. When the gold boom subsided, Armour moved to Milwaukee and continued to prosper until his empire of packing and slaughtering houses *(below)* became the foremost meat suppliers in the entire nation.

One of the millions of Americans who dreamed of taking off for the great gamble in California was this Minnesota schoolteacher, who festooned himself with full miner's kit for the hometown photographer —but never made it out of Minnesota.

tered $2,500 worth of window glass; but as always, Sam Brannan cheerfully paid for everything.

As another harsh expression of his volatile sentiments, he spent $1.5 million on Mexican bonds to support Benito Juárez in the struggle against France's colonial oppressions—and he personally equipped and supported a company of American volunteers to fight with Juárez. Meanwhile at home Brannan bought land in the Napa Valley—eventually about 3,000 acres—on which he began building a resort that he named Calistoga (California-Saratoga). Blooded horses and merino sheep grazed the hills. Vines and orchards flourished and a distillery turned out 90,000 gallons a year of brandy made from Brannan grapes. One of the many bubbling hot springs on the estate even produced a natural potion which Brannan insisted tasted like soup (and he always had salt, pepper and soda crackers near the spring so that passersby could enjoy it).

For all his high-flying exuberance, however, Sam Brannan began to stagger under a pair of burdens, either one of which by itself might have brought him to earth. One was an affinity for whiskey; like the ill-fated John Sutter, Sam rarely was able to rouse himself out of bed before noon, and he was seldom sober after that.

Brannan's other curse was his wife, who scolded him incessantly for his profligate ways—and then proceeded to spend baskets of his money on liveried coachmen and a long sojourn in Europe, which she undertook "for the good of the children." After 13 years abroad, the difficult Mrs. Brannan returned to the Brannan home in San Francisco to discover Sam cozily wrapped up with another lady. In 1870, Mrs. Brannan declared her intention to seek a divorce, and Brannan stormed out of the house, never to return.

The property settlements (about $500,000) that the courts awarded to her amounted to roughly half the cash value of Sam's estate—and cash was precisely what she demanded. Faced with a scramble for money, Brannan—again reminiscent of Sutter—found himself with his credit badly extended; and he careened into bankruptcy. The Calistoga property had to be sold, and soon other properties as well. By 1876, Sam Brannan was broke, or nearly so.

Still game to gamble for another fortune, he dug out his old Mexican bonds, went to Mexico and secured in exchange for them a grant of two million acres of land in the northwestern part of the country. But the local Yaqui Indians objected fiercely to this use of their ancestral land, which in their opinion, the Mexican government had no right to turn over to Brannan. Nor was Mexico, at this point, in a mood to provide Brannan with military protection for his holdings.

Helpless, and now semiparalyzed from drink, Brannan again lost everything. He drifted back to California, where for a time he tried selling real estate in the southern part of the state. In the mid-1880s, an unexpected $49,000 came to him from the Mexican government in a belated and diminished settlement of his $1.5 million in bonds. With this windfall Brannan managed to pay off his remaining debts before he died, sober, penniless and almost forgotten, in 1889.

In many ways Sam Brannan's story, with its dizzy rise and tragic fall, summed up the gaudier aspects of the era of the forty-niners. But there was yet another element in the gold rush saga—less eye-catching but far more valuable than all the glittering millions grabbed up

English financier Joshua A. Norton lost a fortune trying to corner the San Francisco grain market. Dazed by the disaster, he bought a fancy uniform, declared himself Emperor of North America, and reigned over local barrooms for the next 26 years.

Long after the bonanza had passed, gold fever lingered in Sierra towns like Grass Valley *(below)*. When its main street was paved, citizens turned out to pick through the gravel, hoping to find gold flakes.

or fumbled away by the high rollers. It became apparent in the ultimate fortunes of nearly 400,000 hopeful emigrants who had crowded into California in the decade after the find at Sutter's Mill. The vast majority of these men (even after 10 years, California still had woefully few women) neither prospered greatly nor starved, neither suffered unduly nor died at the diggings. For them the gold rush was a great adventure that, no matter the cost, they would not have missed for the world. In fact, many of them never did get over their excitement in scrambling for gold; and when the California diggings tapered off, they packed up and headed elsewhere, to new strikes in other beckoning gold fields, some of them half a world away.

They sang "Farewell, Old California, I'm going far away, Where gold is found more plenty, in larger lumps they say"; and they took off for Australia, for the Fraser River in British Columbia, for Oregon, Idaho, Montana, for the Comstock in Nevada, for Colorado, for the Black Hills of Dakota Territory. And wherever they went, the expertise they had acquired in California, either working for themselves or for others, earned them deep respect as "Old Californians," men whom it would be wise to follow if you wanted to find out where the rich ore lay hidden.

Many more forty-niners, after repeated efforts at mining, settled down in California and made new and happy lives for themselves. Franklin Buck of Bucksport, Maine, tried his hand at storekeeping, mining—and then at trading, hotel keeping, waiting on table, tending bar and milling lumber. Finally an old friend, John Benson, persuaded him and his wife to come and settle on a farm in Napa Valley.

"It will be a humdrum slow business," Buck wrote to his sister back East, "picking grapes and milking cows and raising chickens. But on the other hand we are getting along in life and we had better take a certainty of having a good living than the uncertainty of making money. I have given up the idea of ever finding a rich mine or making a fortune. I have given it a fair trial and such things are not for me so I am setting out trees and fixing myself comfortably. I don't know where you can find such a beautiful climate and valley, cloudless skies, warm as May, the hills and valley all green. Wheat is about two inches high; the almond trees just ready to burst into bloom. Roses and lilacs are leafing out. I am adept at making butter. It is gilt edged, yellow as gold."

Still other men, after a healthy taste of the diggings, simply packed up and went back home, for the most part looking back with fondness on California and their experience scratching for gold. They lovingly preserved their miners' garb—the cracked boots, ragged trousers, faded flannel shirts, greasy broad-brimmed hats—as mementos of the great adventure. Before setting sail for home they bought gold-headed canes for themselves and Chinese silks for their mothers, wives and sweethearts. And once home they talked with increasing nostalgia of the times, only recently past, when the challenges of each day had outweighed the disappointments. If they had not become rich they could, at least, take satisfaction in the saying that "no coward ever set out in the gold rush and no weakling ever survived it."

Dr. William McCollum, after returning to Lockport, New York, confessed that he had not found much gold in California. Nevertheless, he wrote: "Should I never revisit it, I shall hope always to hear of its prosperity and of the well being and happiness of the brave, noblehearted men I knew and left there. May success, health, wealth and comfort, be with them who remain."

And Enos Christman, the young printer who had sailed around the Horn in 1849 to seek his fortune, managed in three years to scrape up barely more than 100 ounces in gold dust. But it was enough. It paid his passage back to West Chester, Pennsylvania, balanced off his small debt to the man who had financed his trip West, and ultimately enabled him to marry Ellen Apple, the girl with whom he had faithfully corresponded all during his stay in California.

On May 8, 1853, Enos and his bride went to the Pine Street wharf in Philadelphia to look at the *Europe,* the sailing ship on which he had gone to California four years earlier.

"The old craft," Christman wrote to a friend soon afterward, "does not look much the worse of the wear. I almost felt as though I were being greeted by an old and tried friend. Memory carried me back to the day that I turned my face towards a land of golden promise. What trying times were those that followed. How easy it was to walk into trouble. But the thought of the dear burthen on my arm broke in upon these musings and reminded me that all was well with me. Indeed my hopes have been gratified and I have realized a fortune."

Gilt-edged mementos of the great adventure

For most forty-niners, the lasting significance of the gold rush was the proud memory of having been on the spot, and being able to boast about it ever afterward. Fortunately for this pleasant exercise, the art of portrait photography, in a process invented by the Frenchman Louis Daguerre in 1837, reached California just in time for the forty-niners to make use of it.

The miners loved daguerreotypes. While still at the diggings they would get themselves "pictured off" in convivial groups *(right)* or staunchly alone *(following pages)*. The rare examples on these pages show men in work clothes and in frock coats, bearing the tools of their trade or a mean-looking revolver tucked into a belt. Still, the real character of these anonymous miners is not expressed in the details of their costume or equipment, but in their faces, which reveal the resolute hardiness or high good humor of the men who searched for gold.

Mounted in ornate frames, pictures like these became treasured possessions. Sometimes the bright gilding of the frames formed a symbol of success; more often, it was the nearest thing to precious metal a miner ever saw. But whatever a sitter's luck, his portrait became a proud memento of his days in the gold fields, and certain proof to the folks at home that he had truly been out there and had seen the elephant.

230

PICTURE CREDITS

The sources for the illustrations in this book are shown below. Credits from left to right are separated by semicolons, from top to bottom by dashes.

Cover: Herb Orth, TIME-LIFE Picture Agency, ©1972, Time Incorporated, courtesy Collection of the National Cowboy Hall of Fame and Western Heritage Center, Oklahoma City. 2—Courtesy the private collection of Mr. and Mrs. Philip Kendall Bekeart, San Francisco. 6,7—J. R. Eyerman, courtesy collection Carl Shaefer Dentzel. 8,9—Courtesy of the E. B. Crocker Art Gallery, Sacramento, Calif. 10,11—Courtesy Pioneer Museum & Haggin Galleries, Stockton, Calif. 12,13—J. R. Eyerman, courtesy Stanford Univ. Museum of Art, gift of Jane L. Stanford. 14, 15—Frank Lerner, courtesy Everett L. Millard. 16—Courtesy Calif. Historical Society, San Francisco/San Marino. 17—Courtesy The Bancroft Library. 18—Courtesy Economics and Public Affairs Div., The New York Public Library, Astor, Lenox and Tilden Foundations. 19—Courtesy Kahn Collection, The Oakland Museum. 20,21—Courtesy The Huntington Library, San Marino, Calif. (HM 322). 22—Courtesy The Society of Calif. Pioneers. 23—Benschneider, courtesy Gold Discovery Museum, Marshall Gold Discovery State Historic Park, Calif. 24,25—Courtesy Prints Div., The New York Public Library, Astor, Lenox and Tilden Foundations. 27—Courtesy The Bancroft Library. 28—Reproduced by permission of The Director, The Bancroft Library. 30, 31—Courtesy Calif. Historical Society, San Francisco/San Marino. 33—Frank Lerner, courtesy The New-York Historical Society. 34,35—Courtesy Economic and Public Affairs Div., The New York Public Library, Astor, Lenox and Tilden Foundations. 36,37—Frank Lerner, courtesy The New-York Historical Society. 38—Courtesy *The Hartford Courant.* 39—Courtesy Melville Collection, Suffolk Museum and Carriage House, Stony Brook, N.Y. 40,41—Courtesy Museum of the City of New York. 42—Courtesy Rare Book Div., The New York Public Library, Astor, Lenox and Tilden Foundations. 43—Courtesy The New-York Historical Society. 44,45—Courtesy The Oakland Museum. 46—Courtesy The Huntington Library, San Marino. 48—Courtesy The Huntington Library, San Marino (HM 8044)—courtesy Western Americana Collection, Beinecke Library, Yale Univ. 49—Courtesy The Huntington Library, San Marino (HM 8044). 50—Courtesy Western Americana Collection, Beinecke Library; Yale Univ.—courtesy The Huntington Library, San Marino (HM 8044). 51—Courtesy The Huntington Library, San Marino (HM 8044). 54—Mark W. Sexton, courtesy Peabody Museum of Salem, except top right, courtesy The New-York Historical Society. 56,57—Courtesy The Mariners Museum, Newport News, Va. 58,59—Reproduced by permission of The Director, The Bancroft Library. 60—Courtesy the Federal Reserve Bank of San Francisco. 62,63—Reproduced by permission of The Director, The Bancroft Library. 64,65—Courtesy The New-York Historical Society, inset drawn by Rafael Palacios. 66—Courtesy General Research and Humanities Div., The New York Public Library, Astor, Lenox and Tilden Foundations. 68—Courtesy Library of Congress. 70,71—Courtesy I. N. Phelps Stokes Collection, Prints Div., The New York Public Library, Astor, Lenox and Tilden Foundations. 72,73—Courtesy Wells Fargo Bank History Room, San Francisco. 74,75—Reproduced by permission of The Director, The Bancroft Library. 76,77—Courtesy Calif. Section, Calif. State Library, Sacramento. 78—Courtesy Calif. Historical Society, San Francisco. 79—Courtesy San Francisco Public Library, Special Collections Dept. 80,81—Courtesy Wells Fargo Bank History Room, San Francisco. 83—Harry B. White, courtesy Calif. Dept. of Parks and Recreation, Columbia State Historic Park. 84,85—Courtesy Calif. Dept. of Parks and Recreation. 87—Courtesy The Oakland Museum. 89—Courtesy The Huntington Library, San Marino (HM 19088). 90—Reproduced by permission of The Director, The Bancroft Library. 91—Courtesy Calif. Section, Calif. State Library, Sacramento. 92—Drawings by Nicholas Fasciano. 93—Drawings by Nicholas Fasciano—Benschneider, courtesy Wells Fargo Bank History Room, San Francisco, except far right, courtesy Calif. Div. of Mines and Geology, San Francisco. 94—Courtesy The Bancroft Library. 96,97—Carleton E. Watkins, courtesy Robert Weinstein Collection. 99,100—Courtesy The Huntington Library, San Marino (HM 322). 103—Courtesy Calif. Section, Calif. State Library, Sacramento. 107—Courtesy Wells Fargo Bank History Room, San Francisco. 108,109—Courtesy Library of Congress. 110, 111—Reproduced by permission of The Director, The Bancroft Library. 112, 113—Courtesy The Bancroft Library. 114,115—Reproduced by permission of The Director, The Bancroft Library. 116, 117—Courtesy Wells Fargo Bank History Room, San Francisco. 118, 119—Courtesy Library of Congress. 120, 121—Courtesy Wells Fargo Bank History Room, San Francisco. 122—Courtesy The Bancroft Library. 123—Courtesy Rare Book Div., The New York Public Library, Astor, Lenox and Tilden Foundations. 124—Courtesy American History Div., The New York Public Library, Astor, Lenox and Tilden Foundations. 126, 127—Courtesy American Heritage Publishing Company, from Gene Autry Collection. 128, 129—Courtesy Rare Book Div., The New York Public Library, Astor, Lenox and Tilden Foundations. 130—Courtesy The Huntington Library, San Marino. 132, 133—J. R. Eyerman, courtesy Marguerite Hoxsie, Folsom, Calif. 135—Courtesy The Huntington Library, San Marino. 136—Courtesy The Bancroft Library. 138—Courtesy Museum of the City of New York. 140, 141, 143—Courtesy Calif. Historical Society, San Francisco/San Marino. 144—Reproduced by permission of The Director, The Bancroft Library. 145—Courtesy Wells Fargo Bank History Room, San Francisco. 146 through 149—Courtesy The Huntington Library, San Marino. 150—Courtesy Leo Stashin. 151—Courtesy The Society of Calif. Pioneers; Jon Brenneis, courtesy Calif. Historical Society, San Francisco. 152—Courtesy Calif. Section, Calif. State Library, Sacramento; courtesy The Huntington Library, San Marino (2). 153—Courtesy Culver Pictures; courtesy Harvard Theatre Collection. 154, 155—Courtesy The New-York Historical Society. 156, 157—Harry Baskerville, TIME-LIFE Picture Agency ©1972, Time Incorporated, courtesy Roger D. Lapham Jr. 158, 159—Courtesy The New-York Historical Society. 160, 161—Courtesy Kahn Collection, The Oakland Museum. 162—Courtesy The New-York Historical Society. 163—Frank Lerner, courtesy Newspaper Collection, The New York Public Library, Astor, Lenox and Tilden Foundations. 164—Reproduced by permission of The Director, The Bancroft Library. 166, 167—Reproduced by permission of The Director, The Bancroft Library. 168, 169—Courtesy The New-York Historical Society. 170, 171, 172—Courtesy Calif. Historical Society, San Francisco. 174—Courtesy The Bancroft Library. 175—Courtesy Calif. Historical Society, San Francisco/San Marino. 176, 177—Courtesy The Bancroft Library; courtesy I. N. Phelps Stokes Collection, Prints Div., The New York Public Library, Astor, Lenox and Tilden Foundations. 180, 181—Courtesy The Society of Calif. Pioneers. 183—Courtesy The Bancroft Library—J. R. Eyerman, courtesy James R. Briggs, Director, Fred Coops and Company, San Bernardino, Calif. 184, 185—Courtesy The Huntington Library, San Marino. 186, 187—Reproduced by permission of The Director, The Bancroft Library. 188—Courtesy The Bancroft Library. 190, 191—Courtesy Calif. Historical Society, San Francisco. 193—Courtesy Calif. Historical Society, San Francisco. 194, 195—Harry Baskerville, TIME-LIFE Picture Agency, ©1972, Time Incorporated, courtesy The Society of Calif. Pioneers, San Francisco. 196, 197, 198 — Courtesy The Bancroft Library. 200, 201 — Courtesy Calif. Historical Society, San Francisco. 202,203 — Courtesy The Oakland Museum. 204,205 — Courtesy The Oakland Museum. 206 — Courtesy The New-York Historical Society. 207 — Frank Lerner, courtesy Newspaper Collection, The New York Public Library, Astor, Lenox and Tilden Foundations. 208,209 — Courtesy The Huntington Library, San Marino (HM 36347). 212,213 — Courtesy The New-York Historical Society — courtesy I. N. Phelps Stokes Collection, Prints Div., The New York Public Library, Astor, Lenox and Tilden Foundations. 216 — Courtesy Brown Brothers. 217 — Courtesy General Research and Humanities Div., The New York Public Library, Astor, Lenox and Tilden Foundations — courtesy The New York Public Library, Astor, Lenox and Tilden Foundations. 219 — Courtesy Brown Brothers — courtesy Indiana Historical Society. 220,221 — Courtesy Levi Strauss & Co. except top left, courtesy The National Archives. 223 — Courtesy *Chicago Today* — courtesy American History Div., The New York Public Library, Astor, Lenox and Tilden Foundations. 224 — Courtesy Minnesota Historical Society. 225 — Courtesy Wells Fargo Bank History Room, San Francisco. 226 — Courtesy Calif. Historical Society, San Francisco. 228 through 231 and 233 — Reproduced by permission of The Director, The Bancroft Library. 232 — Courtesy International Museum of Photography, George Eastman House.

TEXT CREDITS

For full reference on specific page credits see bibliography.

Chapter 1: Particularly useful sources for information and quotes in this chapter were: *Anybody's Gold,* Joseph Henry Jackson, Chronicle Books, 1970; *California Gold,* Rodman W. Paul, Univ. of Nebraska Press, 1969; "California Gold Mania," Ralph P. Bieber, *Mississippi Valley Historical Review,* Vol. 35, No. 1, June 1948; *The Elephant As They Saw It,* assembled by Elisabeth L. Egenhoff, Calif. Div. of Mines and Geology, 1949; *One Man's Gold,* Enos Christman, Whittlesey House, 1930; *Sutter's Fort: Gateway to the Gold Fields,* Oscar Lewis, Prentice-Hall, Inc., 1966; 23 — Marshall quote excerpted from Bancroft, p. 70; 26 — Sutter quotes excerpted from Bancroft, pp. 70-71; 32 — *Californian* quote excerpted from Bean, p. 112; *California Star* quote excerpted from Loomis, p. 29. Chapter 2: Particularly useful sources were: *The Diaries of Peter Decker,* Peter Decker, Helen S. Giffen, ed., The Talisman Press, 1966; "The Panama Route," John Haskell Kemble, *Univ. of Calif. Publications in History,* Vol. 28, Univ. of Calif. Press, 1943; *Sea Routes to the Gold Fields,* Oscar Lewis, Alfred A. Knopf, 1949; 43 — Downie quote, Downie, p. 9; 46 — caption excerpted from Ware, pp. 10, 22-23; 47 — Gold rush verse, Paul, *Mining Frontiers,* pp. 14-15, Gardiner verse, Gardiner, p. 16; 67 — McCollum quote, McCollum, p. 89, Taylor quote, Taylor, pp. 17-18; 68 — Smith letter, Berthold, p. 39; 69 — Branch quote, Berthold, p. 51. Chapter 3: Particularly useful sources were: *Annals of Tuolumne County,* Thomas Robertson Stoddart, Carlo De Ferrari, ed., Tuolumne County Historical Society, 1963; *The Gold Hunters,* J. D. Borthwick, Internat'l Fiction Library, The Macmillan Company, 1917; *Hunting for Gold,* Major William Downie, American West Publishing Co., 1971; *In Pursuit of the Golden Dream,* Howard C. Gardiner, Western Hemisphere, Inc., 1970; *John Doble's Journal and Letters from the Mines, 1851-1865,* John Doble, Charles Camp, ed., Old West Publishing Co., 1962; *Memoirs of Elisha Oscar Crosby,* Charles Albro Barker, ed., The Huntington Library, 1945; *Six Months in the Gold Mines,* E. Gould Buffum, Lea Blanchard, 1850, 1959 editions; *Three Years in California,* William Perkins, originally published by the University of California Press, reprinted by permission of The Regents of the University of California, 1964; 94 — McCollum quote excerpted from McCollum, p. 133, Taylor quote, Taylor, p. 87; 95 — song, Paul, *Mining Frontiers,* p. 17, Leeper quote excerpted from Leeper, p. 105; 104 — song, Paul, *Mining Frontiers,* p. 26, food quote excerpted from Canfield, p. 3, Helper quote excerpted from Helper, pp. 123-124; 104-105 — doctor quote excerpted from O'Brien, *California Called Them,* p. 39; 105 — Buck quote excerpted from Buck, pp. 1, 215. Chapter 4: 124 — verse, Paul, *Anybody's Gold,* p. 99; 125 — Doble quote, Doble, p. 35; 125 — Gillespie quotes excerpted from DeNevi, pp. 153-156; 126, 128, 129 — Shirley quotes, Clappe, pp. 29, 22-25, 45; 131 — advertisement, Paul, *Anybody's Gold,* pp. 101-102, Blair quote excerpted from Gulhorn, pp. 11-14; 134 — Perkins quote excerpted from Perkins, pp. 101, 105-107, 131, 252; 135, 137 — bull-and-bear contest, Borthwick, pp. 276-277; 140 — Doss quote, The Donald Segerstrom Collection, Sonora, Calif.; 142 — Bucroft letter, O'Brien, *California Called Them,* p. 56; Buffum quote excerpted from Fisher & Holmes, p. 278. Chapter 5: Particularly useful sources were: *The Annals of San Francisco,* Frank Soulé, John H. Gihon and James Nisbet, D. Appleton & Co., 1854; *City of the Golden Fifties,* Pauline Jacobson, Univ. of Calif. Press, 1941; *History of the San Francisco Committee of Vigilance of 1851,* Mary Floyd Williams, Da Capo Press, 1969; *The Madams of San Francisco,* Curt Gentry, Doubleday & Co., 1964; *Reminiscences and Incidents of "The Early Days" of San Francisco,* John H. Brown, Mission Journal Publishing Co., 1886; *This Was San Francisco,* Oscar Lewis, David McKay Co., 1962; 185 — fire quotes, Baldwin, pp. 13-14; 186 — fire quote, Marryat, pp. 32-33; 199 — San Francisco quotes excerpted from Richard Henry Dana, pp. 409-410, 429, Helper, p. 55. Chapter 6: Particularly useful sources were: *James W. Marshall, A Biography,* Theressa Gay, The Talisman Press, 1967; *Sutter's Fort: Gateway to the Gold Fields,* Oscar Lewis, Prentice-Hall, Inc., 1966; *Sam Brannan: Builder of San Francisco,* Louis J. Stellman, Exposition Lochinvar, 1953; 210 — Carson quote, Buckbee, pp. 64-65, song, Rourke, p. 30; 214 — Sutter quote excerpted from Olmsted, pp. 183-184; 218 — McKinstry quote excerpted from Julian Dana, pp. 138-139, Churchill quote, courtesy Mrs. W. Murray Smith, Warner Springs, Calif.; 222 — fire engine quote excerpted from Stellman, pp. 161-162; 227 — Buck quote excerpted from Buck, pp. 276, 284-286, McCollum quote, McCollum, p. 82; Christman quote excerpted from Christman, p. 278.

ACKNOWLEDGMENTS

The editors give special thanks to the following persons who read and commented on portions of the book: Dr. Rodman W. Paul, The Edward S. Harkness Professor of History, California Institute of Technology, Pasadena, Calif.; Carlo De Ferrari, County Clerk and Historian, Tuolumne County, Sonora, Calif.

The editors also acknowledge the assistance of Albert Baragwanath, Senior Curator, Museum of the City of New York; Mr. and Mrs. Philip Kendall Bekeart, San Francisco; Brenda Boswell, Information Section, State of California Department of Parks and Recreation, Sacramento; James R. Briggs, Director, Fred Coops and Co., San Bernardino, Calif.; Susan Burns, Assoc. Researcher, Charles Lokey, Curatorial Assist., The Oakland Museum, Oakland, Calif.; Lee L. Burtis, Librarian, Photographs and Genealogy, Maude K. Swingle and Jay Williar, Reference Librarians, California Historical Society, San Francisco; William B. Clark, Geologist, California Division of Mines and Geology, Sacramento; Maud Cole, Rare Book Room, The New York Public Library; Carl S. Dentzel, Director, Southwest Museum, Los Angeles; Wilson G. Duprey, Jan B. Hudgens, Evelyn Raskopf, The New-York Historical Society; Merrilee Gwerder, Director, Elaine Gilleran, Assist. Director, Wells Fargo Bank History Room, San Francisco; Raymond W. Hillman, Curator of History, Pioneer Museum & Haggin Galleries, Stockton, Calif.; Gladys Hansen, Archivist, Department of Special Collections, San Francisco Public Library, San Francisco; Jerry Kearns, Head of Reference Prints and Photographs Division, Library of Congress, Washington, D.C.; Anthony M. Knapp, Elise Rea, Interpretive Collections Section, State of California Department of Parks and Recreation, Sacramento; Irene Lichens, Librarian, The Society of California Pioneers, San Francisco; Jim McDonald, Public Relations, Levi Strauss & Co., San Francisco; Olga K. Melko, Acting Curator, The Old Mint, San Francisco; Kirby R. Morgan, Elizabeth Smart, Sutter's Fort, Sacramento; Kenneth I. Pettitt, Head Librarian, Miriam Pike, Librarian, California Section, California State Library, Sacramento; Winifred E. Popp, The Huntington Library, Art Gallery and Botanical Gardens, San Marino, Calif.; Neil Power, Area Manager, Columbia State Historic Park, Columbia, Calif.; Elizabeth Roth, Prints Division, The New York Public Library; The Donald Segerstrom Collection, Sonora, Calif.; Mrs. W. Murray Smith, Warner Springs, Calif.; Dr. John Barr Thompkins, Curator of Pictorial Collections, Suzanne H. Gallup, Reference Librarian, The Bancroft Library, Berkeley; Louise R. Vessell-Fiellen, Assist. to the Director/Registrar, E. B. Crocker Art Gallery, Sacramento; Robert A. Weinstein, Los Angeles; James Woodson, Curator of Exhibits, Catherine Hoover, Assist. Curator, California Historical Society, San Francisco.

BIBLIOGRAPHY

Baldwin, Jos. Glover, *The Flush Times of California*. Richard E. Amacher and George W. Polhemus, eds. University of Georgia Press, 1966.

Bancroft, Hubert Howe, *California Inter Pocula*. Vol. XXXV. The History Company, 1888.

Barker, Charles Albro, ed., *Memoirs of Elisha Oscar Crosby: Reminiscences of California and Guatemala from 1849-1864*. The Huntington Library, 1945.

Bean, Walton, *California: An Interpretive History*. McGraw-Hill Book Co. Inc., 1968.

Berthold, Victor M., *The Pioneer Steamer California 1848-1849*. Houghton Mifflin Co., 1932.

Bieber, Ralph P.:
  "California Gold Mania," *Mississippi Valley Historical Review*. Vol. 35, No. 1, June 1948.
  "The Southwestern Trails to California in 1849," *Mississippi Valley Historical Review*. Vol. 12, No. 3, pp. 342-375.

Borthwick, J. D., *The Gold Hunters*. International Fiction Library, The Macmillan Company, 1917.

Brown, John H., *Reminiscences and Incidents of "the Early Days" of San Francisco*. Mission Journal Publishing Co., 1886.

Buck, Franklin, *A Yankee Trader in the Gold Rush: The Letters of Franklin A. Buck*. Katherine A. White, ed. Houghton Mifflin Co., 1930.

Buckbee, Edna Bryan, *The Saga of Old Tuolumne*. The Press of the Pioneers, Inc., 1935.

Buffum, E. Gould, *Six Months in the Gold Mines*. Lea and Blanchard, 1850, 1959 editions.

Canfield, C. L., *Dairy of a Forty-Niner*. Houghton Mifflin Co., 1920.

Caughey, John W.:
  Gold is the Cornerstone. University of California Press, 1948.
  Rushing for Gold. Pacific Coast Branch of the American Historical Association special publication No. 1. University of California Press, 1949.

Chidsey, Donald Barr, *The California Gold Rush: an Informal History*. Crown Publishers, Inc., 1968.

Christman, Enos, *One Man's Gold*. Whittlesey House, 1930.

Clappe, Louise, *The Shirley Letters from the California Mines 1851-1852*. Carl I. Wheat, ed. Alfred A. Knopf, Inc., 1970.

Coblentz, Stanton A., *Villains and Vigilantes*. Wilson-Erickson, Inc., 1936.

Colton, Walter, *Three Years in California*. S. A. Rollo & Co., 1850.

Dana, Julian, *The Sacramento River of Gold*. Farrar & Rinehart, Inc., 1939.

Dana, Richard Henry, Jr., *Two Years Before the Mast*. Random House, Inc., 1936.

Decker, Peter, *The Diaries of Peter Decker*. Helen S. Giffen, ed. The Talisman Press, 1966.

Dempsey, David, and Raymond P. Baldwin, *The Triumphs and Trials of Lotta Crabtree*. William Morrow & Co., Inc., 1968.

DeNevi, Donald. *Sketches of Early California*. Chronicle Books, 1971.

DeQuille, Dan, *The Big Bonanza*. Alfred A. Knopf, Inc., 1947.

Doble, John, *John Doble's Journal and Letters from the Mines 1851-1865*. Charles L. Camp, ed. Old West Publishing Company, 1962.

Downie, Major William, *Hunting for Gold*. American West Publishing Co., 1971.

Egan, Ferol, *The El Dorado Trail*. McGraw-Hill Book Co., Inc., 1970.

Eldredge, Zoeth Skinner, *The Beginnings of San Francisco*. Vols. I and II. John C. Rankin Co., 1912.

The Elephant as They Saw It. Assembled by Elisabeth L. Egenhoff. California Division of Mines and Geology, 1949.

Federal Writers' Project:
  California: A Guide to the Golden State. American Guide Series, Hastings House Publishers, Inc., 1943.

San Francisco: A Guide to the Bay and Its Cities. Gladys Hansen, ed. Hastings House Publishers, Inc., 1973.

Fisher, Vardis, and Opal Laurel Holmes, *Gold Rushes and Mining Camps of the Early American West.* Caxton Printers, Ltd., 1968.

Gardiner, Howard C., *In Pursuit of the Golden Dream.* Western Hemisphere, Inc., 1970.

Gay, Theressa, *James W. Marshall, a Biography.* The Talisman Press, 1967.

Gentry, Curt, *The Madams of San Francisco.* Doubleday & Co., 1964.

Greever, William S., *Bonanza West.* University of Oklahoma Press, 1963.

Gulhorn, Jane B., *A California Gold Rush Miscellany.* Grabhorn Press, 1934.

Hannon, Jessie Gould, *The Boston-Newton Company Venture.* University of Nebraska Press, 1969.

Helper, Hinton, *Dreadful California.* Bobbs-Merrill Co., Inc., 1948.

Hittell, John S., *History of the City of San Francisco.* A. L. Bancroft & Co., 1878.

Hulbert, Archer Butler, *Forty-Niners: The Chronicle of the California Trail.* Little, Brown and Co., 1949.

Jackson, Joseph Henry:
Anybody's Gold. Chronicle Books, 1970.
Gold Rush Album. Bonanza Books, Crown Publishers, Inc., 1949.

Jackson, Joseph Henry, ed., *The Western Gate.* Farrar, Straus and Young, Inc., 1952.

Jacobson, Pauline, *City of the Golden 'Fifties.* University of California Press, 1941.

Kemble, Edward C., *History of California Newspapers.* Plandome Press, 1927.

Kemble, John Haskell, "The Panama Route," *University of California Publications in History.* Vol. 28, University of California Press, 1943.

Leeper, David Rohrer, *The Argonauts of 'Forty-Nine: Some Recollections of the Plains and the Diggings.* J. B. Stoll & Co., Printers, 1894.

Lewis, Oscar:
San Francisco: Mission to Metropolis. Howell-North Books, 1966.
Sea Routes to the Gold Fields. Alfred A. Knopf, Inc., 1949.
Sutter's Fort: Gateway to the Gold Fields. Prentice-Hall, Inc., 1966.
This Was San Francisco. David McKay Co., Inc., 1962.

Loomis, Noel M., *Wells Fargo.* Clarkson N. Potter, Inc., 1968.

MacMinn, George R., *The Theater of the Golden Era in California.* Caxton Printers, Ltd., 1941.

Marryat, Frank, *Mountains and Molehills.* Harper & Bros., 1855. Also Stanford University Press, 1952 edition.

Mathews, Mitford M., ed., *A Dictionary of Americanisms on Historical Principles.* University of Chicago Press, 1951.

McCollum, William, *California As I Saw It.* Dale Morgan, ed. The Talisman Press, 1960.

Mulford, Prentice, *Prentice Mulford's Story.* F. J. Needham, 1889.

Nadeau, Remi, *Ghost Towns and Mining Camps of California.* Ward Ritchie Press, 1965.

O'Brien, Robert:
California Called Them: a Saga of Golden Days and Roaring Camps. McGraw-Hill Book Co., Inc., 1951.
This Is San Francisco. Whittlesey House, 1948.

Olmsted, R. R., ed., *Scenes of Wonder and Curiosity from Hutchings' California Magazine, 1856-1861.* Howell-North Books, 1962.

Quaife, Milo Milton, ed., *Pictures of Gold Rush California.* The Lakeside Press, R. R. Donnelly & Sons Co., 1949.

Paul, Rodman W.:
California Gold. University of Nebraska Press, 1969.
The California Gold Discovery: Sources, Documents, Accounts and Memoirs Relating to the Discovery of Gold at Sutter's Mill. The Talisman Press, 1966.
Mining Frontiers of the Far West, 1848-1880. The University of New Mexico Press, 1963.

Perkins, William, *Three Years in California: William Perkins' Journal of Life at Sonora, 1849-1852.* University of California Press, 1964.

Read, Georgia Willis and Ruth Gaines, eds., *Gold Rush: The Journals, Drawings, and Other Papers of J. Goldsborough Bruff,* Vols. I and II. Columbia University Press, 1944.

Riesenberg, Felix Jr., *Golden Gate.* Alfred A. Knopf, Inc., 1940.

Rolle, Andrew F., *California: A History.* Thomas Y. Crowell Co., 1963.

Rourke, Constance, *Troupers of the Gold Coast or the Rise of Lotta Crabtree.* Harcourt, Brace and Co., 1928.

Royce, Josiah, *California.* Alfred A. Knopf, Inc., 1948.

Scherer, James A. B., *The First Forty-Niner and the Story of the Golden Tea-Caddy.* Minton, Balch & Co., 1925.

Secrest, William B., *Juanita.* Saga-West Publishing Company, 1967.

Shinn, Charles H., *Mining Camps.* Rodman W. Paul, ed. Harper & Row, 1965.

Soulé, Frank, John H. Gihon and James Nisbet, *The Annals of San Francisco.* D. Appleton & Co., 1854.

Stellman, Louis J., *Sam Brannan: Builder of San Francisco.* Exposition-Lochivar, 1953.

Stewart, George R.:
The California Trail. McGraw-Hill Book Co., Inc., 1962.
Committee of Vigilance. Houghton Mifflin Co., 1964.

Stoddart, Thomas Robertson, *Annals of Tuolumne County.* Carlo De Ferrari, ed. Tuolumne County Historical Society, 1963.

Sutherland, C. H. V., *Gold: Its Beauty, Power and Allure.* McGraw-Hill Book Co., Inc., 1959.

Taylor, Bayard, *Eldorado: Adventures in the Path of Empire,* Vols. I and II. Lewis Osborne, 1968.

Ware, Joseph E., *The Emigrants' Guide to California.* Reprint of 1849 edition, Da Capo Press, 1972.

Wellman, Paul I., *Gold in California.* Houghton Mifflin Co., 1958.

Williams, Mary Floyd, *History of the San Francisco Committee of Vigilance of 1851.* Da Capo Press, 1969.

Young, Otis Jr., *Western Mining.* University of Oklahoma Press, 1970.

INDEX *Numerals in italics indicate an illustration of the subject mentioned.*

A
Ah Toy, 179
Alta California: on lawlessness, 193; on Joaquin Murieta, 144
American River, 17, 18, 23, 37, 82, 214; diversion of, 108; miners, *96-97,* 142
American Theatre, 163
Angels Camp, 82, 83
Annals of San Francisco, quoted, 165, 179
Armour, Philip D., *222, 223*
Arrastra, 95, 98

B
Baker, Col. E. D., 165
Baker, Isaac, journal, *58, 59*
Barnum, P. T., 46
Bateman, Kate and Ellen, 149, *152*
Beach, John: chart of voyage, *60,* 61
Beale, Edward F., 36, 46
Bear market, 137
Bear River, 37
Bennett, Charles, 28
Bidwell, John, 83, 209-210
Bidwell's Bar, 82, 83
Bierce, Ambrose, 216
Big Annie, 131
Big Rich Bar, 102
Bigler, Henry, 26, 27, 28; diary, *22, 23,* 27
Blair, I. M., letter, 131, 134
Blonde Burlesques, 153
Booth family, 138
Borthwick, J. D.: painting by, *124;* quoted, 105, 135, 137
Boston & California Joint Mining & Trading Co., 52, 65
Boyle, Charles, 61; diary, 58
Branch, Stephen H., quoted, 69
Brannan, Sam, 28-29, *172;* decline, 218, 224; farming, 224; and gold find, 29, 32, 169; and Mexico, 224; in San Francisco, 172, 193, 196, 222, 224; store, 29, 37; success, 222; and Brigham Young, 29
Broderick, David, 189
Browere, Alburtis, painting by, *14-15*
Brown, John Henry, 165, 169; quoted, 154
Browns Bar, 102
Bruff, Joseph Goldsborough, 48-51; drawings and paintings, 48-51
Buck, Franklin, 227; quoted, 105, 134, 146, 227
Bucroft, John, letter, 141
Buffum, Edward Gould, 79, 104, 142; quoted, 142
Bull-and-bear fight, 135
Bull fights, 137
Bull market, 137
Bullards Bar, 101
Burt, Benjamin, Jr., 53

C
Calaveras Chronicle, quoted, 94
Calaveras River, 88
California: emigration from, 227; female population, 129, 131, 134; Golden State, 209; laws for non-U.S. citizens, 68; and Marshall, 214; and Mexico, 19, 21-22; origin of name, 21; population growth, 207, 227; pregold-rush emigration to, 53; and Spain, 21; state seal, *212-213;* statehood, 207, 209, 213; and Sutter, 215
California (steamship), 67, 69
California Gold Mining Association of Philadelphia, 65
California Police Gazette, 188
California Star, 29; reports of gold, 29, 32
Californian, reports of gold, 17, 29, 32
Camerer, Eugene, painting by, *10-11*
Cape Horn, voyage via, *40-41,* 55, *56-57, 58, 59, 60,* 61, *64-65*
Carson, James H., 210; quoted, 210
Carson Creek, strike near, 82-83
Carson Hill, 82, 210
Casey, James P., *196, 197, 198,* 199
Chinese, 68, 106, 144; tongs, 143
Christman, Enos, 46, 65, 88, 95, 227; on homesickness, 106-107; letter to fiancée, 17, 19; trek to diggings, 86, 88
Churchill, Charles W., 218
Churchill, Mendall, quoted, 218, 220
Claims: law, 83, 89, *91,* 95; size, 95, 102
Clappe, Fayette, 126
Clappe, Louise Amelia Knapp Smith, 126. *See also* Dame Shirley
Clarke, George P., voyage, *64-65*
Clemens, Samuel, 216
Coffin, George, 186; quoted, 186
Coleman, William T., 199
Coloma, *24-25,* 125, 211
Colton, Walter, 178; book, *33;* quoted, 104, 134-135
Columbia, 131, 218
Columbus & California Industrial Association, 55, 58, 61, 131
Comet (ship), *56-57*
Committee of Vigilance. *See* Vigilantes
Consumnes River, 37, 82
Council Bluffs, Iowa, 53
Coyote and Deer Creek Water Company, *103*
Coyote Hill, water supply, 103
Crabtree, Lotta, 138, 139, 149, *151;* family, 139
Cradle, 6, 7, *73, 74-75,* 92, 95
Crime and punishment, 141-142, 144, 146; in San Francisco, *156-157, 164,* 165, 172, 183, 189, 193, *196-198,* 199. *See also* Law
Crocker, Charles, 220
Currier, Nathaniel, lithographs by, *202-203, 204-205*
Cuteye Foster's, 82, 101, 218

D
Dame Shirley, 126; quoted, 126, 128-129
Dana, Richard Henry, quoted, 199
Dashaway Society, 192
De Russailh, Albert Benard, diary, 179
Decker, Peter, diary, 55, 58, 61, 131
Delaware (Ohio) Company, 58
Diggings, 19. *See also* Mining camps; Prospecting
Diseases, 55, 63, 67, 104
Doble, John, 88; quoted, 125
Donner party, 53
Doss, James E., 140
Downie, William, 101, 209; gold fever, 43; gold strike, 98, 101, 114; quoted, 43, 114; trip west, 98
Downieville, 101, 138; growth, 114; justice, 144, 146; women, 129, 131

E
E Clampus Vitus, 140
Economic effects of gold rush: abandonment of production, 32, 37, 43; depression, 197-198; guesses about, 45; local inflation, 19, 32, 33, 37, 88, 154, 172-173; effects on nation, 22, 43; in Panama, 67; value of gold production, 19, 32, 37, 207, 210. *See also* Sacramento; San Francisco
Eldredge, Zoeth Skinner, quoted, 33
Elephant symbol, *78,* 79-80
Elton, Robert, cartoon, *206,* 207
Entertainment, 135, 137-139, *148-153,* 182, 185
Escobar, Rafael, *146-147*
Everett, Edward, 52

F
Fairy Stars, 138
Farnham, Eliza W., 129, 131
Feather River, 17, 37, 82, 214, 215; strikes near, 83, 102, 104, 125
Felton, John, 178
Fire companies, volunteer, 189, 192, 197, 222; equipment, 189, 222
Flaxhead, 165, 168
Flying Cloud (ship), *64;* private flag, *174*
Fool's gold. *See* Pyrites
Fort Gunnybags, *194-195,* 198, 199
Forty-Mile Desert, 61
Forty-niners, 61; caricatures, *16, 44-45, 162, 202-206;* distrust among, 105; emigration from California, 227; entrepreneurs, *219,* 220, *221, 222, 223,* 224; homesickness, 106-107, 175, 176; non-U.S. citizens, 32, 68, 69, 95, 105, 134, 140, 142, 143, *169;* number of, 19, 37, 68, 106, 207; number via land, 53; number via Panama, 67, 69; portraits, *96-97, 228-233;* quickness to move, 98; saga of, *208,* 209; San Francisco spree, 178; successful, 209-210, 220; types of men, 17, 52, 53, 104-106, 125, 199;

238

unsuccessful, 210-211, 214-215, 218, 220, 222, 224; vocabulary, 124, 203; and women, 129, 131, 134, *136, 138*
Frémont, Jesse, quoted, 178-179
French Gulch, 104

G

Galloway, Mrs. James, 129
Gambling, 123, *124,* 125, 134, 135, 140, 154, *173,* 178
Gardiner, Howard C., 88-90, 123
Gardiner, John D., quoted, 47
Gauly claim, 89
Geography of gold district, 82; place names, 82, 114
George, Henry, 216
Gilbert, Eliza, 138. *See also* Montez, Lola
Gillespie, Charles B., on Sunday in Coloma, 125
Godey's Lady's Book, 140
Gold: bar measures of value, 125; discovery at Sutter's mill, 17, 23, 26, 28-29, 32; discovery in 1842, 21; first nugget, *28;* forms, 17, *93,* 98; in history, *20-21;* largest U.S. nugget, 210; lectures on, 45; minimum sustaining output, 98; minting, *183;* newspaper announcements of discovery, *17,* 29, 36, *38;* official reports, *34-35, 36-38;* output in 1853, 207; output in 1852, 19, 207; output in 1848, 32; output over seven years, 203; output over 25 years, 210; placer deposits, 21, 36, 90, 95, 119, 197, 207; price, *93, 183;* in quartz, 10, 95, 98, 119; regions, *18, 34-35,* 82; in San Francisco, *165, 183;* tests for, 23, 95; unusual discoveries, 82-83, 86, 90, 101, 102, 125, 137, 209, 210; uses, 20
Gold fever: in 1848, 29, 32-33, 36-38; in 1849, 43-52; promotion of, 43-46
Gold rush: decline, 207; events leading to, 22-23, 26-29, 32; growth, 32; by non-U.S. citizens, 68; out of California, 227; and San Francisco, 32, 169, 172; and U.S. expansion, 207, 209. *See also* Travel

Goose Lake Hunt, 102
Grass Valley, *118-119;* after boom, *226;* and Lola Montez, 139, 149; strike at, 83
Greeley, Horace, quoted, 43
Guidebooks, *46*

H

Hall, Sam, 178
Hangtown, 116, 124, 125, 142. *See also* Old Dry Diggings, Placerville
Harte, Bret, *216; The Luck of Roaring Camp, 217*
Hartford Union Mining and Trading Company, 52
Hawkins' Bar, 88, 89, 140
Health conditions: at diggings, 104, 218; medicines, 46, 55; on overland route, 55, 58; in Panama, 43, 67; on ship, 64
Helper, Hinton Rowan, quoted, 104, 135, 199
Hittell, John S., quoted, 220
Hopkins, Mark, 209, 220
Hovey, John, 98; diary, *99-100;* painting by, *20-21*
Hall, Patrick Purdy, 139
Huntington, Collis, 209, 210
Hutchings, J. M., 131; "The Miners' Ten Commandments," *130*

I

Illustrated California News, 79
Independence, Mo., 53
Indian Bar, 102
Indiana Girl, The, 128
Indians: encounters with travelers, 58; and Marshall, 23, 211; rights, 28, 211; and Sutter, 23, 26-27, 211; treatment by miners, 105-106, 211; in Yerba Buena, 168
Iron City Rangers, 58

J

James, George, 106
Jacksonville, 94
Jeems Pipes of Pipesville, 137
Jenny Lind Theaters, 182, 185
Jewitt, William S., 24
Johnson, J. Neely, 199
Jones, Thomas Ap Catesby, report on gold find, 33, 36
Josefa, 144, 146
Juárez, Benito, 224
Judah, Sophia, *150*

K

Kemble, Edward, 29, 32
Kern, Edward, 218
King of William, James, *196,* 198-199
Knickerbocker Five, 189, 192

L

Larkin, Thomas O., reports, 36
Law: at diggings, 83, 89, *91,* 95; lawyers, 104; and Mexican land grants, 215; and non-U.S. citizens, 28, 105-106, 142, 211; in San Francisco, 193, 196-199. *See also* Crime and punishment
Leeper, D. R., quoted, 98
Lees, Isaiah, *164*
Little Rich Bar, 102
Loeser, Lucien, 38
Long tom, 73, *76-77,* 92, *93,* 95
Love, Harry, 142, 144

M

McCabe, James, 179
McCollum, William, 94; quoted, 47, 94, 227
McCready, Irene, 179
McKinstry, George, Jr., 218; letter, 218
McKnight, George, 83
Maguire, Tom, 182, 185
Mail, 67, 106-107, 114, 139, 175, 176
Malakoff mine, 108, *112-113*
Mariposa Diggings, 86, 94, 218
Market Street, 190
Marryat, Frank, 186; lithographs by, *154-155;* quoted, 186
Marshall, James Wilson, *23, 27,* 210-211, 214; decline, 210-211, 214; gold find, 23, 26, *28;* quoted, 211
Mason, R. B., reports, 33, *34-35,* 36-38
Massett, Stephen C., 137, 182
Meiggs, Henry (Honest Harry), 197-198
Menken, Adah Isaac, 182
Merced River, 17, 18, 82
Mexico, 21; and Brannan, 224; and California, 19, 21-22; and French, 224; and Sutter, 23, 214, 215
Michigan Bluff, 220
Miners. *See* Forty-niners
"Miners' Ten Commandments, The," *130,* 131
Mining camps and towns, *114-121, 132-133;* civic and fraternal organizations, 140, 143; crime and punishment, 141-142, 144, 146; entertainment, 135, 137-139, *148-153;* growth, 114, 123, 125, 139-140; life in, *8-9, 12-13,* 90, 104-107, 123-126, 128, *129,* 131, 134, 135, 137-142, 144, 146; names, 82; newspapers, 140-141; religion, *8-9,* 125, 140; schools, 140; Sunday in, *8-9,* 125, *129;* tongs, 143; and type of gold deposit, 119; and women, 129, 131, 134, *136, 138*
Mining equipment: advertisements, 46, *122;* basic, *6-7,* 46, *72-73, 74-75, 76-77, 92-93,* 95, 98, *107;* caricature, *16;* mechanized, 46, 95, *108-113;* prices, 32, 95, *173*
Mint, United States, *183,* 216
Mission Dolores, 187
Missouri Bar, 82, 102
Mokelumne River, 18, 82, 88
Montez, Lola, 138-139, *148-149, 150,* 222
Montgomery, John B., 169
Montgomery St., 173
Monumental (Big) Six, 189, 192
Mormon Island, 123, *132-133,* 218
Mormons, 23, 28, 29, 36, 33, 123
Mount, William, painting by, *39*
Muggins Bar, 102
Murderers Bar, 82, 211
Murieta, Joaquin, 142, *144,* 145
Murphy, John and Daniel, 209

N

Nahl, Charles: engravings by, *128, 129;* paintings by, *8-9, 144*
Native Sons of the Golden West, 214
Neall, James, Jr., 193
New Helvetia, 23
New York Herald, 36, 69; quoted, 45
New York Tribune, 43; quoted, 67, 94
Niantic (ship), *158-159, 173*
North Bloomfield, *112-113*
Norton, Joshua A., *225*

239

O

Oakes, George J., 193
Old Dry Diggings, 82, 98, 142
Oregon, 209, 211
Oriental Hotel, *172*
Overland trails, travel on, 53, 55, 58, 61

P

Pacific Mail steamers, 67, 69, 175, *176;* flag, *174*
Pacific Star, quoted, 144
Page, Henry, quoted, 176
Panama, voyage via, 40, *62-63, 64-65, 66,* 67, 69; by rail, 134
Pans, 73, *74-75, 92,* 95; prices, 32, 173
Panama City, 67
Parker House, 168, 178
Peasoup Bar, 102
Peck, William D., *87*
Pellet, Sarah, 131
Perkins, William, quoted, 105, 134
Price, Hiram, quoted, 19
Pikes, 105
Placerville, *116-117,* 142, 219, 222, 223
Polk, James K., 35, 38, 43
Porter, Rufus, 53
Portsmouth Square, 173, 178, 179, 196
Poverty Bar, 82, 102
Pownall, Joseph, quoted, 94
Prevost, Victor, painting by, *30-31*
Prospecting, 86, 88-90, 94, 98, 101-104
Pyrites, 23, 95

R

Rabbit Creek, 139
Railroad, transcontinental, 220; transisthmian, 134
Raspberry, Bennager, 83, 85
Reid, Hugo, quoted, 106
Rich Bar, 102, 125-126, 128, 139
Richardson, William H., 163-165, 198
Riley, Bennet, 18
Robinson, Charles, quoted, 192
Robinson, Dr. David "Yankee," 138, 182
Robinson, Sue, 139
Rose, John, 98, 101
Rose's Bar, 101

Routes west, 52-53; by Isthmus, *60, 66;* by land, 53; by sea, *60,* 61, 64-66

S

Sacramento, *212-213,* 218; as capital, 213; growth, 80; Lola Montez in, 149; as staging area, 82; and Sutter, 215
Sacramento River, 79, 82, 214
St. Francis Hotel, 178
St. Joseph, Mo., 53
Salting mines, 26, 173
San Francisco: alcohol in, 179, 182; building of, 154, *158-159, 170-171, 172;* center for gold rush, 32, 80, 82, 165, 172; crime and punishment, *156-157, 164,* 165, 172, 183, 189, 193, *196-198,* 199; depression, 197-198; financial center, 173, 209; fire companies, 189, 192, 222; fires, *160-161,* 163, 179, *180-181,* 185-186, 189, 192; first newspapers, 29, *30-31,* 32; first photograph of, *166-167;* food, 178; gambling, 154, 173, 178; pregold rush, 169; land fills, *158-159,* 173, 190; name, 28, 31, 168, 172; population, 163, 168, 169, 172; prices, 154, 172-173, 178; prostitution, 179, *188,* 189; seaport, *70-71, 166-167, 190-191;* stage entertainment, 182, 185; streets, 168, 173
San Joaquin River, 79, 82
Santley, Mabel, 149, *153*
Schultz, Charles, 192
Scott, Winfield, *68*
Seamon, Victor, painting by, *90*
Seeing the elephant, *78,* 79-80
Seeing the Elephant, 138-182
Sherman, William Tecumseh, 37; quoted, 32, 33
Ships: abandoned by crews, 69, *70-71,* 159, *190-191;* advertisements, *54,* 55, 61; beached in San Francisco, *158-159,* 173; for Cape Horn trip, *40-41,* 61; clipper, 40, 55, 64; flags, *174;* on Panama-California run, 66, 67, 69, 175, *176;* in storms, *56-57*
Sierraville, *114-115*
Simpton, 193, 196

Slater, William, 101
Sluice, 92, *93*
Smith, Persefor F., letter, 69
Smith's Bar, 102
Society of California Pioneers, 222
Songs, 46, 47, 61, 124, 137; quoted, 47, 95, 124, 192, 210, 227
Sonora, *120-121,* 134, 140
Sonora Herald, 140
Spain, quest for gold, 21
Spanish American forty-niners, 32, 68, 69, 95, 106, 134, 142
Springfield, mining law, 91
Stanford, Leland, 209, 220
Stanislaus River, 17, 18, 82; strikes near, 83, 209
Steamer Day, 182
Steamer Union, 123
Stoddart, Thomas Robertson, 101-102
Stone, John A., 137
Strauss, Levi, 220, *221,* 222
Stuart, English Jim, *156-157,* 197
Studebaker, John M., *219,* 222
Sullivan, John, 83, 209
Sullivan's Creek: store, 123; strikes at, 83, 90, 209
Sutter, John Augustus, 19, 22-23, 26, 28, 209; decline, 214-215, 218; farming, 23, 26, 37, 214; fort, *20-21,* 23, 37, 215, 218; and Indians, 23, 26-27, 211; land rights, 23, 214, 215; in politics, 215; profits from mining, 27, 214; quoted, 26, 211; and Sacramento, 80; sawmill, 23, *27,* 28, 210-211; secret of gold find, 26, 28
Sydney Ducks, 189, 193, 197

T

T.K.L. Company, accounts, 89
Taylor, Bayard, quoted, 67, 94
Taylor, Mart, 139
Taylor, Zachary, *68*
Taylors Bar, 102
Telegraph Hill, *170-171,* 175
Three-fingered Jack, 106, 144
Tongs, 143
Travel in gold district, 80, 82, 86, 88; in 1850s, 139
Travel to California, 40, 51; advertisements, *54,* 55, 61;

cartoon, *44-45;* cost, 53, 66, 67; after 1855, 135; length, 40, 53, 61, 64; overland, 53, 55, 58, 61, 81; by sea, 40, 55, 57, *58, 59,* 60, 61, 64-66, 80; via Panama, 40, *60, 62-63, 64-65,* 66, 67, 69
Trinity River, mining near, 73
Trommels, *110-111*
Tuleburg, 82
Tuolumne River, 17, 18, 82; strikes near, 82, 88-89; towns near, *120-121,* 134, 140
Twain, Mark, *216; The Jumping Frog of Calaveras County, 217*

U

United States Army: desertion for gold fields, 33; pay, 79

V

Vallecito, map, *94*
Vigilantes, *156-157,* 193, *194-195,* 196, *197,* 198, 199, *200-201,* 222
Vocabulary of miners, 124, 131, 203

W

Ware, Joseph E., 46; guidebook, *47*
Washington Daily Union, quoted, 45
Water supply, 103; in San Francisco, 189
Watson, Captain, 169
"We Miss Thee, Ladies," 135
Weaver's Creek, 79, 125
Weaverville, 134, *140-141;* tong war, *143*
Weller, John D., 144, 146
Western, Helen, 149, *153*
Western Emigration Society, 53
Wimmer, Jenny, 23, 28, 210; children, 26, 28
Wittmer, Jacob, 28, 29
Women in mining region, 124, 128-129, 131, 134, 135, *136,* 137; non-U.S. citizens, 134, 179; in San Francisco, 178-179, *188*

Y

Yerba Buena, 28, *30-31,* 168, 173
Yuba River, 17, 37, 82, 218; strikes in and near, 83, 86, 101, 102, 114